A GARDEN GREW

A GARDEN GREW

KATHLEEN PICKARD-SMITH

Edited and Introduced by Richard Baker

Copyright © 2025 Kathleen Pickard-Smith
Copyright © 2025 Richard Baker

Appendix B – A Downland Gardener, Copyright © held by Alan Edenborough.
Permission has been granted to use the material.

Front cover: Watercolour painting dated 1904 by Wilfred Ball of the property that would become 'Harveys'.
Rear cover: An elderly Kathleen Pickard-Smith in the garden at 'Harveys' (Andrew Lusted - with permission).

The moral right of the author has been asserted.

Apart from any fair dealing for the purposes of research or private study, or criticism or review, as permitted under the Copyright, Designs and Patents Act 1988, this publication may only be reproduced, stored or transmitted, in any form or by any means, with the prior permission in writing of the publishers, or in the case of reprographic reproduction in accordance with the terms of licences issued by the Copyright Licensing Agency. Enquiries concerning reproduction outside those terms should be sent to the publishers.

Troubador Publishing Ltd
Unit E2 Airfield Business Park
Harrison Road, Market Harborough
Leicestershire LE16 7UL
Tel: 0116 279 2299
Email: books@troubador.co.uk
Web: www.troubador.co.uk

ISBN 9781836285274

British Library Cataloguing in Publication Data.
A catalogue record for this book is available from the British Library.

The manufacturer's authorised representative in the EU for product safety is Authorised Rep Compliance Ltd, 71 Lower Baggot Street, Dublin D02 P593 Ireland (www.arccompliance.com).

Printed and bound by CPI Group (UK) Ltd, Croydon, CR0 4YY
Typeset in 11pt Minion Pro by Troubador Publishing Ltd, Leicester, UK

With Special thanks to Barbara Abbs

CONTENTS

Introduction		1
Chapter 1	The Setting	27
Chapter 2	The Planning	30
Chapter 3	The Shrub Border (1)	34
Chapter 4	The Shrub Border (2)	41
Chapter 5	The Herbaceous Border	47
Chapter 6	The Rock Wall	53
Chapter 7	The Upper Lawn	58
Chapter 8	The Main Lawn and Side Path	63
Chapter 9	The Bulbs (1)	70
Chapter 10	Propagation	77
Chapter 11	The Animals (1)	84
Chapter 12	The Animals (2)	93
Chapter 13	The Sink Gardens	101
Chapter 14	The Screes and Sand Beds	106
Chapter 15	The Greenhouse (1)	112
Chapter 16	The Greenhouse (2)	118
Chapter 17	The Greenhouse (3)	124
Chapter 18	The Greenhouse (4)	130
Chapter 19	The Greenhouse (5)	135
Chapter 20	Change in the Herbaceous Border	140
Chapter 21	Change in the Salad Bed	150

Chapter 22	The Shrub Border (3)	157
Chapter 23	The "Bantam" Border	163
Chapter 24	The Bulbs (2)	170
Chapter 25	The Small Greenhouse	179
Chapter 26	The Nursery and the Rose Beds	185
Chapter 27	From the Bamboo to the Garage	193
Chapter 28	The Upper Lawn (2)	199
Chapter 29	The Peat Bed	207
Chapter 30	L'Envoi	212

Appendix A: Living with Reptiles — 214
Appendix B: A Downland Gardener — 218
Appendix C: Kathleen Pickard-Smith Papers, etc. Held by East Sussex and Brighton and Hove Record Office at The Keep — 224
Appendix D: Queenwood Ladies' College — 228
Appendix E: Advert for the Brighton School of Music c1936/37 — 234
Appendix F: Handbill of Opening Times at Harveys — 235

Bibliography — 236
Botanical Glossary — 238
Acknowledgements — 240
Index of Common Plant Names — 242
Index of Latin Plant Names — 253

INTRODUCTION

I first became aware of Kathleen (Katie) Pickard-Smith when I was at junior school back in the 1960's. Every Saturday morning my father would take me and my two brothers to the Carnegie Library[1] in Crosby; a suburb of northern Liverpool. There I discovered a copy of her book *Living with Reptiles*, published in 1961 (see Appendix A). As I was interested in keeping reptiles and amphibians at that time, and still am, the book was a revelation. In contrast to the rather dry textbooks then available it described the author's day-to-day experiences in keeping these animals, and much of it was devoted to keeping the hardier species outdoors, which is what I was doing at the time, albeit on a much smaller scale.

I subsequently bought a second-hand copy of the book, and as I became more affluent, obtained increasingly better copies. In more recent years I carried out some basic research on the Internet to learn more about the author, and in 2014 discovered an obituary in the *Independent* online newspaper, written in 1998 by well-known gardening writer Barbara Abbs.[2] This mentioned an unpublished book about Katie's garden at Harveys; a Tudor house located in the village of Glynde in East Sussex. In 2023 I decided to track down the manuscript with a view to getting it published. Barbara Abbs was obviously the person to contact, but this proved difficult until I discovered that her daughter was the multi-award-winning writer Annabel Abbs.[3] A e-mail to Annabel quickly put me in touch with her mother, and I discovered that she was in possession of the unpublished typescript of Katie's book, which was titled *A Garden Grew*. Katie had entrusted this to

Barbara so that she could use extracts as the basis for an article published in *My Garden* magazine in 1994 (Appendix B). Barbara was happy to send me the typescript, as it had always been her wish to see it published in full.

Katie

What do we know about Katie? To discover more about her I have relied heavily upon information supplied by her friend Barbara Abbs, local historian Andrew Lusted, and papers, etc. kept in the East Sussex and Brighton and Hove Record Office at The Keep (Appendix C). With regard to the latter, the most important source has been a recording of an interview with Katie made by Andrew Lusted in December 1991. However, Katie was aged 89 at the time of this recording, and her memory was hazy on some points, so where possible I have used alternative sources to confirm or refute statements made.[4]

Kathleen Nora Irene Pickard was born in the old farmhouse (Home Farm) on the Glynde Estate on 25 March 1902.[5] Her father was Thomas William Pickard, born around 1863.[6] Tom was the Steward of Glynde and apparently a formidable character; a trait which his daughter inherited.[7] Her mother was Caroline Martha Higgs Pickard (nee Woodley), also born around 1863.[8] Both Tom and Caroline were heavily involved in the local community.[9] A son, Eugene Cuthbert Llewellyn Pickard, had been born on 23 September 1889,[10] so thirteen years before Katie. He is commonly referred to as Cuthbert, for example in Katie's Obituary in the *Independent* newspaper,[11] and in the December 1991 interview with Andrew Lusted, so presumably this was the name by which he was known. He played cricket for Glynde, attended Steyning Grammar School, and was studying to become a chartered surveyor when World War One intervened.[12] On 6 June 1917, aged 27, he married Elsa Schen aged 24, whose occupation was teacher of domestic economy.[13] Her father was a brewery manager.[14] Cuthbert was a captain in the Royal Engineers, involved in building coastal defences during World War One, and so did not get involved in the fighting overseas.[15] He died in Norfolk on 24 November 1918, aged only 29, during the influenza outbreak which followed the war.[16] It's very sad that he survived the war but died two weeks after it ended, and must have been devastating for a 16-year old Katie, who probably regarded him as a father figure because of the age difference. He was buried with full military honours, including a firing party of twenty soldiers, and two buglers sounding the 'Last Post', at St. Mary's

INTRODUCTION

Cuthbert, Mother (Caroline), and Kathleen – probably taken by Tom Pickard
(Andrew Lusted – with permission)

Elsa and Cuthbert – probably taken by Tom Pickard
(Andrew Lusted – with permission)

Church, Glynde on 28 November 1918,[17] and is recorded on the two village war memorials.

Katie's schooling started with governesses. At the age of 11 (~1913) she went to Queenwood Ladies' College, Eastbourne. She boarded there until 1916, then attended as a day girl for a couple of years; travelling by train every day. She was captain of the netball team and played tennis. She left the school around 1918 (see Appendix D).

Katie went looking for wild flowers with her brother at a very early age. As she got older she went plant hunting all over the UK with members of the Botanical Society of Great Britain, and often stayed with members.[18] She was often in the company of eminent botanists, including George Claridge Druce.[19] Her initials (KP) occur in many pages of *Flora of Sussex* (1937) by Lt. Col. A. H. Wolley-Dod,[20] and there is a letter to Katie written in 1926 from Henry Salt[21] which thanks her for her instructions for finding the small hare's ear (*Bupleurum baldense*) and stating "I doubt if I could have found it without your directions".[22]

Katie gained her LRAM (Licentiate of the Royal Academy of Music),[23] after she became a student at the Brighton School of Music,[24] then located in the Athenaeum Hall,[25] and later would go on to become its principal and owner.[26] Katie was a student at the Brighton School of Music between 1919 and 1924, and then became a teacher there. Around 1936 she bought the School from its owner, Sidney Harper, and ran it until 1955.[27] It is apparent from an advert for the School that Katie, although owner, was not always director. The advert (Appendix E), from 1936/37, identifies James Ching[28] as director at that time, although his tenure only ran from 1936 to 1939. It seems possible that Katie then took over as director upon his departure. Teachers were employed there on a casual basis, and one was the mother of Herbert Menges, the well known conductor and composer.[29] Rather strangely, she makes no reference to music in *Living with Reptiles* or *A Garden Grew*, and Graham Gough, a trained musician who helped in the garden at Harveys during the early 1980s, reports that music was not discussed.[30] However, we have some snippets of information about her life in music. There is a 1931 newspaper report that Kathleen Pickard of Glynde was placed third with 87 marks in the contralto oratorio song competition for over 18's in the Brighton Music Festival. The test piece was '*Inflammatus*' from Dvorak's '*Stabat Mater*'.[31] Later, in 1936, there is a newspaper report of a Christmas party in which Mrs. Currey sang, accompanied by Miss K. Pickard.[32] This indicates that Katie was an accomplished piano player. Finally, in a 1998 newspaper obituary it is reported that Katie played the church organ when necessary.[33] In the December 1991 interview with Andrew Lusted Katie states that she played piano, and played the viola a bit. She also states that she sang, but couldn't carry a tune, which led to her failing an oral test and thus not gaining a diploma from the Royal College. It is difficult to reconcile this with her performance at the 1931 Brighton Music Festival.

On 25 August 1921 the War Memorial at Glynde was unveiled. It listed the seventeen men of Glynde and Beddingham who had lost their lives as a result of the Great War, including Katie's brother Captain Eugene Cuthbert Pickard.[34] A second War Memorial, in the form of a plaque, was added later to commemorate those killed in both World Wars.

In the early 1920s Tom Pickford bought Harveys, then called Grapevine Cottages, with a view to moving in upon his retirement. He bought the properties from Harvey Smith, and when he evicted the tenants, and moved in during the 1930's with his wife and daughter, he converted the properties into a single residence and named it after the person from whom he bought it.[35] Katie's comments regarding the greenhouse in the opening paragraph of Chapter 15 – The Greenhouse (1) suggest the move may have taken place as late as 1939, and Katie later states that it happened in the spring of 1939.[36] In support of this there is a brief newspaper article from 1938 about her parent's golden wedding anniversary which gives their address as Caburnside, Glynde.[37] Another supporting fact is that Tom Pickard retired in 1939, so this would be a natural point at which to move house.

Around 1930 Katie was working on producing a book about wild flowers, possibly to be titled *Wild Flower Days*. We know this from a set of 96 pages of handwritten notes, mostly double-sided, kept at the East Sussex and Brighton and Hove Record Office at The Keep (see Appendix C). For some unknown reason this project never came to fruition.

In 1933 Katie joined the Alpine Garden Society.[38] For a couple of years she wrote a column about wild flowers for Sussex County magazine, and was paid a penny per line.[39] This possibly arose from Katie knowing local personality E. J. Bedford.[40] She also carried out wild flower exhibitions at Glynde Library every week, and sometimes in Brighton too.[41]

On 5 July 1943 Katie's mother, Caroline Pickard, died from natural causes at the age of 80.[42]

In the December 1991 interview with Andrew Lusted Katie recounts how, during the Second World War, Canadian soldiers were billeted in Sussex, including at Glynde. Whilst walking her dogs in the dark one night in 1941 Katie met Frank Smith whilst he was on sentry duty, and romance blossomed. Frank was later sent to France, so that would have been after D-Day on 6 June 1944. There he was injured by blast whilst unloading shells, and sustained rib and facial injuries. He was sent home by boat in August. The boat was torpedoed, Frank ended up in the water, but was picked up. He went to a hospital in Haslar, Portsmouth, where he was visited by Katie. He was then transferred to Bramshott Hospital near Liphook, where Katie visited him over a long period of time, travelling by bike. Frank was finally taken back to Canada on Boxing Day.[43] Two interesting items are omitted from the interview, but documented elsewhere. In the first, it is recounted that the initial encounter with Frank was brought about when one of Katie's dogs bit him.[44] In the second, it is stated that Frank sustained a leg injury (presumably from the accident described above) and thereafter walked with a limp.[45]

Frank returned to the UK after the war, and on 19 August 1952, married Katie at a Register Office in Chelsea,[46] when she was 50 years old, and he was two years younger. The lengthy delay in getting married was caused by legal complications arising from Frank's previous marriage in Canada.[47] His profession at this point was manufacturer's agent (salesman?).[48] There are two curious aspects relating to the Marriage Certificate; both concerning the addresses of the participants. Somewhat unexpectedly, Katie's address is given as 137 Sloane street, Chelsea![49] It has been suggested that Katie's father was opposed to the marriage, and this would explain the marriage in London and the use of a London address – possibly a temporary address or the address of a friend.[50] The second curious aspect is that Frank's address is given as 3 St. Peter's Place, Brighton, Sussex, which is the address given for a Miss K. Pickard on a receipt for tuning a Bechstein grand piano in 1948,[51] and which Katie states to be one of the the addresses of the Brighton School of Music as it moved from one location to the next over the years.[52] Frank had been born in Canada on 26 February 1904.[53]

In 1955[54] Katie sold the Brighton School of Music and retired from work so that she could look after her ailing father.[55] He died on 2 June 1955 at Harveys at the age of 92.[56] Rather oddly, perhaps because of her father's reservations about Katie's husband, Frank, Harveys was left 'in trust' to Katie, and the trustees would regularly visit to make checks.[57] It was after

Katie's departure from the Brighton School of Music that the garden at Harveys really began to blossom.[58]

In the February 1961 edition of *She* magazine there was an article about Katie and Frank and their menagerie of animals. The article, titled *Skink on the Hearth*, mentioned the forthcoming book (*Living with Reptiles*), so was good publicity.[59] Katie's book *Living with Reptiles* was published on 5 October 1961 (see Appendix A), and further publicity was provided by a brief article titled *Snakes alive* in the *Sussex Express* dated 13 October 1961. The article refers to an appearance by Katie on Southern Television's *Day by Day* programme on Thursday of the previous week, which would have therefore have been 5 October 1961.[60] The round of publicity for the book concluded on 13 November 1961 when Katie took part in a BBC Home Service radio programme *For Your Bookshelf*.[61] Katie explains in the December 1991 interview with Andrew Lusted that the book came about as a result of a man visiting her garden when it was open to the public. He visited the following year, and it transpired that he was an editor at Nelson Publishing Company, presumably impressed with Katie and her collection of reptiles and amphibians, and wanted her to write a book about them.

In the East Sussex and Brighton and Hove Record Office at The Keep can be found a handbill advertising Harveys as a visitor attraction (see Appendices C and F). The attractions listed include a picturesque Tudor house, garden of botanical interest, and tame reptiles. The East Sussex and Brighton and Hove Record Office at The Keep have attributed a date of c1960 to this item, but '67' has been added in pencil to the handbill, which may refer to a date of 1967. Reference is made to an iguana, and we know that Ig died in 1961 (see Note 59). However, it is likely that Ig was replaced with another iguana.[62] The handbill cannot therefore be dated with any certainty, but we do know that at some point the garden was open to the public.[63]

At some point in the 1960's, possibly around 1969, Katie completed the draft of *A Garden Grew*. We know it was completed after 1962 because she mentions in the book the severe winter of 1962/1963. What we don't know is why it was never published. I have not seen any evidence, such as rejection letters, that it was ever submitted for publication, and she informed her friend and well known gardening writer Barbara Abbs that she was "pipped at the post" by Margery Fish,[64] presumably referring to the latter's book *We Made a Garden*. However, this can't be correct, as the timing is wrong; *We Made a Garden* being published in 1956. Katie would have been in her

90s when this information was imparted, and may have been confused. As described below, the draft of *A Garden Grew* was not sufficiently 'polished' to submit for publication, and it may well be that she simply never got around to completing the project. Who knows what might have transpired if the book had been published? She may not have been in the same league as Margery Fish, Rosemary Verey or Beth Chatto, but she may have become a minor gardening celebrity.

Katie was married to Frank until his death in Cuckfield Hospital on 6 March 1975 at the age of 71. The hospital is located about 14 miles north-west of Glynde, and presumably it is a coincidence that it was taken over by the Canadian Medical Unit in 1942, and handed back at the end of the war. Rather intriguingly Frank's occupation is listed as "Journalist (retired)".[65] Does this refer to his occupation before the Second World War, or was he in employment after the war, or even after he married Katie? Potential employers could have been the *Brighton Argus* (now *The Argus*) or the Lewes-based *Sussex Express*. Katie makes no mention of Frank being in employment in either *Living with Reptiles* or *A Garden Grew*, but it is conceivable that he worked until 1969, when he reached retirement age.

In addition to the original script for *A Garden Grew*, Barbara Abbs was able to provide me with a typescript of Katie's other book, *Living with Reptiles*. Accompanying this script are notes and letters which indicate that in 1981 Katie was seeking to get the reptile book reissued, possibly as a paperback. Katie relates that this was because book dealers were anxious for it to be re-published. She brought it up to date, and sent a draft to Collins. Unfortunately, that publisher was going through a difficult period at this point and had to reject it, and Katie didn't pursue the matter further.[66]

In 1994 Barbara Abbs liaised with Katie to get some of the material from *A Garden Grew* published in a magazine called *My Garden*. This now defunct magazine was re-created in 1993 by Alan Edenborough, based on Theo A. Stephen's original *My Garden* magazine, which ran from 1934 to 1951. The article, titled *A Downland Gardener*, is in two parts. The first consists of a biography of Katie, and the second is an account of Katie's greenhouse plants, based loosely upon chapters 15 to 19 of *A Garden Grew* (see Appendix B).

Katie was interviewed by local historian Andrew Lusted in December 1991, and the recording is available on the East Sussex Record Office website.[67] See also Appendix C.

Katie and Frank at Harveys in 1961. *Living with Reptiles* Plate 1 (Probably a *She* magazine image – with permission)

In her final years Katie was confined to one room of her house, and all her reptiles and amphibians had either died or been re-homed. She was left with her dogs, and a pair of robins which she would feed by scattering mealworms over the carpet, much to the dismay of her carers.[68] Barbara Abbs knew Katie from approximately 1978 until her death; visiting every week, and twice a week in her final year.[69] Katie had a heart attack on the evening of 23 November 1998, and Barbara, who was present, reports that she flirted with the ambulance crew who attended.[70] Katie died of heart failure later that night at the age of 96 in the Royal Sussex County Hospital, Brighton.[71] The funeral took place at St. Mary's Church, Glynde on 2

December 1998, followed by cremation at Woodvale Crematorium. Her ashes were scattered over her parents grave at St. Mary's Church, Glynde, and the following inscription added to the gravestone in accordance with her wishes – 'also of their beloved daughter Kathleen 25 March 1902 – 23 November 1998'.[72]

Summary of Events

1863	Approximate date of father's birth (Tom Pickard). Approximate date of mother's birth (Caroline Woodley).
1889	Brother (Eugene Cuthbert Pickard) born 23 September.
1902	Kathleen Nora Irene Pickard born 25 March.
1904	Husband (Frank Edgar Smith) born 26 February.
1913	Possible year in which Katie joins Queenwood Ladies' College.
1917	Marriage of brother (Eugene Cuthbert Pickard) on 6 June.
1918	Possible year in which Katie leaves Queenwood Ladies' College and becomes a student at the Brighton School of Music. World War One ended 11 November. Death of brother (Eugene Cuthbert Pickard) 24 November. Katie gains LRAM?
1921	Unveiling of Glynde War Memorial 25 August. Grapevine Cottages (later to become Harveys) bought by Tom Pickard.
1924	Katie becomes teacher at Brighton School of Music
1929	Alpine Garden Society formed.
1930	Possible date Katie working on book about wild flowers.
1933	Katie joins Alpine Garden Society.
1936	Start of Katie's tenure as owner at the Brighton School of Music.
1939	Probable year in which Pickard family move into Harveys. Possible year in which Katie takes over as Director of Brighton School of Music.
1943	Death of mother (Caroline Pickard) 5 July.
1952	Marriage of Katie to Frank Smith 19 August.
1955	Katie sells the Brighton School of Music and retires. Death of father (Tom Pickard) 2 June.

INTRODUCTION

1961	*She* magazine article *Skink in the Hearth* published in February. *Living with Reptiles* book published 5 October. Appearance on Southern Television's *Day by Day* programme on 5 October. *Sussex Express* article *Snakes alive* published 13 October. Participation in BBC Home Service radio programme *For Your Bookshelf* on 13 November.
1969	Approximate date when draft of *A Garden Grew* completed.
1975	Death of husband (Frank Smith) 6 March.
1981	Katie seeks to get *Living with Reptiles* book re-issued.
1991	Recorded interview with Katie by local historian Andrew Lusted in December.
1994	Article by Katie and Barbara Abbs appears in *My Garden* magazine.
1998	Death of Katie 23 November. Katie's funeral 2 December.

What is the correct format for Katie's married name? The title page of the original typescript for *A Garden Grew*, and a draft letter of Katie's, dating from 1981, seeking to get *Living with Reptiles* re-issued, use Kathleen Pickard Smith. However, the title page of the original typescript for *Living with Reptiles*, the book *Living with Reptiles*, and her Death Certificate use Kathleen Pickard-Smith, i.e. with a hyphen. Katie thus appears to have used the two formats interchangeably. In this book I have adopted the latter format.

What sort of person was Katie? We have already noted above that her father Tom was a formidable character, and that Katie had inherited this trait. In addition, it has been said in her obituary that she did not mellow with the years.[73] We therefore have the impression of a woman who did not suffer fools gladly and who probably spoke quite bluntly. However, she was said to have a mind like a razor, even in old age, and a kindly but wicked wit.[74] She was also rather eccentric. We have already learnt that in her old age she would scatter mealworms on the carpet to feed robins, and her obituary[75] relates the following story originating from Elizabeth Strangman.[76] At a meeting of the Royal Horticultural Society at Vincent Square in London Katie was seen in the ladies' toilet with a number young terrapins swimming in a hand basin. She then proceeded to dry them one by one and pop them into her bra, explaining that they had not long hatched, and could not be left at home all day. A variation on this story is contained in a pen picture of Katie in David Lang's book.[77]

We know from her will that Katie had an extensive book collection, and two titles are specifically mention; these being *The Encyclopaedia of Plants* (1829) by John Loudon,[78] and *On the Eaves of the World* (1917) by Reginald Farrar.[79] She also had a copy of the previously-mentioned *Flora of Sussex* (1937) by Lt. Col. A. H. Wolley-Dod.[80]

Glynde and Harveys

Katie lived in the small village of Glynde,[81] which lies about 3 miles east of Lewes, 8 miles north-east of Brighton, and 5 miles from the coast in the county of East Sussex. It sits on the flank of Mount Caburn, a 159 metre hill topped by an Iron Age hill fort. The 1971 Census revealed a population size of 217, which had risen to 312 by the 2011 Census. It is perhaps most famous for Glynde Place, an Elizabethan manor house built in 1569. It is built of Sussex flint and stone from Caen, and is a Grade I listed building; one of 27 listed buildings in the village.

The parish church of St Mary the Virgin was dedicated in 1765, and the war memorial, unveiled in 1921 to commemorate those lost in World War One, is of Portland stone and stands at the bottom of the churchyard. An updated memorial plaque is displayed at the entrance to the lych gate to commemorate those lost in both World Wars.[82]

There is a railway station in the village, and an unusually large number of small businesses, including a staircase manufacturer and a weighing machine manufacturer. There is also a teashop, a forge, and a paragliding and hang-gliding centre. The village pub, the Trevor Arms, reopened in 2025. Just over a mile to the north lies Glyndebourne; an English country house and the venue for the annual Glyndebourne Festival Opera.[83]

The village is linear in shape, arranged along a road connecting the A27 with Ringmer about one and a half miles to the north. At the south end, as well as the rail line, is an offshoot of the Sussex Ouse called Glynde Reach, which used to be a transport route for heavy goods such a coal. The village possesses a very attractive cricket ground, and some picturesque houses of mixed design, mostly dating from the nineteenth century. The history of these properties is very well described in a 2008 booklet by Andrew Lusted titled *A Guided Tour of Glynde Street*. Various editions of an undated booklet called *Glynde Place, Sussex: An Illustrated Guide* are available, and

INTRODUCTION

Grapevine Cottages, later to become Harveys (Pre-1940 postcard)

Harveys in September 2024 (Richard Baker)

the history of the village is described in *A Glimpse of Glynde* written by Anthony Hampden in 1997.

Katie lived in Harveys, an L-shaped 16th century timber framed house which is Grade II listed. The building has cream plaster infilling between the timber frame and the red brick at ground floor level. At some point in the nineteenth century it was converted into two labourers' cottages, known as Grapevine Cottages, but after Katie's father, Tom Pickard, bought the properties in 1921 he had them converted back into a single residence and renamed it Harveys – the name of a previous owner.[84] A double garage has been added recently. The property lies on the west side of the main road which runs through the village. Because of its striking appearance the house has been photographed many times over the years, sometimes for postcards, and painted by famous artist Wilfred Ball in 1904.[85]

A few words about the original manuscript

The original manuscript consists of a cardboard cover containing the book tile (*A Garden* Grew) and Katie's name (given as Kathleen Pickard Smith), two pages listing the contents, followed by two hundred pages contained within thirty chapters. The paper used is very flimsy, almost like tracing paper, in UK Quarto size (10" x 8"). It is possible that it dates from the Second World War, or the period immediately afterwards, when quality paper was in very short supply or unavailable.

The text has been typed using a typewriter. Simple amendments or additions have been added in block capitals using a ball-point pen, and are easy to read, but longer ones have been written in longhand, and are difficult to decipher. In some cases I have had to omit them because the handwriting is illegible. Page numbers have been added in biro. The script was thus, when Katie left it, not in a condition to be submitted to a publisher. Perhaps the work involved in re-typing some of the pages was a contributing factor in the failure to publish. The script required 'polishing' by an editor, and I attempted to perform that function.

Also provided was a handwritten script of the first twelve chapters, contained on both sides of 37 sheets of lined, A4-size paper. The handwriting is mostly legible – more legible than the handwritten corrections and additions on the typewritten script – and was done with a blue biro. Corrections and additions have been done with a red biro, as was the book title on page 1. Katie has underlined Latin plant names, which is the correct procedure – something she neglected to do with the typescript. It is not known whether the handwritten version of chapters 13 to 30 are missing, or whether Katie skipped this stage and composed them on her typewriter.

As a general principle I have decided to make as few changes as possible to the original typescript, deeming it preferable to leave it as Katie intended. Her spelling was excellent, and very few corrections were required; an exception being a handful of plant names. She did have a tendency to under-punctuate, and as I have a tendency to over-punctuate I have tried to strike a happy medium. One consistent error that crops up regularly is that when Katie writes a plant's Latin name she uses a capital letter to start the specific epithet. For example she writes the dawn poppy as *Eomecon Chionantha*, when it should of course be written *Eomecon chionantha*. We must remember that Katie was an amateur and had no formal training in botany, if we discount the basic botany lessons taught at her school. She does, however, use some technical terms that the lay reader may be unfamiliar with, and I have therefore included a botanical glossary at the end of the book.

It is the convention that when writing in longhand, or using a basic typewriter, Latin plant names are underlined to signify that they should be in italics. Katie did not adopt this approach, but as she used an upper case letter to start a common name we do not know, in instances where the common name is the same as the Latin generic name, e.g. *Clematis* what was intended. I have used my best judgement to resolve such issues.

In many cases a plant's common name is not provided, and I have addressed this by adding them in square brackets where they exist, and I should state at this point that anything else in square brackets is material I have added.

Almost sixty years have elapsed since the script was written, and in that time many of the plants' Latin names have changed as botanists have developed a better understanding of the plant kingdom. This is likely to be on on-going process now that we can use DNA to establish the relationship between plants, as it is a more reliable technique than a visual examination of a plant's morphology. Some plant names have also been updated because the original name used was incorrect. I have added notes at the end of each chapter to identify name changes. My main sources for doing this were *RHS Plant Finder 2023* for plants in cultivation, and *The Wild Flower Key* by Francis Rose for wild plants. Some plants are not listed in *RHS Plant Finder 2023*, either because Katie was collecting very rare plants, or because some plants of the 1960's have gone out of fashion. In these cases the plants can usually be found listed on the Internet.

Thousands of new cultivars have, of course, been created since the original script was written, and replaced older ones in popularity. The popular Mexican orange cultivar *Choisya* 'Sundance' for example was not introduced until 1986. Also, trends in plants come and go, and as an example, tree ferns (*Dicksonia antartica*) are now very popular, but don't get a mention in Katie's book.

What did Katie's garden look like? The impression formed by reading her book is that her primary interest was the plants, particularly rare or unusual ones, and overall appearance took second place. The garden was probably not in the same league, from a design perspective, as Beth Chatto's garden near Colchester, or Christopher Lloyd's 'Great Dixter' near Rye. This view is supported by Barbara Abbs, who describes it as pleasant and well kept, but not of outstanding design.[86] Unfortunately, Katie's typescript did not include a plan of her garden, nor is one available from any other source.[87] In addition, the author has been denied access to see the garden as it is today.[88] It is therefore rather difficult to navigate our way around the garden as Katie describes it chapter by chapter. In the opening sentence of Chapter 1 Katie describes it as being three quarters of an acre in area, and from mapping, which shows the shape of the garden, we can calculate that its approximate dimensions are 80 yds by 50 yds. A rough, incomplete plan of the garden as it was in the 1960's, based upon information supplied in the typescript, is provided below.

Throughout the book Katie makes frequent use of the word "we", implying that she is writing on behalf of her husband, Frank, as well as herself. However, I get the impression that the driving force was Katie, and that perhaps Frank only got involved when heavy manual labour was involved. He seldom gets a mention in the book, which is in stark contrast the Margery Fish's husband Walter, who crops up on almost every page of her book *We Made a Garden* as she hilariously describes their skirmishes on just about every aspect of gardening. Katie mentions at the start of Chapter 23 that outside help was becoming increasingly difficult to obtain, indicating that she had some help in the early years. In later years she must have been kept very busy tending a three quarter acre garden, two greenhouses, a pond, two reptile and amphibian outdoor enclosures, a house full of exotic reptiles and amphibians, and walking two dogs. In Chapter 23 she also mentions

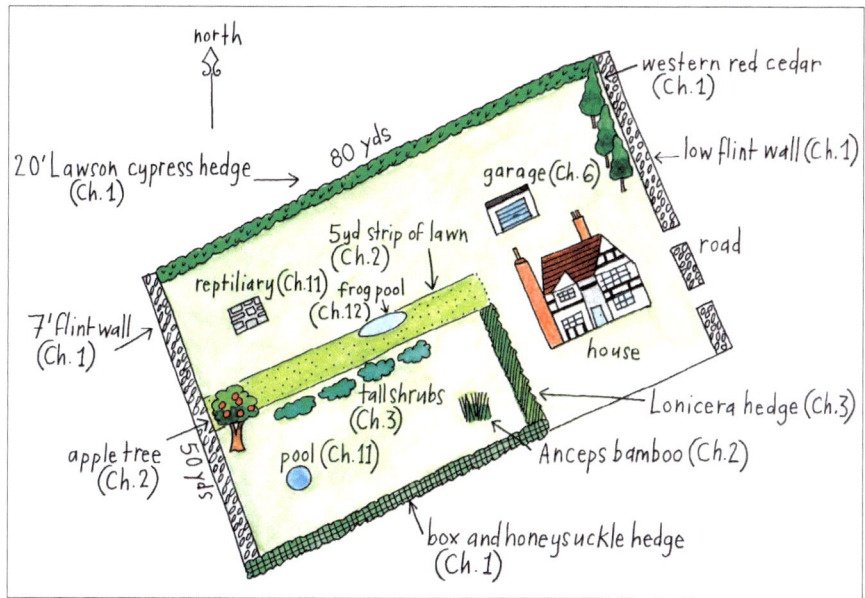

Possible plan of garden at Harveys (Sophie Harding)

an allotment! In her book *Living with Reptiles* she makes reference to using public transport, both bus and train, but never mentions a car.[89] However, she did own a car at one point, a 1936 Ford bought by her father around 1936 or 1937. It was nick-named Henrietta (derived from Henry Ford's name?), and was probably sold before Frank's death in 1975 and never replaced.[90] Acquisition of garden supplies and plants would have been more difficult once the car had gone.

Finally, it should be born in mind that Katie's garden at Harveys was located on chalk, and this dictated what she could, and could not, grow. However, as she explains in Chapter 3, the situation was ameliorated to some extent by the presence of a deep layer of domestic ash.

A few words about taxonomy

It might be helpful to say a few words about taxonomy, ie. the naming of living organisms. I have based this information mainly upon guidance provided by the Royal Horticultural Society (RHS)[91] and used UK orchids as examples.

The binomial system, comprising two names, was devised by Carl Linnaeus (1707-1778). Every organism is given two names. The first is the genus name, and this is written with a capital first letter. The second is the specific epithet, and this is written with a lower case first letter. The pyramidal orchid is thus written *Anacamptis pyramidalis*. Note use of italics. Where lists of organisms in the same genus are involved, the genus name is often abbreviated, thus *Anacamptis pyramidalis, A. laxiflora, A. morio*. Sometimes an organism becomes geographically separated, for example on an island, and individuals evolve slightly from the norm. These are designated as subspecies and given a third component to their name. So, for example, specimens of the fen orchid found only in South Wales are named *Liparis loeselii ovata* (sometimes written as *Liparis loeselii* subsp. *ovata*). Placed below subspecies in the taxonomic hierarchy are varieties. These are specimens which differ from the norm, but often occur throughout the geographical range of a species. Thus, for example, can be found specimens of the bee orchid which have an elongated flower which looks more like a wasp. These are named *Ophrys apifera* var. *trollii*.

Different organisms can sometimes interbreed, and the offspring are known as hybrids. For example, the dark-red helleborine (*Epipactis atrorubens*) has been known to hybridise with the broad-leaved helleborine (*Epipactis helleborine*). The resultant offspring are written in the following format: *Epipactis atrorubens* x *E. helleborine*. Sometimes a new name is given to such a hybrid, so, for example the aforementioned hybrid is known as *E.x schmalhausenii*.

Cultivars, an abbreviation of cultivated variety, are plants created by man as a result of selective breeding. In these cases the species name (in italics) is followed by the cultivar name (without italics, with a capital first letter, and in inverted commas). Thus a particular cultivar of the common spotted orchid is written as *Dactylorhiza fushsii* 'Eleanor'.

The family name of a species is always written in italics, thus the orchid family is written *Orchidaceae*. Finally, for common names there is no international consensus, but the RHS recommends use of lower case letters throughout, except where a word is a personal or geographic name. Thus frog orchid, Pugsley's marsh orchid, and Lindisfarne helleborine. I can't say I'm entirely happy with this approach, as it can lead to confusion. For example, if the word "common" is written before something that is obviously a plant name, is it being used as a noun or an adjective?

Richard Baker
2025

INTRODUCTION

Notes

1. Carnegie libraries were built with money donated by Scottish-American businessman and philanthropist Andrew Carnegie (1835-1919). A total of 2509 libraries were built between 1883 and 1929, including 660 in the UK. The library in Crosby opened in 1905, and closed in 2013.
2. Barbara Abbs is a gardening writer and garden historian. Her books include *French Gardens: A Guide* (1994), *The Conservatory Month-by-Month* (1997), *Gardens of the Netherlands and Belgium* (1999), and *Choosing and Using Climbing Plants* (2003). She has also, as Ros Glancy, written a novel about the problems of ageing. She founded the Lewes & District Garden Society, of which she was Secretary and Chairman, and started the *Speaker's Register*, a national list of speakers on horticultural subjects. She also helped to set up the Sussex Gardens Trust.
3. Annabel Abbs is a writer of fiction, e.g. *The Joyce Girl* (2016) and non-fiction, e.g. *The Language of Food* (2023) and has been published internationally in 30 languages.
4. There are three obvious errors made by Katie during the interview. The first is the claim that the majority of the animals she kept had a vegetarian diet. Whilst this was true of the tortoises, it was not true of the frogs, toads, salamanders, terrapins and green lizards, for example, which all fed on invertebrates. Katie seems to be implying in the interview that any diet other than a mammalian one equates to a vegetarian diet! The second refers to how she persuaded a monitor lizard to start feeding. In the interview she claims this was brought about when someone gave her a number of slow worms, which she used to break the fast of the monitor, but in her book, *Living with Reptiles*, she writes that this was achieved with one slow worm from Toad Hall (one of the two reptile and amphibian enclosures in the garden) and a group of common lizards donated by a workman. The latter account is more likely to be true as it would have been written only a few years after the event. The third example is that Katie states that her school was located in Rusington Road, Eastbourne, when it was actually located in Darley Road (see Appendix D). However, we shouldn't be critical, as Katie was 89 when the interview was conducted. I am 20 years younger than she was then, and struggle to remember what day of the week it is!
5. Date from Katie's Birth Certificate. Location from David Lang's book *Wild Orchids of Sussex* 2001). Andrew Lusted advises that Home Farm was also known as Seven Acres (pers.comm September 2024).

6. Katie's Birth Certificate and Tom Pickard's Death Certificate.
7. David Lang's book *Wild Orchids of Sussex* (2001).
8. Katie's Birth Certificate and mother's (Caroline Smith) Death Certificate.
9. A newspaper article dated 22 April 1938 in the *Sussex Express*, covering the golden wedding of Tom and Caroline Pickard, and a further article in the same newspaper dated 6 April 1939 about Tom Pickard's retirement after fifty years, provide much information about his involvement in the local community. I am indebted to Andrew Lusted for drawing my attention to these. Tom Pickard was: Chairman of the Ouse Navigation Trustees and of the Ouse Catchment Board, member of Adur Catchment Board, Vice-chairman of the Chailey Rural District Council, Chairman of Glynde Parish Council, Manager of the Glynde and South Heighton schools, and President of the Glynde and Beddingham Working Men's Club. His wife, Caroline, was also an active lady, being a member of the Lewes Branch of the Royal Surgical Society, chair of the School Attendance Sub-committee, and President of the Glynde and Beddingham Women's Institute. A plaque recording Tom Pickard's sixty-three year service as churchwarden between 1892 and 1955 can be seen in the lych gate at St. Mary's Church, Glynde.
10. Brother's (Eugene Cuthbert Smith) Death Certificate, and December 1991 interview with Andrew Lusted.
11. Obituary in the *Independent* online. Retrieved May 2014.
12. December 1991 interview with Andrew Lusted.
13. Cuthbert's Marriage Certificate. In the December 1991 interview with Andrew Lusted Katie states that Elsa was Austrian, lived in the UK following Cuthbert's death, and died several years ago. She further states that she accompanied Elsa to Switzerland to visit Elsa's parents, presumably at some point after Cuthbert's death. She does not explain why the visit was to Switzerland when Elsa was said to be Austrian. Katie states that Elsa's half-sister was Athene Seyler CBE (1889-1990) – a well known English actress whose German-born grandparents had moved to the UK.
14. Cuthbert's Marriage Certificate. No indication of Elsa's nationality is provided on the Marriage Certificate. Her address is given as New Malden (a London suburb), and her occupation as teacher of domestic economy.
15. Pers. comm. Andrew Lusted September 2024. In the December 1991 interview with Andrew Lusted Katie states that Cuthbert suffered from asthma, and this was exacerbated by the requirement to ride a horse whilst in the army. She also believed that Cuthbert's asthma contributed to him contracting the flu

16. Cuthbert's Death Certificate. There is no field for next of kin on this particular certificate, so no indication that he was married, although we know that he was.
17. *Sussex Daily News* 29 November 1918.
18. December 1991 interview with Andrew Lusted. Barbara Abbs, in *My Garden* magazine (1994) (see Appendix B) states that Katie was a member of the Wild Flower Society. Was Katie a member of both societies, or has confusion crept in?
19. Barbara Abbs. *My Garden* magazine (1994). See Appendix B. George Claridge Druce (1850-1932) was, by profession, a pharmacist who ran a chemist shop in Oxford. He was the mayor of Oxford 1900-1901, a Fellow of the Royal Society, and a Justice of the Peace. He was the author of *The Flora of Oxfordshire* (1886), *The Flora of Berkshire* (1887), *The Flora of Buckinghamshire* (1926), and *The Flora of West Ross* (1929).
20. Barbara Abbs. *My Garden* magazine (1994). See Appendix B. Anthony Hurt Wolley-Dod (1861-1948) was a British soldier and botanist who collected plants in California, Gibraltar and South Africa, as well as in the British Isles.
21. Henry Shakespear Stephens Salt (1851-1939) was a writer, naturalist, and campaigner for social reform.
22. David Lang's book *Wild Orchids of Sussex* (2001).
23. Barbara Abbs. *My Garden* magazine (1994). See Appendix B. The LRAM is a professional diploma in voice, keyboard, orchestral instruments, guitar, conducting, and other musical disciplines. This reference gives a date of 1918 for Katie gaining the LRAM, but in the December 1991 interview with Andrew Lusted she states that she started at the Brighton School of Music in 1919! There is very little information available about the Brighton School of Music. It is not known when it was created, but we know that it occupied the Athenaeum Hall from 1892. It was located at 148a North Street, and its concert room could seat 500 people. Just before World War Two it moved to 5 Marlborough Place, and then St. Peter's Place. After the war, around 1951, it moved again to 90, Montpelier Road. Katie tells, in the December 1991 interview with Andrew Lusted, that Evelyn Laye CBE (1900-1996) – also known as Evelyn Lay – opened the School when it moved into the Marlborough Place address. She was an actress and singer known for performances in operettas, musicals,

radio and TV. She was still working at the age of 92. Katie bought the Brighton School of Music in 1936 from Sidney Harper, and during his tenure it was also known as the Sidney Harper School of Music. Even less is known about the school after Katie sold it in 1955. At some point it became the Brighton School of Music and Drama, and it continued as such into the 1970's, when the principal was a Miss Best.

24. Barbara Abbs. *My Garden* magazine (1994). See Appendix B.
25. Incorrectly called the Aeolian Hall in David Lang's book *Wild Orchids of Sussex* (2001).
26. www.glynde.info website.
27. December 1991 interview with Andrew Lusted.
28. James Ching (1900-1962) was a pianist, music teacher, and author of many books, mostly about music and playing the piano. Further information can be found on the website www.jamesching.co.uk.
29. December 1991 interview with Andrew Lusted. Herbert Menges OBE (1902-1972). His mother, Kate, founded the Brighton Symphony Players in 1925.
30. Pers. comm. May 2024.
31. A report on Glynde in the *Sussex Express* dated 15 May 1931.
32. A report on Glynde in the *Sussex Express* dated 21 February 1936. I am indebted to Andrew Lusted for drawing my attention to this.
33. *Sussex Express* dated 4 December 1998.
34. Captions on the floral tributes for Katie's brother were: "In ever lasting and most loving memory of my husband, Captain Cuthbert Pickard, RE." and "In ever loving memory of a dear son and brother, from dad, mum, and Kathleen."
35. www.glynde.info/history/property/harveys. Retrieved 25 May 2014.
36. December 1991 interview with Andrew Lusted.
37. Article in the *Sussex Express*. 22 April 1938. I am indebted to Andrew lusted for drawing my attention to this.
38. Obituary in the *Independent* online. Retrieved 23 May 2014.
39. December 1991 interview with Andrew Lusted.
40. Edward John Bedford (1865-1953) was a Lewes artist, photographer, teacher and museum curator specialising in railway locomatoves, nature, and the cultural life of the local area. The circumstances of his death are unusual. Police made a forced entry into his house and found his body on an upstairs landing, and the body of his housekeeper in a basement kitchen.
41. December 1991 interview with Andrew Lusted.
42. Mother's (Caroline Pickard) Death Certificate.

43. December 1991 interview with Andrew Lusted.
44. Obituary in the *Independent* online. Retrieved May 2014.
45. Pers. comm. Andrew Lusted September 2024.
46. In the December 1991 interview with Andrew Lusted Katie explains that the marriage took place in the Chelsea Registry Office near Harrods.
47. December 1991 interview with Andrew Lusted.
48. Marriage Certificate.
49. In the December 1991 interview with Andrew Lusted Katie Katie tells how the marriage was followed by a wedding meal at the flat of the son of a Mrs. Brand. Could this be the Sloane Street address that appears on the Marriage Certificate?
50. Pers. comm. Barbara Abbs, May 2024.
51. Catalogue of perennials in the garden of Harveys, Glynde. Document Number ACC7854/4 held at East Sussex and Brighton and Hove Records Office at The Keep (see Appendix C).
52. December 1991 interview with Andrew Lusted.
53. Husband's (Frank Smith) Death Certificate.
54. In a news item titled 'Surprised' in the *Sussex Express* dated 28 June 1963 it is reported that Katie ran a school of music in Brighton between 1936 and 1955.
55. www.glynde.info/history/property/harveys. Retrieved 25 May 2014.
56. Father's (Tom Pickard) Death Certificate.
57. Pers. comm. Barbara Abbs. September 2024.
58. December 1991 interview with Andrew Lusted.
59. *She* was a monthly magazine for women which ran for 56 years from 1955 to 2011. The article about Katie (*Skink on the Hearth*) was very brief, and written by Pam Massingham. It included seven photos by Don Smith of Katie, Katie and Frank, a tame robin in flight, and various reptiles and amphibians. An unusual feature of the article is that it includes three photos of 'Iggy' the green iguana (*Iguana iguna*) who featured so prominently in the book *Living with Reptiles*, but mentions that he died when six years old. The animal must therefore have died between the photoshoot and publication of the article. His death is not mentioned in *Living with Reptiles*, published later in the same year, so presumably production of the book was too advanced to make any amendments.
60. Southern Television ran from 1958 to 1981. Enquiries in October 2024 revealed that no recording of this TV programme is available. One of the presenters on the *Day by Day* programme was the well-known Cliff Michelmore (1919-

2016), but it is not known whether he was involved in Katie's interview. Katie reveals in the December 1991 interview with Andrew Lusted that she was accompanied by her husband and one of her tortoises during the programme.

61. www.waicblog.wordpress.com/2014/11/14/living-with-reptiles. Retrieved 31 May 2017. A listing for this radio programme can be found online in the BBC Programme Index (genome.ch.bbc.co.uk). Retrieved September 2024. It shows that the programme aired at 1715 hrs on Monday 13 November 1961, and that Katie was interviewed by David Lloyd James. An enquiry with the BBC Archive in September 2024 revealed that there is no extant recording of this broadcast. *For Your Bookshelf* was a brief programme typically running for 20 minutes on Monday evenings, starting at either 1715 hrs or 1730 hrs. The BBC Home Service ran from 1939 to 1967, and was replaced by BBC Radio 4.

62. Pers. comm. Barbara Abbs September 2024 who recalls seeing a lizard climbing on the curtains at Harveys during the period she knew Katie (1978-1998), which may well have been an iguana. In addition, Graham Gough (pers.comm. May 2024), who helped Katie in the garden in the early 1980s, reports seeing an iguana on the TV set. It therefore seems fairly certain that the original iguana, Ig, was replaced by at least one other lizard of that species.

63. December 1991 interview with Andrew Lusted.

64. Obituary in the *Independent* online. Retrieved May 2014. Margery Fish (1892-1969) was an English gardener and gardening writer. She is famous for the cottage garden style of her garden at East Lambrook Manor in Somerset, which has Grade 1 listed status and is open to the public. She wrote eight gardening books; the most well known of which is *We Made a Garden*, and contributed to others.

65. Husband's (Frank Smith) Death Certificate.

66. December 1991 interview with Andrew Lusted. A pattern of failure to see writing endeavours to a conclusion is emerging. First there was the failure in the 1930s to progress the wild flower book (possibly titled *Wild Flower Days*), then there was the failure to finish *A Garden Grew* in the 1960's, and finally, in 1981, the decision to make no further progress with getting *Living with Reptiles* reissued after only one rejection. The latter is inexplicable, as it is unrealistic to expect any book to be accepted by the first publisher to be approached. For example, Thor Hyerdahl's 1948 book *Kon Tiki* was rejected by 20 publishers, but went on to sell 50 million copies. Perhaps completion of the *Living with Reptiles* book in 1961 was due to it being a commission from the publisher.

67. www.thekeep.info. Item ACC8631/1/7.

INTRODUCTION

68. Obituary in the *Independent* online. Retrieved 23 May 2014. Katie left a will, dated 1989, and two codicils, dated 1993 and 1996. Her reptile and amphibian collection is mentioned in the 1989 will, not applicable in the 1993 codicil, and omitted from the 1996 codicil. We can therefore deduce that the animals had either all died, or been given away, between 1993 and 1996. As far as the financial aspects are concerned, the estate was split into six equal shares between four friends, the Church, and Sussex Trust for Nature Conservation.
69. Pers. comm. Barbara Abbs. September 2024.
70. Pers. comm. Barbara Abbs. September 2024.
71. Katie's Death Certificate. Rather unusually, it states that she was to be cremated. It is not common practice for such information to be provided on a Death Certificate.
72. Katie's will dated 7 February 1989, and confirmed by Marjorie Holloway at Cooper & Sons Funeral Directors, Lewes. It would be more usual for Katie's ashes to be reunited with those of her husband, who had died in 1975. I do not know what became of Frank's ashes, if indeed he was cremated (he left no will). It seems unlikely that his ashes were scattered over the grave of Katie's parents. Did Katie have a deeper attachment to her parents than to her husband?
73. Obituary in the *Independent* online. Retrieved May 2014.
74. David Lang's book *Wild Orchids of Sussex* (2001).
75. Obituary in the *Independent* online. Retrieved May 2014.
76. Elizabeth Strangman ran the renowned Washfield Nursery in Kent, which closed in 1999. She then bought a Grade II listed cottage in East Sussex. She is co-author of the book *The Gardener's Guide to Growing Hellebores* (1993).
77. David Lang' book *Wild Orchids of Sussex* (2001).
78. John Claudius Loudon (1783-1843) was a Scottish botanist, garden designer and author of more than 15 books.
79. Reginald Farrar (1880-1920) wrote over twelve books on plants and exploration. *On the Eaves of the World* describes a two-year expedition to Tibet and surrounding areas.
80. Pers. comm. Barbara Abbs September 2024.
81. Further information about Glynde (rhymes with mind) can be found in Andrew Lusted's booklet *A Guided Tour of Glynde Street*.
82. The report of the unveiling ceremony in the *Sussex Express* dated 28 August 1921 identifies 17 men commemorated on the war memorial. However, the more recent plaque lists 21 men (and one woman) killed during World War One. It identifies a further 8 killed during World War Two.

83. Information on Glynde obtained from Wikipedia. Retrieved 29 April 2024.
84. Andrew Lusted's book (2008).
85. Wilfred Williams Ball (1853-1917) was a watercolour artist of rural and marine landscapes. He had two books published: *Sussex: Painted by Wilfred Ball* (1906), and *Hampshire: Painted by Wilfred Ball* (1909). During World War One he served as an administrator for the British army in Africa, and died in Khartoum of heat stroke.
86. Pers. comm. October 2024.
87. The East Sussex and Brighton and Hove Record Office at The Keep holds many records relating to Kathleen Pickard-Smith (see Appendix C). These have been examined, and although there are numerous lists of the plants in the garden at Harveys, the date they were obtained, and their provenance, there is no plan of the garden. Also, no photos of the garden were found.
88. Three letters written between April and August 2024 to the current owners went unanswered. The house was visited in September 2024 with the intention of arranging a viewing of the garden on the following day in the company of Barbara Abbs, but this was denied, as was a viewing on any other date. One can well imagine what Katie would have said about this in view of the fact that she was happy to open her garden to the public! Little can be seen of the rear garden from areas to which the public have access, but satellite images from Google Earth show that it may be considerably overgrown with large shrubs and trees, and this supposition is supported by the overgrown nature of the front garden, which can be seen from the road. The probability is that the garden Katie created has been lost forever. It should be noted that in the second codicil to Katie's will, dated 1996, a married couple were bequeathed "such of my plants as they may select", but whether this had any impact on the garden is unknown. Another friend was bequeathed "the choice of one of my greenhouses in the garden".
89. Katie made extensive use of a bicycle, and may have taken it on the train when commuting to work at the Brighton School of Music (Pers.comm. Andrew Lusted September 2024).
90. December 1991 interview with Andrew Lusted. Katie states in the interview that she had seen the car two years previously, and Andrew Lusted replies that it was still in the area.
91. *The Royal Horticultural Society Botany Advisory Service. Recommended Style for Printing Plant Names.* January 2004.

Chapter 1

THE SETTING

Our first introduction to the three quarters of an acre of ground which might now be described as a mature garden, took place just thirty years ago, on a dreary afternoon. A cluster of bronze chrysanthemums at the far end did their best to enliven the scene, but for the rest a few scattered fruit trees, a well used hen run complete with derelict wire netting, a tumble-down pigsty, and row upon row of staggering Brussels sprouts completed the picture. How often have we wished we had taken a series of photographs as the various stages came about.

The outline of the garden is quite simply an oblong running east and west.[1] The north boundary consists of a twenty foot high hedge of *Chamaecyparis lawsoniana* [Lawson cypress] planted some years earlier, when the property was acquired. The western boundary is a lovely old flint wall seven feet high, and the southern has graduated from a chain link fence to a substantial hedge of the dull, but ubiquitous, small-leaved honeysuckle, *Lonicera nitida* [also known as box honeysuckle or Wilson's honeysuckle]. The house stands in the south-eastern corner, facing the village street from behind a low wall, again of flints, with a rounded top, and the remainder of the eastern boundary is a continuation of this wall behind which, on the upper side of the entrance gate, a row of dark blue-green *Thuya plicata* [western red cedar] stand guard against the north and east winds.

Further protection for both house and garden are provided by the sharp rise to the north of the downland slope close to the foot of which the village lies. Opposite the house is a steep bank thickly planted with daffodils, which is one of the sights of Sussex in spring time. Fortunately – although as always with these old houses, it faces due east and west to avoid the miasma supposed to arise from the marshlands – this house is built sufficiently far up the hill to be just above the region of mists which, particularly in fine weather, drift over these marshes, or brooks as they are known hereabouts, and consequently the garden lies between the two areas of more severe frost at the higher and lower levels of the steep village street.

The house is a showpiece in itself, genuine 15th Century Tudor with the Tudor Rose at the base of the north wall, and many original bricks still visible. The whole front is brick built to the level of the first floor after which beams, very large old ship's timbers, and plaster take over. The windows are all leaded lights, some more modern than others (with untold hundreds of corners to keep clean!). An outward leaning gable at the north end of the house points to its having been built around 1490 though no date has ever come to light on the actual structure.

The massive central chimney rises above a tiled roof which on the western side slopes down to little more than six feet from the ground – a beloved haunt of house martins basking in the autumn sun while awaiting the call of migration. Several of the upper floors are of polished elm boards with generous gaps between them, woe betide a dropped collar stud or more

Grapevine Cottages, later to become Harveys (very old postcard)

precious treasure! In one of the attics a patch of genuine wattle and daub[2] can still be seen. The wide chimney with its built-in ovens fills a surprisingly large area of the centre of the house, and tapers slowly through the three storeys.

No stone has been left unturned to learn the history of the building but without success, though there seems little doubt that it was a dower house[3] attached to the manor house, an Elizabethan building standing on the site of an older one. There is a strong suspicion that it has housed quite a lot of contraband in its time, to which theory the deep wine bins in the cellar, cut from solid chalk, lend considerable colour.

When it was purchased in the nineteen twenties for a now incredibly small sum the vendors were the local brewers who had kept it in their hands in case they ever needed to open a public house in the village, so it was accordingly named "Harveys" after them.

Notes

1. The H.M. Land Registry map for this area of Katie's village, Glynde, shows the garden to be rectangular with the long axis orientated WSW-ENE.
2. A building method in which a woven lattice of wooden strips called wattle is daubed with sticky material usually made from some combination of wet soil, clay, sand, animal dung and straw.
3. A moderately large house available for use by the widow of the previous owner of a large estate. Cognate with dowager.

Chapter 2

THE PLANNING

Here then was the canvas – now for the picture. We were lucky in that the distance between our former home[1] and the new one was less than a mile, and that there had been plenty of time in advance to propagate many of the larger trees and shrubs which would have to be left behind. Herbaceous and rock plants presented no problem from this point of view of course. But before a planting scheme could even be considered the essential requirement was an attempt at garden design – a sealed book as far as we were concerned, though we were aware that the element of surprise was very desirable in that one should not be able to see the whole of such a garden at a glance. On the other hand simplicity had to be the keynote, and it would have been out of character to try to achieve an element of mystery with wandering paths in such a small area. What seemed necessary was a series of smaller gardens within the greater whole, with practical paths of easy maintenance interlinking them.

The first necessity was to separate entirely the piece of ground behind the house from the strip running the whole length of the upper side of it, and to make the former escape proof for pets of any kind, particularly dogs. To this end a few more thuyas were planted running north and south parallel with the end of the garage, and the remaining space filled with more quick growing *Lonicera*, and a gate to allow access to this front area, which lies at a considerably higher level owing to the contours of the land. Two more gates and more chain link fencing to re-inforce all the hedges admirably fulfilled the safety requirements.

The original rectangle was now to all intents and purposes divided in half, with an enormous apple tree known to be at least one hundred years old sited practically in the centre near the west wall, which obviously had to be the focal point.

Shrubs were to play a large part in the garden we planned – with a view to ease of maintenance in our later years – also an herbaceous border and a lawn were essential.

A slight incline from the north east corner towards the south west, however, made it obvious that to get any sort of level, these features would have to run east and west, and although this would curtail their length it would ensure that in their maturity the shade of the shrubs would not fall in the wrong places.

Bearing in mind all these factors we now set to work with paper and pencil to work out how much space could be allotted to each item to produce a balanced whole. There had to be a path all round the boundary to provide access, not only to the north west corner where there was to be a gate leading to the Vicarage garden over the wall,[2] but also to the south west corner where a place under the same wall was to be reserved for the game bantams who were to provide our breakfast eggs for many years to come.

The south bound path was obviously going to take the most wear and tear, so cement blocks were laid end to end as far as the chicken run, and from there household ashes took over. Small cinders are pleasant to walk on, dry quickly in wet weather, are easy to keep free of weeds and were always in good supply prior to storage heating days – what could have been better? Actually, I was brought up with gravel paths, lovely to look at when they have just been raked over, but the noise they make under one's feet earned them my undying detestation, apart from the fact that a certain amount of beach usually finds its way on to the bed or border. Now that we can no longer supply our own, or even obtain, ashes we have followed the line of least resistance, and allowed most of the paths to grass over, though this does necessitate more frequent attention with the mowing machine.

It was quite quickly established that a strip of lawn five yards wide with the veteran apple tree in the centre, all flanked by another five yards of shrub border on the left, and an equal amount of herbaceous border on the right, would make a very adequate basic plan. This would leave an almost similar strip on each outer edge for the salad crops and a rose bed, this latter to be separated from the more practical portion by another planting of shrubs. Besides the apple tree the only other fruit trees we inherited were a quite large quince tree [*Cydonia oblonga*] opposite to, but at just the right distance from, the back door, and near the northern boundary two plum trees with the most luscious blue fruit – a souvenir of a Herefordshire holiday – and with an eye to the future presented to the former tenants for planting so that they were mature before we took possession. One or two other very elderly one-time espalier apple trees have made excellent supports for rambler roses.

In case it is felt that the vegetable section was strangely inadequate for a country garden, it should be explained that we had been invited to use part of the enormous adjoining vicarage garden for this purpose, to the benefit of the incumbents as well as ourselves. There, too, we were able to establish

Arundinaria anceps/Yushania anceps (Wikimedia Commons – Daderot)

a cutting garden for many plants that quickly outgrew their quarters on this side of the wall.

Having been a garden long before the days of dustbins and refuse collections the chief repository for broken glass and pottery was a large mound against the southern boundary. Literally cartloads were removed from here and from the rest of the garden, and for many months it was a common thing for a dog to appear with a nasty cut on its foot, or for a careless weeder to find an undetected piece of glass the hard way. The best way to make that particular corner safe seemed to be to introduce a strongly growing plant to fill the two-fold purpose of acting as a windbreak, and making an impenetrable cover for the dangerous shards.

At first we did not realise what an excellent choice we had made when we selected *Arundinaria anceps*[3] [anceps bamboo], a slender leaved "bamboo" which has flourished without taking too many liberties – and these are easily curbed – for it has done all that was required of it even though it dislikes very bad weather, which occasionally kills all the leaves, but it soon recovers. For the last three years it has been flowering spasmodically, which is rather alarming as bamboos are said to flower all over the world at the same time and then to die. So far there is no sign of this and even the flowering branches are still surviving, but we are watching anxiously such a valuable source of shelter. There seems a possibility that this fate befalls the clump-forming species rather than one such as this with its creeping stolons.

Notes

1. Probably Caburnside – stated in an article in the *Sussex Express*. 22 April 1938. I am indebted to Andrew Lusted for drawing my attention to this.
2. In Katie's time the vicarage was located at Hampden House in Glynde, with its extremely large garden to the west of Harveys. The vicarage has now moved to the nearby village of Firle.
3. Now called *Yushania anceps*.

Chapter 3

THE SHRUB BORDER (1)

So here we were all ready for the adventure of a brand new garden – our very first planting was the bamboo – what next? The shrub border seemed to be next in importance, but this was going to take a good deal of thought and planning and was, in any case, going to look rather peculiar for quite some times as many of the would-be inhabitants were still only two or three year old cuttings. We were exceptionally lucky in that – as the move was so short – we were able to fetch a batch of plants, place them where we wanted them and return at our leisure for another load. Most of the plants we intended to transfer had been propagated and potted, so that when we had finished, the old garden showed no signs of our departure, which is as it should be.

The major operation was removal of the strawberry tree (*Arbutus unedo*) which appeared to settle remarkably well, but which died quite suddenly some years later, possibly because of the site which lacked the admixture of the heavier loam of its original home. Not only does the slight overall slope of the garden ensure good drainage, but it makes it very difficult to find the damp spots which so many desirable plants appreciate. Lying as it does at the base of the South Downs the basic soil is of course alkaline, but here the long period of its cultivation has stood us in good stead, as there is a deepish layer of more neutral soil over the whole area consisting mostly of domestic ash, which often makes it possible to grow plants which one would not expect to see on the chalk.

Planting a shrub border from scratch certainly provides plenty of problems to trap the unwary, and it would hardly be human to evade them all. Only an experienced planner plants his shrubs far enough apart, for the novice cannot visualise their probable size after a few years' growth. Then there is the ratio of deciduous shrubs and evergreens to be considered – here we failed badly in not planting enough evergreens, and even to this day this failure has not been entirely overcome, one obstacle being that of finding evergreen shrubs of suitable size which will not object to the chalky soil. If there is sufficient space the ideal is probably one evergreen to every pair of flowering shrubs, these latter being, if possible, shrubs that flower at different periods. Further problems arise with the vexed questions of contrast in foliage colour and texture, not to mention relative heights and flowering periods. So once more the only answer was recourse to pencil and paper and with a list of the available material at hand to make a plan which, at first, seemed as though it would prove an insoluble riddle. One has to remember too, that if one is an inveterate collector there will certainly be further additions at any moment for which space will have to be found.

My actual introduction into the joys of gardening came suddenly and unexpectedly in my late teens. My mother had always been keen and I grew up surrounded by a fairly wide selection of plants which would nowadays, I fear, be considered rather dull. Besides, like a good many other young people, I was inclined to look on gardening in general as an essential chore, and not as an inviting method of spending one's time and energy. My interest in natural history, and wild flowers in particular, had always been strong and had been fostered by several eminent botanists whom I had had the good fortune to meet, so that I had covered a good deal of Britain in search of them. This botanical training has always stood me in good stead, both in the unravelling of Latin names and in family identification. Not one but two dedicated gardeners came into my life during this period, and played a considerable part in shaping my future by giving me treasures such as I had never dreamed it was possible to grow in one's own garden.

Capitulation eventually came when I went, in early May, to spend a weekend near a large general nursery. Sheer chance (or was it fate?) led my steps along the path by the alpine plunge beds, and the temptations there offered were my final undoing, when I discovered that any one of them could be mine for the now trivial sum of nine-pence.[1] *Gentiana acaulis* [stemless gentian] with its wide trumpets of vivid blue was the first selection, then *Androsace sarmentosa* [rock jasmine] with its soft pink clusters, *Vitaliana primuliflora*[2] a grey mound covered with yellow primroses (how did they do it? It is a shy flowerer), *Antennaria dioica* [mountain everlasting], that delicious native with bright pink flower heads over silver carpets, and *Arenaria balearica* [mossy or Corsican sandwort] which, if it likes you, will fill a cool spot with softest green and star it with dainty white flowers – alas! there is not a spot in this garden it will even consider at present, try as we may.

Such then were the beginnings from which all the rest has sprung, just as the hedgehog led us to iguanas! – but that is another story.[3] An appetite was whetted which will obviously never be appeased. In fact the war intensified the hunger, for it was no longer possible to visit new plants, so the only way to see fresh faces was to acquire them as seeds, cuttings or plants from any available source.

Incidentally, the other (better?) half of the "we" stands for my husband[4] who was drawn into the gardening fold after the war more or less in spite of himself, but who is always an aider and abettor, and after some training has become a useful asset, particularly where muscle is required!

In those far off days there were several fruitful sources from which new contributions frequently came. Instead of the seeds to which a Royal Horticultural Society's member is now entitled on application, one used to fill in a short questionnaire as to the type of plant which suited one's conditions, and in due course an exciting parcel of plants and cuttings was received, many of them normally unobtainable by an amateur – an event much to be regretted when it had to be discontinued.

Another treasure house on which it was wise to keep a watchful eye – and for that matter it still is, though without quite such notable results – was Woolworths.[5] Many a rare, and now expensive, shrub still happily growing here was bought there between the wars for the noble sum of sixpence.[6] In fact, from here came what is now our tallest and most beautiful tree, *Gleditsia triacanthos,* the honey locust, with its dainty ferny foliage, yellow flowers, and the really wicked three pronged thorns which give it its specific name, and which are capable of impaling a bird unlucky enough to fly against one.

One of the people who was so influential in my gardening career was the incumbent of a neighbouring parish and an equally ardent plantsman,[7] though in his case there was no consideration at all of aesthetic values, everything was planted in straight rows beside the garden paths as if in an open air museum. Every few weeks we visited each other's garden to inspect any new acquisitions. The great thing was that while he could only cope with rooted specimens, I could have any propagating material that appealed to me. Needless to say every advantage was taken of this wonderful opportunity, and to the fact that his tastes were very catholic a good many plants here bear witness to this day.

As we planned to make our lawn as much like an outdoor room as possible we planned to put the taller shrubs along the southern side of the allotted space to make a screen, as the sharp fall of the ground behind then meant that the boundary hedge was inadequate for this purpose. Shorter shrubs were then to be arranged in two large curves meeting at the centre front, forming sheltered nooks for the smaller plants which appreciate such a position, and also bearing out the principle of surprise. As a corner piece, and to soften the junction of bed, lawn and path, a prostrate *Juniperus sabina* 'Tamariscifolia' [Savin juniper] was planted at each end – these fulfilled their purpose admirably for a good many years, but unfortunately eventually fell victim to the die-back disease to which they are apparently prone, even in the wild, and had to be removed.[8] As the eastern end of the border seemed to need more definition another *Lonicera* hedge was planted to run from the edge of the lawn southwards well down past the quince tree [*Cydonia oblonga*] and the bamboo, and this proved a very satisfactory move.

Gledistia triacanthos (Wikimedia Commons – Kevmin)

Shrubs of any size were, of course, very much at a premium among such a collection of youngsters, so that the first step was to erect a rough trellis of poles most of the way along the back of the potential border and to plant several strong climbing roses, including such well tried favourites as 'Dorothy Perkins', 'Hiawatha' and 'Evangeline', whose enormous clusters of pink roses always reminded us of Alexandra Day,[9] and a dainty little climbing China rose [*Rosa chinensis*] whose buds are as exquisite as those of the better known bush type.

A place of honour at the far end of the back row was given to a bird cherry (*Prunus padus*) raised from seed personally collected in Scotland, where I never saw it making more than a large bush twelve to fifteen feet high. Here, however – probably due in part to its proximity to the site of the ancient pigsty – in a few years it achieved its normal height of about forty feet, and annually fills the whole garden with its scent during its all too brief period of blossoming in May. An interesting point about this tree is the extraordinary contrast between the intense fragrance of its flower (or is there a faint hint of shoe polish?) and the noxious odour of its wood when it is cut – in fact Frenchmen refer to it as "stinking wood". Actually, the tree could not have been better placed for it gives welcome shade over a wide area throughout all the hottest hours of sunlight, besides breaking the force of the south west gales with its resilient twigs. And how the birds love its fruit which are always cleared long before they are anything more than green marbles.

Next to this and seemingly far enough away we put a maidenhair tree (*Ginkgo biloba*) which had been languishing in a large pot for some years. Now after thirty years it is just overtopping the bird cherry [*Prunus padus*], and in spite of its rather fastigiate growth shows that it would have been much better planted several feet further away. We have never been able to prove the sex of the tree but it is very beautiful in autumn when its foliage – each leaf the exact shape of a single giant pinna of the fern from which it takes its name – turns to pure gold. In sharp contrast the next planting was the darkest obtainable buddleia [*Buddleja*] with intensely silver leaves – a family having the merit of speedy growth.

The centre positions of the row were given over to sturdy specimens of both male and female sea buckthorn (*Hippophae rhamnoides*), another splendid wind resistant shrub with narrow silver leaves, and as both sexes were planted, masses of bright orange berries which are usually disdained by birds. Although rather too free with suckers – one purpose of their lives being to fix

Hippophae rhamnoides (Wikimedia Commons – gbohne)

sand dunes – these were most satisfactory for a good while until a particularly vicious wind twisted the by then sizable trunk of the female, and split it right to the ground, a treatment which not even this stalwart could survive. As not even a sucker was left the male was finally removed for something more choice. Between these two, but in front of them to gain contrast, the deep green *Berberis* x *stenophylla* [golden barberry] was introduced, but this too threatened to annex the whole border, and in spite of it undeniable beauty when wreathed with its yellow flowers this suffered the same fate.

Having by this time become aware of the value of winter flowers, the next two plantings were *Lonicera fragrantissima* and *Viburnum fragrans*[10] – [winter] honeysuckle and Guelder rose[11] respectively. The latter, if not pruned too severely, makes a graceful bush whose every twig is tipped in quite early autumn by dainty pink clusters of scented flowers, which can make an unforgettable picture against the limpid blue of an October sky. But the former? – it took more than twenty years to make up our minds that its room would be preferable to its company. Heresy no doubt, but it makes a gaunt old bush which is very difficult to prune successfully, and quite often the birds or frost deprive one of the rather small though admittedly wonderfully scented flowers which hide in pairs under the heavy leaves.

There are two near relatives to be recommended *Lonicera standishii*[12] and *L. x purpusii*,[13] but having grown them all only the latter remains, and that is banished most unkindly to an inhospitable corner, which treatment it suffers quite unmoved.

Notes

1. This, of course is nine old pence under the pre-decimal £sd system, which ended in 1971. Equivalent to four 4 new pence.
2. Now known as *Androsace vitaliana*. It does not appear to have a common name.
3. Told in her book *Living with Reptiles* (1961).
4. Frank Smith (1904-1975). The likelihood is that Katie took possession of the garden in 1939. The "we" therefore cannot refer in all instances to her husband, whom she didn't meet until 1941, and who didn't move into Harveys until their marriage in 1952. She could be using "we" to refer solely to herself, or she could be referring to herself and her mother – Caroline Pickard, who lived with her until her death in 1943, and/or her father – Tom Pickard, who lived with her until his death in 1955.
5. A chain of nationwide general stores that closed in 2009.
6. Converts to three new pence.
7. Arthur George Gregor (1867-1954). He was the vicar of nearby Firle, and a Fellow of the Linnean Society.
8. This is probably a reference to the rust fungus *Gymnosporangium sabinae*.
9. The Alexandra Rose Day is a charitable fund raising event held in June in the UK since 1912 by Alexandra Rose Charities. It was launched on the 50th anniversary of the arrival of Queen Alexandra from her native Denmark to the UK.
10. Some publications state that *V. fragrans* is a synonym of *V. farreri*, but *RHS Plant Finder 2023* lists them as separate species.
11. The Guelder rose is *Viburnum opulus*. The common name sometimes used for *Viburnum farreri* is Farrer viburnum.
12. One cultivar is 'Budapest'.
13. One cultivar is 'Winter Beauty'.

Chapter 4

THE SHRUB BORDER (2)

Amongst the melange of more ordinary shrubs which were put in to fill the rest of the available space, a few stand out for special mention, and three major errors crept in unawares of which two are still with us. *Cornus mas*, or Cornelian cherry, first came to our notice as an unassuming bush of about six feet, and of course made an instant appeal with its little ruff of yellow stars in earliest spring, so one was obtained and planted close to the foot of the bird cherry [*Prunus padus*] as being a warm sunny corner where the amber fruits, from which it takes its name, might ripen. Ever since that day we have been struggling to prevent its becoming a sizable tree which it just cannot be allowed to do, though we have not been able to harden our hearts sufficiently to annihilate it altogether, always supposing such a thing were possible with such a willing grower.

The second mistake was to introduce a rooted sucker of that very lovely dark lilac *Syringa* 'Souvenir de Louis Spaeth', which would have formed a complete copse if it had not been banished after considerable effort. Never, never plant a lilac that is not grafted unless you want to spend your life rooting out suckers long after the parent has gone, at any rate on alkaline soil.

The third misfortune was the acceptance of an innocent seeming plant of one of the larger polygonums – relatives of the dock family – about which, far too late, we were given several warnings. We believe the species in question to be *Polygonum cuspidatum* [Japanese knotweed].[1] For a number of years it stayed in a neat clump, then, alas, it started to suffer from territorial aggression, and to send up strong shoots everywhere, though regular mowing has so far prevented it from actually crossing the lawn. On the credit side there is no doubt that it is one of the most striking plants of the winter garden. It makes a branched clump of stout stems about four feet high, every twig festooned with almost translucent flowerets similar to those of the very well known Russian vine (*Polygonum baldschuanicum*).[2] In October the leaves, branches and seed pods turn to an arresting and most unusual shade of bright cinnamon brown which catches every gleam of winter sunlight. No weed killer seems to have the slightest effect on the outlying suckers so we just keep digging away at a nuisance we would not really like to be without.[3]

Kerria japonica, both the seldom seen and most attractive single flowered species, and the ever popular jew's mallow with its golden tuffets,[4] Chaenomeles red and white, berberises, hardy hibiscus in various colours, and hebes were some of the commoner fry scattered along the border and keeping company with them were three rather special spireas which are a real standby on chalky soils, and which certainly rank among our most freely flowering shrubs. One of the most charming, *Spiraea thunbergii* [spirea], which is often forced by florists for the early spring markets, utterly refuses to have anything to do with chalk. However, *Spiraea* 'Arguta' fully lives up to its name of "Foam of May" to be quickly followed by *S. x vanhoutei* which, though slightly more leafy, is just as effective. The third, another still later flowerer which makes a particularly shapely bush of tall, arching wands thickly set with neat clusters, is *S. veitchii*.

Flowering currants, *Ribes sanguineum* and its varieties, too do well here and like the spireas have not so far suffered from bud damage, possibly owing to their strong scent which some people cannot abide. Their tassels come in shades of pink and red and never fail to make a show. They also have the merit of opening their buds in water if the branches are pricked in tight bud – even though the resultant flowers are nearly white they are doubly welcome on a bleak spring day. The *piece de resistance* of this family, which has proved quite hardy in these parts, is the Californian species *R. cruentum*[5] [Sierra gooseberry] which deludes many people into thinking it is a fuchsia when the arching stems are crowded with the small scarlet pendent blooms amongst the fresh green foliage – a closer look soon reveals the relationship to the gooseberry. This, by the way, makes an excellent wall shrub.

Two more items among the taller ranks at the back which would be very

THE SHRUB BORDER (2)

Ribes sanguineum (Wikimedia Commons – Patrice78500)

much missed should accident befall them are very different in character. The first is the May flowering tamarisk (*Tamarix pentandra*),[6] which has slender upright branches, fine, almost heather-like foliage, and large plumes of pink flowers. This is a Mediterranean relation of the familiar seaside species whose August flowers are a much less striking colour. The other notability is a rather uncommon Chinese shrub, *Decaisnea fargesii* [blue sausage shrub], belonging to a most unusual genus,[7] and seemingly indifferent to sun and shade, with greyish stems like those of an ash reaching a height of six feet or more, with very large pinnate leaves ideal for screening. Its green petalled flower clusters appear in late April or May, when a late frost will often ruin one's chances of the fruits which are its chief claim to fame. These consist of long solid pods – reminiscent of broad beans – which ripen to a curious metallic blue, and contain rows of dark shiny flattened seeds (which germinate easily) deeply embedded in a very adhesive translucent mucilage.

Two of the three front line shrubs which have given particular pleasure over the years also started life here as sixpenny[8] bargains from the famous store. One is a constant reminder of happy days in the Swiss Alps, and has the distinction of being the only dwarf rhododendron which will grow on alkaline soil without help, *Rhododendron hirsutum*, the rosy red Alpine rose [also known as hairy alpenrose]. This veteran began to look rather aged two or three years ago and was treated to a thorough watering with the chemical mixture of iron, Sequestrene,[9] with the immediate result of an almost entire rejuvenation and an absolute mass of bloom. This is now a regular treatment as a spring tonic.

The second of the pair is a member of a genus which has been curiously neglected – though recently more frequent mention of these has cropped up in the gardening press – sweet box – *Sarcococca confusa*. A low-growing sturdy evergreen of about three and a half feet high, quite indifferent to shade, and whose white flowers consisting chiefly of microscopic petals and conspicuous stamens, will fill the whole garden with the fragrance of vanilla – or some say honey – from Christmas onwards for several weeks. An absolute must for those who appreciate a scented garden, and a trouble-free plant which obliges with self-sown seedlings all ready to make an excellent low hedge. The equally sweet *S. hookeriana* var. *digyna* [Himalayan sweet box] has a rather more warmly attractive appearance on a cold January day on account of the mauve anthers and pinkish purple tint of the willowy young growths.

Tamarix pentandra/Tamarix ramosissima (Wikimedia Commons – Sten Porse)

The last shrub of the original planting which is of particular interest is a New Zealander, a low growing stiffly-branching semi-evergreen, *Hymenanthera crassifolia*[10] [thick-leaved mahoe], which has the distinction of belonging to the violet family [*Violaceae*]. Its flowers almost need a magnifying glass to appreciate the perfection of the tiny mauve pansies which cluster thickly along the undersides of the branches and which are followed by the small matt white berries much beloved of harvest mice.

Two or three large shrubs had been reserved for the partition between the roses and the utility bed nearer the greenhouse. The choicest of these was a sturdy specimen of the Japanese bitter orange [better known as trifoliate orange] – now called *Poncirus trifoliata*[11] but then known as *Aegle*, whose curiously jointed growth and stout spines would deter even the most determined entrant if it were used as a hedge. This covers itself in spring with large rather ragged white flowers and generally manages to ripen a good crop of purely ornamental small velvety oranges about the size of a golf ball, which in a warm season will produce enough pips to raise another generation. Its companions were *Ceanothus* [California lilac] 'Gloire de Versailles', whose colour is a little too pale to be really effective in such a spot, and another spirea[12] – known as *Holodiscus discolor* [oceanspray] – whose long, drooping, lacy plumes of creamy white always attract attention in July.

It is now time to turn our attention to other parts of the garden, but as a final gesture and as a substitute for the shrub screen which we were eagerly anticipating, as well as to provide shelter to encourage its growth, we planted a row of Jerusalem artichokes [*Helianthus tuberosus*] right along the south side of the shrubs, which fulfilled its purpose magnificently – besides providing some winter vegetables – and was easy to remove when it had done its bit.

Notes

1. Now called *Reynoutria japonica*. It is not listed in RHS Plant Finder 2023, which is hardly surprising as it is an offence under section 14(2) of the Wildlife and Countryside Act 1981 to plant or otherwise cause to grow in the wild any plant listed in Schedule 9, Part II of the Act, which includes Japanese

knotweed. The species is also classed as "controlled waste" under part 2 of the Environmental Protection Act 1990, and therefore requires disposal at a licensed landfill site. Some owners are unable to sell their homes because of Japanese knotweed in their gardens. The threat from this plant was not fully appreciated at the time *A Garden Grew* was being written.

2. Now called *Fallopia baldschuanicum*.
3. Glyphosate is reported to be effective against Japanese knotweed, although it can take several years to fully eradicate it.
4. It is the single-flowered species *K. japonica* that seems to be referred to as jew's mallow, with the double-flowered cultivar *K. japonica* 'Pleniflorum' being called batchelor's buttons.
5. The correct name is *R. roezlii var. cruentum*.
6. Some authorities, including *RHS Plant Finder 2023* provide the alternative name *T. ramosissima*.
7. And belonging to a most unusual family – *Lardizabalanceae*.
8. Converts to three new pence.
9. Presumably a trade name for sequestered iron – a mixture of ferrous salts and EDTA (Ethylenediaminetetraacetic Acid). On chalky soils a lime-induced chlorosis can occur in which leaves produce insufficient chlorophyll. Sequestered iron is used as a tonic to counter this. If ferrous salts alone are used they become insoluble due of the presence of lime, and are thus unavailable to plants. EDTA is therefore added to make iron available. This is achieved without adjusting the pH value, as sequestered iron has a near neutral pH.
10. Now called *Melicytus crassifolius*.
11. Now called *Citrus trifoliata*.
12. Not, strictly speaking, a spirea.

Chapter 5

THE HERBACEOUS BORDER

The Herbaceous border seemed to be the next section to tackle so that a clearance could be made of some of the many boxes, pots and even piles of plants laid on the ground, and their contents could be settling down to a new season's growth. Incidentally we had moved into the house in the first days of January which could have not been more convenient from a gardening point of view. Here again a careful plan was prepared to try to get the right balance of height, colour and spread, though there was no room to follow the counsel of perfection to put in more than one specimen of the many plants for which we needed accommodation, but we did our best to avoid the "spottiness" which often results from such an omission. Do not forget this is a collector's garden!

Such purely perennial borders are now more or less a thing of the past but at that time we did our best to live up to the traditional pattern of graded heights, early flowers and late, and as many contrasts of bloom colour and foliage texture as could be managed. Had space allowed, our taste would have run to an all white or pale yellow border, to the reds of oriental poppies or phlox, or to the blues of delphiniums, echinops and scabious with silver foliage plants, but these dreams were not to be realised. The very name herbaceous border really underlines its limitations for of course this means that except for the often attractive outlines of the withered stems, especially when rimed with frost, there is little or nothing to be seen in the winter months, as the plants have fulfilled their yearly cycle of growth between spring and autumn.

The first step was to mark the limits of the back row by planting a 4 foot bush of *Chamaecyparis* [false cypress] 'Fletcheri' at each end, a decision we are only beginning to regret now that they are showing signs of the ravages of time in that their glorious blue has been burned by hot sun and also by frost and snow, and that they are beginning to fall apart at the tips. It will leave a sorry gap if they have to be removed – the space would be welcome but they are popular bird sanctuaries apart from anything else.

This bed was not as long as its shrubbery counterpart, as a little grass path was made from the boundary to the lawn about two thirds of the way along, in pursuit of the policy of breaking up the formality of the area as much as possible. The bed beyond the path housed our small collection of soft fruits and also two apple trees [*Malus domesticus*] we thought would be desirable acquisitions – Lane's Prince Albert as a general purpose fruit, and a Laxton Pippin[1] for dessert. The former flourished but the latter, in spite of all advice received and acted upon, from reducing the rooting area to extra careful pruning, refused to do anything but send up long whippy shoots with never a sign of producing fruit so it was finally removed. Actually, the veteran tree at the bottom of the garden often produces more fruit than we can use, even though the apples will keep round to the next March, so it is not really important. We also imported a conference pear [a cultivar of *Pyrus communis*] but this only does itself justice about once in every five years – if the bloom is not frosted, then wasps or birds spoil the fruit long before we realise that it should have been protected weeks earlier. At the moment its fate is very much in the balance, although it may be reprieved as a support for clematis species.

Anyway, back to the herbaceous border where rudbeckias or cone flowers, red hot pokers, heleniums, the giant golden rod [*Solidago gigantea*] and the blue flowered globe thistle (*Echinops*) made a sufficiently imposing background. Delphiniums were indispensable – two large clumps of mixed shades – Michaelmas daisies [*Aster*] and monk's hoods [*Aconitum*], the large gold plate achillea [a cultivar of *Achillea filipendulina*], soft pink sidalceas and shasta or moon daisies [*Leucanthemum* x *superbum* and *L. vulgare* respectively], single or double, and phlox in many colours, paeonias, irises and erigerons [fleabane], silvery artemisias, the golden daisies of anthemis, *Anemone japonica* [Japanese anemone] in pink and white for early autumn,

Solidago gigantea (Wikimedia Commons – Pethan)

oriental poppies [*Papaver orientale*] and mullein (*Verbascum*), lovely primrose 'Gainsborough', 'Pink Domino' and terracotta 'Cotswold Queen',[2] these and many others made a colourful picture.

Campanulas of the peach-leaved (*persicifolia*) type are almost a weed on this soil, but very pleasant with their stiff spikes of clear white and shaded blue saucers. They play an important part in linking the various sectors of the garden into a whole. Another subject seldom seen nowadays which comes into this category, and which sows itself about mildly into what are generally ideal places, is the old-fashioned sweet rocket (*Hesperis matronalis*) both white and pale lavender, which fills the garden with its unmistakeable sweetness. Still another of similar habit, but alas! without the scent, is an equal favourite of the country garden, honesty (*Lunaria annua*), here in white, a rather sad pink, and what might almost be called magenta, making a wonderful contrast with the brilliant greens and yellows of May. If the clusters of young seed heads are picked while still green and preserved by standing in glycerine and water for a few weeks they are nearly as lovely for winter decoration as their silvery skeletons when they are ripe.

Here and there among these more usual denizens of such a border several plants outstanding for their size or shape were introduced to counteract any impression of monotony. *Lavatera cachermeriana*[3] is a handsome pink-flowered mallow with stout six to seven foot stems and lasting in flower for weeks at a time. An equally impressive clump was made by *Buphthalmum speciosum* – the yellow ox-eye from Hungary with bold heads of orange suns.

Centaurea macrocephala [giant knapweed] precedes this with lemon yellow powder puffs enclosed in calyces of gleaming coppery scales. Towering above them all to a height of ten feet or so nearly every year was a chance seedling of the giant hogweed (*Heracleum mantegazzianum*) whose cartwheel umbels of dull white florets are often two feet or more wide, making it an outstanding addition to any garden. True, the basal leaves are rather large but they can be quietly removed one at a time, and it is not any more generous with its seedlings than any other member of the parsley family [*Apiaceae*]. Recently this plant, which is, in any case only a biennial, has achieved notoriety as a source of dermatitis, but it does not seem to

Centaurea macrocephala (Wikimedia Commons – Dwight Sipler)

qualify for our blacklist as we have handled it with impunity at every stage of its development as have other friends. Possibly the danger time is in really hot weather when one's pores are all open to receive the poison which is also more active under such conditions.[4]

No such border would have been complete without at least a few clumps of soft mauve catmint (*Nepeta* x *faassenii*) to mask the edge where lawn and border meet, in company with clumps of 'Mrs. Sinkins' [a *Dianthus*] and other pinks which revelled in the southern aspect – as did a colourful selection of rock roses [*Helianthemun*] – 'Wisley Primrose' with silvery foliage, double pink 'Rose of Leeswood', 'Butter and Eggs' in soft yellow, and others in brick red, flame, orange, cream and white. About a yard away from the front edge a little service path meandered the shorter growths of dwarf Michaelmas daisies [*Aster*], tradescantias [spiderwort] with their unending supply of three-petalled flowers, soft rose-purple saucers of *Sedum spectabile* [ice plant] for the butterflies, heucheras [coral bells] and the like. But this little path lead to an experiment which failed.

It has often been mooted as a good idea to plant paving stones or paths with various thyme species and varieties intermingled to make a tapestry of colour and a warm coverlet for some of the smaller bulbs such as crocuses, and also as a suppressor of weeds, besides adding to the fragrance so much to be desired. The theory is exciting but in practice several snags arose. For the first year or two everything worked perfectly and then the thymes which are, after all, prostrate shrubs, began to develop tough woody trunks and wiry roots which made competition very hard for the bulbs, and the ever-lengthening creeping and rooting branch tips began to invade and strangle the less sturdy growth within their reach, besides providing wonderful cover for a large proportion of the garden's slug population. Finally, after a battle royal, for they are certainly aggressive colonisers, they were finally ejected. Possibly they would not take such determined possession on acid soils as they are natives of our South Downs.

But what a lot of work this border entailed, for to be really effective such a plot has to be kept in apple-pie order. We had tried to choose varieties which did not need staking – almost the most distasteful chore of all – but there were always wilful plants which had to be restrained. The dead stems had to be cut down in autumn or left for winter furnishing and removed in spring, and every two or three years everything had to be dug up and parted, or else even with constant attention to feeding there was a diminution of vigour. So gradually there began the infiltration of plants which were really rather more suitable for the type of garden into which this was developing, and one by one most of the original inhabitants were transferred to the vegetable garden where, planted in straight rows, their maintenance was immeasurably easier.

But more of this anon – there is still the rest of the garden to plant.

Notes

1. Not listed in *RHS Plant Finder 2023*, or on the Internet.
2. To clarify, Gainsborough, Pink Domino and Cotswold Queen are all cultivars of *Verbascum*.
3. Now called *Malva cachermeriana*.
4. Contact with the sap of this plant prevents the skin from being able to protect itself against sunlight, leading to phytophotodermatitis – a serious skin inflammation.

Chapter 6

THE ROCK WALL

Two or three years before we came here to live a large wooden shed had been acquired as a garage, and placed at the north west corner of the house, necessitating the removal of a large quantity of earth to make a way in. This left a sharp cliff some four feet high along the south side of the strip of ground running from the back garden to the front boundary. Would we have known then as much as we know now about building dry walls for no doubt we could have channelled the procedure into the right direction. This has certainly not been a case of ignorance being blessed! Not until too late by many years did we realise that the facing of stone slabs of all sizes and shapes which were placed against it was far from pleasing to the critical eye, and that much of the material could have been used to greater advantage. We have always wanted to rebuild it, turning at least the front half into two tiers, but a good many favourite plants are very well established in it, or in the border at the top, and many of the stones would be too heavy for us to handle personally, so we have regretfully given up the idea, and try to keep the worst faults well covered with plenty of vegetation.

The drive itself and the area in front of the house was paved with large stones, but unfortunately, in order to protect the cellar below, shallow gutters had to be made against the house so that a limited number of climbing plants could be allowed, charming though they would look against such a backdrop. A good many plants have found themselves happy homes in the crevices and at one time *Crocus tommasinianus* [early crocus] outlined the slabs with mauve every February, but now, alas! an unknown marauder plays such havoc with them that they might just as well not be there at all. At first the blame fell on the sparrows though yellow flowers are more often their target, but it has been suggested recently that it may be the work of wood pigeons which seem yearly to become more daring. The devastation is almost too complete all over the garden to implicate blackbirds or even mice, which in any case prefer to dig for the bulbs themselves. It would of course have been easier to cement between the stones but this would have been out of character. Actually, we would like to see a greater variety of plants established but visiting cars discourage the use of a large portion of this area.

The dainty little blue-eyed grass (*Sisyrinchium bermudiana*) – actually a native of Canada – makes a charming picture when numerous starry flowers open in the sunshine in company with white *Sedum album* [white stonecrop] and the fluffy pink heads of the Cornish variety of the native kidney vetch, known as *Anthyllis vulneraria dillenii*.[1] *Thymus nitidus*[2] [thyme] finds both the wall and the paving very much to its liking, seeding itself about and making shapely compact one foot high bushes of fine dark foliage which literally smother themselves in lilac pink flowers. Originally planted by our predecessors on the top of the wall snow-in-summer (*Cerastium tomentosum*) quickly spilled itself down the front and on to the paving just where the overhanging *Cupressus* [cypress] makes a very inhospitable spot but provides the *Cerastium* with a situation in which it revels, and where its silvery masses of foliage literally snowed under with the clear white flowers make an unforgettable sight. After it has flowered we pull handfuls away, and it shows no sign of overstepping its present boundary.

The south side of this paving is shaded by the L-shaped wing of the house. There creeping Jenny (*Lysimachia nummularia*) and the little ferny-leaved *Cotula acaenifolia*[3] [buttonweed] with its creamy buttons, find things very much to their liking. Some day the golden leaved form of creeping jenny will come to join them. *Corydalis lutea*[4] [fumewort or yellow corydalis] makes a ribbon of green and yellow all round the base of the house walls and submits imperturbably to being ruthlessly cleared off two or three times a year.

Vying with the *Corydalis* for pride of place is another almost invincible plant, but one so charming that only when it starts to trespass in real earnest do we take strong measures with it. *Campanula poscharskyana*[5] [Serbian bellflower] to give the villain its true name, sends up the wall – hugging sprays of tender blue about one foot long – these flower for several weeks

Cerastium tomentosum (Wikimedia Commons – Hugo.arg)

after which all the old leaves and stems can easily be pulled away leaving a tidy clump of clear fresh foliage – a welcome sight in late summer. An ideal plant for such a spot. It has also taken possession of the lower shady part of the offending wall, and so long as it does not try to ascend to the summit we rather welcome its attentions as it is now very difficult to introduce new plants where the earth has slipped away behind the facing stones. Our dogs[6] much appreciate this plant as a salad but we have not observed that they particularly avoid the neighbouring rose of Sharon [*Hypericum calycinum*] as they are said to do.

Sharing the sunbaked patch under the evergreens near the front gate with the snow-in-summer are two other rampant growers which now that they are established make a colourful tangle for weeks. The first, the owner of a somewhat formidable name, *Ceratostigma plumbaginoides*, which resolves quite simply into plumbago or leadwort, is a low spreading shrub covered with brilliant blue phlox-shaped flowers throughout the late summer and foliage which takes beautiful tints. It pays for cutting back hard in early spring or it can become straggly. The other is the lovely, but potentially

Convolvulus althaeoides (Wikimedia Commons – Tigerente)

dangerously invasive and consequently rarely seen, *Convolvulus althaeoides* [mallow bindweed] with finely cut silvery foliage, and most eye-catching clear pink trumpets, whose long stems climb up into the trees and hang in festoons among the sombre green. An awkward plant to place in the average garden here it can do no harm.

Another very unusual plant which has flourished in the same corner but which over all the years has always disappointed us of the orange berries it is reputed to produce is the shrubby horsetail (*Ephedra gerardiana* var. *sikkimensis*) which is a low tufted rush-like evergreen shrub, not immediately arresting perhaps, though a good foil to the more colourful trio, but of particular interest to botanists as being the link between conifers and flowering plants. Also competing in this area and helping to keep each other under control are the rambling roots of the rose of Sharon (*Hypericum calycinum*) and the least attractive of the Californian fuchsias (*Zauschneria*)[7] with all too few orange scarlet flowers.

Notes

1. Some sources identify *iberica* as synonymous with *dillenii*.
2. Possibly refers to *Thymus richardii nitidus*.
3. Not listed in *RHS Plant Finder 2023,* nor on the Internet.
4. *Pseudofumaria lutea* appears to be a synonym.
5. Not to be confused with a similar-sounding species *Campanula portenschlagiana*.
6. The dogs appear in a photo in the Introduction, and are described in Chapter 11.
7. A synonym appears to be *Epilobium canum*.

Chapter 7

THE UPPER LAWN

The narrow border along the top of the wall and many of the crevices were packed with a goodly selection of the colourful plants common to such a setting, where they settled down quickly and covered a good deal of the long bare stretch with a coat of many colours. *Aubretia* in shades of mauve and pink, thrift (*Armeria*) in pink and white, or rust red in the case of *A.* 'Corsica', more rock roses [*Helianthemum*], white *Arabis* [rockcress] double and single, *Alyssum* brilliant yellow, soft primrose and in the cultivar 'Dudley Neville' biscuit-buff, *Dianthus* [pinks] large and small – speedwells (Veronicas) and more campanulas in pale blue and dark, Alpine phlox in cool lavender and pinks, and silver and mossy saxifrages [rockfoil] all played their parts.

Alongside the garage a selection of periwinkles (*Vinca major* and *V. minor*) were put in what was virtually a sunless bank and although they have to be ruthlessly trimmed every year their clear blue and white stars are some of spring's earliest harbingers, and their gold and silver variegations stand out clearly amongst the green. We sometimes regret that we did not heed the donor's warning about the vigorous growth of *V. acutiflora*, as it is now taking over under all the hedgerows, though the fresh green of its young growth is especially welcome.

A flight of steps had been made for access to this upper level and at the top of these on the right hand side another *Cupressus* [*lawsoniana*] *fletcheri* [Lawson's cypress] of the same age linked with those of the back garden, and with less exposure to the elements looks considerably less vulnerable.

On the left a plant of the now sometimes despised *Paeonia lutea*[2] [yellow tree peony] has in course of time proved that this was an ideal choice of site, as its modestly hanging flower heads freely produced in its maturity can be appreciated to the full from below. On the same side a prostrate *Juniperus horizontalis* [creeping juniper] clothes the side of the steps with its fine branches which take a purple flush in winter, as on the east side does the old-fashioned candytuft (*Iberis sempervirens*), where, in the shelter of the *Cupressus*, it frequently opens its dazzling white flowers in January. In front of this on the angle of the wall an unusual evergreen from Africa, *Othonnopsis cheirifolia*[3] [Barbary ragwort], with strap-shaped almost succulent smooth grey leaves, has triumphantly endured a good many vicissitudes of snow, frost and burning sun but always covering its scars in an incredibly short time. This has the additional interest of solid yellow blunt-petalled daisy flowers over a long season.

Conspicuous among the plants put into this little border was a collection of colour forms of the pasque flower (*Anemone* now *Pulsatilla vulgaris*) so called because not only does it flower around Easter time, but also because the mauve dye extracted from it was used for colouring the shells of Easter eggs. It is actually a native of some of the chalky upland pastures of Britain and said to have been introduced by the Romans. The type plant has very finely cut leaves much like a carrot and short stems supporting large upturned cups of deepest violet, all of which characters it retains under cultivation, though curiously the best known for gardens is a much stouter plant with foot high stems bearing paler flowers, which does not apparently merit recognition as a separate species though so unlike in appearance. In both cases the flowers are followed by veritable struwwelpeter[4] heads of silky threads clearly showing the relationship with clematis. If these seeds are sown directly they are ripe they germinate readily, but are loath to do so if kept for any length of time. There is a lovely pale pink variety with, unfortunately, a delicate constitution, and various deepening shades of reddish pink, also a white.

There was still some indecision as to what to do with the erstwhile cabbage patch between the rock wall and the *Thuya* [western red cedar] boundary, but there were even yet some rather important shrubs in need of placing, so finally the westernmost corner was marked off diagonally and prepared as another small shrubbery and here was planted the *Gleditsia* [honey locust] mentioned earlier. To keep it company another sixpenny[5]

Pulsatilla vulgaris (Wikimedia Commons – Orchi)

treasure from the same source was put in beside it, *Caragana arborescens* or Siberian pea tree, which is notable for thriving in just such poor dry soil as this spot provided. The yellow flowers are abundant in May and the dark pinnate, rather heavy looking foliage, is a good foil for the feathery sprays above it. At the feet of these, two a small plant of *Daphne mezereum* [mezereon, or February daphne] found the semi-shade it likes.

Prunus x *subhirtella* 'Autumnalis' [winter-flowering cherry] was another homeless waif, so with no more ado a similar treatment was applied to the matching angle at the other end of the lawn, and here again no better site could have been chosen either for protection from the north and east, or for a dark background for the dainty palest pink blossoms which appear at intervals throughout the winter. Midway between these corners an already stalwart *Prunus* 'Kanzan' [flowering cherry] was quickly settled in. Within a month or two a seedling Judas tree (*Cercis siliquastrum*) also joined the assembly. All of them were liable to grow too large for such a small garden where trees, as such, would be kept to a minimum, but this seemed to be the place where they would be least likely to outgrow their quarters to an embarrassing degree.

The gift of a nice young plant of *Juniperus squamata* 'Meyeri' [Himalayan juniper] created another small problem, and there was an up and coming *Picea glauca* var. *albertiana* 'Conica' [Alberta spruce] – a cutting from an old friend's garden, not to mention a really prostrate juniper, possibly true *J. squamata*, which all seemed as if they would make good neighbours and so were finally set at intervals along the back of the little border at the top of the rock wall, where they have created a pleasant diversity of form.

One of the gifts which my father[6] received on his retirement after a lifetime of estate management was a handsome stone sundial, and this was carefully centred on this piece of ground where it makes an imposing focal point. For a short period after the outbreak of World War II an attempt was made to grow vegetables around the sundial but the resulting crops were so poor that later on the whole area was finally grassed down.[7]

Cercis siliquastrum (Wikimedia Commons – Kousvet)

Notes

1. Not listed in *RHS Plant Finder 2023*, nor on the Internet.
2. Now called *Paeonia delavayi*.
3. Now called *Hertia cheirifolia*.
4. German word meaning shock-headed.
5. Converts to three new pence.
6. Thomas Pickard.
7. In 1939 the Ministry of Agriculture urged people to "Dig for Victory" and at one point 40% of the country's vegetables came from home, school and community gardens. These vegetable plots became affectionately known as "victory gardens".

Chapter 8

THE MAIN LAWN AND SIDE PATH

Now that spring was rapidly advancing – it had taken a good three months to sort things out so far – the next important job seemed to be the actual planting of the lawn, now a dejected looking patch of well-trodden soil. As it happened we could not have had more seasonal weather. The site was well dug and raked into a fine tilth in record time, and then sown with the finest mixture of grass seed recommended for an alkaline soil. The whole area was thickly covered with pea boughs over which was thrown an old strawberry net – making a most successful combination against marauders of all kinds. Germination was not only quick but remarkably even and it seemed no time at all before we were able to mow it – the blades set very high – the first time.

There had been some doubt as to whether seed would prove more efficacious than turf as being cheaper, but the means have certainly justified the end as most of the lawns around here that have been turfed soon grow more of the soft golden downland moss than of grass. Our mixture has stood up to very hard usage from both dogs and humans as well as to droughty summers, when, being in full sun from sunrise to mid-afternoon, it has become brown and parched. At one period it developed many unsightly patches of broad-leaved plantain (*Plantago media*) but before we got around to applying weedkiller we took in a homeless Guinea pig who thereafter spent her days on the lawn in a portable run (and her nights in a parrot cage indoors!).[2] She appeared to regard plantains as caviar so that they were constantly nibbled tight down to the taproots, a treatment they did not survive. We missed Squiffles (her greeting was a cross between a squeak and a whiffle) very much when in due course she died at a ripe old age, but so far a lawn cleared of that particular unsightly blemish remains as a memorial to her labours. A selective weedkiller would now be necessary to take the matter in hand.

The only areas which to date had had no attention at all were the square patch directly outside the back door and the path leading from this door down the south side of the house to the back gate. Directly outside the back gate was, and still is, a large and obviously already aged *Berberis darwinii* [Darwin's barberry] with a single trunk and shapely head which covers itself with orange tassels every spring. This veteran appears to have the gift of eternal life having survived the onslaughts of the builders, and the near massacre which is necessary to keep it from completely blocking the light from the window beside it, or in fact from becoming top heavy and falling over as it breaks every kind of tie we have so far devised. Nearly every year it is used as a nesting site by a thrush or blackbird, who evidently think it cat-proof as well as within arm's length of supplementary rations for the family, a lesson they seldom forget in later life.[3]

A narrow border at the base of this wall is edged with a mixture of spring crocuses, and is one of the few real suntraps where *Iris stylosa* (*I. unguicularis*) [Algerian iris] can have its back to the wall to encourage production of winter blooms. The hardy shrubby plumbago (*Ceratostigma willmottianum*) [Chinese plumbago] also revels in the warmth here and produces endless flights of deep blue flowers among the autumn-tinted foliage until quite late in the year. Opposite this, and standing against the safety fence which, with its gate, filled the remaining side of the remaining quadrangle between the coal shed and the neighbour's wall, were placed three tubs containing standard box trees [*Buxus sempervirens*] carefully clipped into globe shapes, which gave us considerable protection before bamboo was really established. Over the years the roots of the two outer ones have obviously made their way through the bases of their tubs and become really handsome specimens which are very popular roosting places, particularly for the blackbirds. The centre one which was stood on an old millstone still retains its original contours.

On the garden side of the fence a *Skimmia japonica* [Japanese skimmia] was introduced and although the glossy leaves are attractive at all times it

Berberis darwinii (Wikimedia Commons – Stan Shebs)

was some years before we acquired the fragrant male-flowered partner which this species has to have before it will produce the clusters of large scarlet berries which, in some gardens, make it really spectacular in early spring. Several members of the family are allergic to chalky soil which probably accounts for the fact that it seldom gives a really first class performance – a good many of the embryo berries fall off soon after they have formed.

A seedling *Clematis tangutica* [golden clematis] came our way later and this was planted against the fence where it makes one of the most breathtaking displays of the garden during the late summer by festooning everything within its reach with myriads of small golden lanterns which in time give place to silvery silky seed heads, both excellent for cutting. This does not in the least mind having the tips of its over-eager shoots nipped back while it is in full flower, in fact it very obligingly lengthens its season of blooms in consequence.

Going from the back door past the *Berberis* we come to another gate and thence down a sloping path to the final gate leading to the road. On the right-hand side going down is a very narrow border under a waist-high wall topped with two feet of wire netting. This border was for some now unknown reason chosen as a suitable spot for the tall white autumn flowering Japanese anemone (*Anemone* x *hybrida*). In the centre a plant of the so-called Russian vine (*Polygonum baldschuanicum*),[4] renowned for its speedy growth, was trained over the netting, whose lacy, silver-white sprays make a combination of the utmost charm with the solid white cups of the anemones. These have found this site – cool and slightly damp – very agreeable, and have been joined by the palest pink and double white cultivars to give a long lasting flowering season.

On the other side of the path the border widens considerably between the bases of the two large chimney stacks and then narrows again. Turning left at the bottom towards the front of the house was another narrow path for easy access to the cellar window at the end of the L-wing for depositing vegetables for winter storage. This path led finally up two stone steps to

Clematis tangutica (Wikimedia Commons – bcanna)

emerge near the front gate. It did not take long to find out that vegetables in the cellar meant a lot of extra work, and also that it was much better to have the front garden entirely separated from this side entrance so that tradesmen were safe from canine attention of however friendly a nature, so this path was blocked where the house is within 3 feet of the front wall. This corner was ideal for the whippy shoots of *Forsythia suspensa* [weeping forsythia] which fall over the wall in a fountain of gold in the years when it does not suffer too many depredations from the birds. It has to be pruned ruthlessly every year, but its long green wands effectively soften the angle of the house.

A knowledgeable friend who had had considerable experience in garden planning advised us to plant a yew tree (*Taxus baccata*) against the lower chimney breast near the gate to act as a windbreak – a piece of advice for which we have been profoundly grateful, for east winds in particular certainly take every advantage of rushing through the narrow passage between the houses. The recess between the yew and the forsythia made an ideal home for a young wintersweet (*Chimonanthus fragrans*)[5] in spite of facing east and therefore not getting much sun. It has rewarded us every year with the piercing sweetness of its purple-lined waxen blooms in the darkest days of winter since we discovered that the flowers are produced on two-year old wood, and that in consequence it needs very special care in the pruning, which is regularly necessary to prevent it from becoming a sizable tree. Just above the yew tree we had found the sturdy and obviously very aged trunks of the hardy grape vine (*Vitis vinifera*) which in good seasons produces numerous bunches of the small green grapes so beloved by the birds. The autumn colour of its handsome leaves draped across the sombre yew is also most welcome.

The angle of the upper chimney seemed a good place to display another gift, the twining *Akebia quinata* [chocolate vine], and we quickly realised we had found a splendid camouflage for the unsightly elements of plumbing which are grouped in that area. This berberid[6] is a strong grower and practically evergreen, and provided it is prevented, by judicious pruning, from becoming too weighty, it threads its way among the pipes and falls down most effectively from the top of the chimney as a loose curtain. The five-lobed leaves are slightly leathery in appearance and each April every leaf joint produces a cluster of chocolate-coloured flowers rather resembling a miniature bunch of grapes of which the larger and darker female blooms at the top are fragrant. Altogether a most satisfactory and worthwhile acquisition although unfortunately it seldom produces its fleshy fruits for which it is said to need cross-pollination – even from another species.

In the remaining angle between the chimney and the top gate one of the Wisley contributions, *Pyracantha crenatoserrata* [Chinese firethorn], has filled the space almost too adequately, especially as the orange-red berries are hardly allowed a tinge of colour before every one is removed [by birds]. As, however, this is another draughty spot, only useful for an equally tough specimen it has been allowed to stay, although it practically doubles its height every year and has to be drastically discouraged.

The bed between these two chimneys seemed just right for a collection of bearded irises [*Iris germanica*] which make an enchanting picture for the short period of their blooming, but which are rather dull between times. Anyway, they increased so speedily and prolifically here that they just had to be moved to a bed in the orchard where they could spread to their hearts' content. Their place was taken by *Alstroemeria ligtu* [Peruvian lily] hybrids which have flourished, particularly relishing the occasional soaking from overflow pipes. Once established these are almost indestructible for their roots gradually pull themselves to unbelievable depths as we found to our cost when we tried to get some out for a friend – we went down eighteen inches and then gave up! Unfortunately, some time later we committed the disastrous error of introducing some of their more plebeian orange and yellow confreres – these multiply so rapidly from seed and division of the tubers that we are beginning to believe this mistake is irremediable. Bushels of tubers have been dug out and – too late – seed heads carefully removed but they still threaten to overpower the aristocrats. We dare not risk weedkiller as they all appear above ground at the same time and are then virtually indistinguishable. One day I believe our patience will be exhausted and that we shall sacrifice all of them for a dose of sodium chlorate.[7]

For some time a handsome specimen of *Solanum crispum* 'Autumnale'[8] [Chilean potato vine] found a happy home against the house in this recess but as it is almost impossible to fix adequate support on such a house an August gale brought it crashing to the ground in full flower and so splintered the main stem that it never even tried to regenerate.

However, two other plants have almost made up for it. A visit to the Channel Islands produced cuttings of a shrub one seldom sees – *Corokea* x *virgata* [wire netting bush] – a New Zealander which has twiggy branches, small dark leathery leaves startlingly white on the undersides, and small starry yellow flowers followed by bright orange berries. A specimen put in the shelter of the yew has now made a handsome shrub completely unruffled by bad winters, until a heavy snowfall in early December did its unsuccessful best to defeat it.

Tucked in between this and the yew a cutting from Glyndebourne of the gloriously scented *Daphne odora* 'Aureomarginata' [golden-edged winter daphne] has made a yard wide bush from which handfuls can be cut to bring indoors from January onwards, though we cannot induce it to flower anywhere else in the garden in seemingly more desirable places. This is one of the few daphnes that does not mind being picked, as every cut grows another two or three shoots, so the more it is cut the more it flowers, though the foliage always looks as if it needs a steady diet of Sequestrene.

Notes

1. Also known as hoary plantain.
2. A shaded area should always be provided when using an outdoor run, as Guinea pigs can suffer from heat stroke, heat exhaustion and dehydration. In addition, we now recognise that Guinea pigs are gregarious animals, and should always be kept in groups. In some countries, for example, Sweden, it is illegal to keep a single Guinea pig.
3. Katie is, of course, referring to the plethora of berries which adorn this species.
4. Now *Fallopia baldschuanicum*.
5. Now *Chimonanthus praecox*.
6. Although both *Akebia* and *Berberis* are in the same Order – Ranunulales, they are in separate Families, with *Akebia* in the Family *Lardizabalanaceae*, and *Berberis* in the Family *Berberidaceae*.
7. The use of sodium chlorate as a weedkiller was banned in the EU in 2009 because of health concerns and its environmental toxicity.
8. Also known as *Solanum crispum* 'Glasnevin'.

Chapter 9

THE BULBS (1)

All this time nothing has been said about the bulbs and their allies which make up such an important part of our garden scene. We have always tried to keep a more or less accurate list of the plants we acquire which, after a number of years, makes very interesting reading. In all humility this once reached the record total of approximately two thousand species and cultivars at a period when we were growing many more of what might loosely be termed "Alpines" than we do now. When war came there was no time for propagation or indeed attention of any sort – a neglect which decimated their ranks and a good many of the casualties have not been replaced. The chief reason for this is that the maturing of the trees and shrubs has very much altered the character of the garden, and therefore suitable sites are much harder to find. Another lesser governing factor is the almost hundred per cent increase in the cost of plants which automatically limited their replacement in such large numbers, not to mention the angle of labour saving.

This catalogue of ours however reveals that at least one sixth of the plants originally brought here consisted of the bulbs, corms and tuberous species whose appeal we always find irresistible to such an extent that it is now impossible to dig up any plant without removing a few bulbs as well. Some like *Crocus tommasinianus* [early crocus] increase rapidly from seed and until three years ago spread a magic carpet each spring, now only a few tattered fragments of mauve betray their presence. The fingered tubers of the mourning widow or snake's-head iris (*Hermodactylus tuberosus*) multiply underground at a great pace, so that their long grassy leaves, which appear in autumn, become quite a nuisance. Unfortunately, they are not nearly so prolific with their charming flowers – silvery grey standards and velvety falls of brown so dark that it appears black – though a warm spot at the base of a wall encourages them to put up a better show.

The first spring that we were here revealed that there were already a good many daffodils and hyacinths in the ground so these were collected and planted all round the edges of the garden where the survivors still multiply. Among them was a very attractive double pink hyacinth often tinted with green in the centre, which is unfailing in its display in any and every situation. Some time ago a survey was held of double hyacinths so we sent specimens hoping the plant might prove to be of historical value, but its only claim to fame seems to be that it has no ovary. Even so it never seems to fail to charm all beholders.

With us we brought a comprehensive collection of crocus species, both spring and autumn flowering, whose increase has been only too well kept in check by the depredations of succeeding generations of the aptly named field mice. Orange *Crocus ancyrensis* 'Golden Bunch', *C. chrysanthus* cultivars in creams and yellows, *C. etruscus* 'Zwanenburg' in pale violet, *C. balansae* 'Zwanenburg' whose golden petals are backed with rich mahogany, mauve *C. sieberi* and bronze *C. susianus*[1] weave a colourful carpet in early spring. A particular favourite is *C. biflorus weldenii* 'Fairy', the outside of whose petals is almost true blue, opening to reveal a cup of purest alabaster.

In September a goodly sprinkling of *C. speciosus* and *C. zonatus*[2] reintroduce touches of mauve in many odd corners, to be reinforced by *C. asturicus* in deep violet, which is followed in its turn by the feathered purple spears of *C. laevigatus* 'Fontenayi' and the slender creamy tubes of *C. ochroleucus* which often hold on to nearly Christmas. Two more uncommon species with mauve flowers do exceptionally well here and both appear to be unattractive to mice. *C. sativus* with its near violet petals and lolling orange-red stigma has had a bad reputation for scanty flowering, but we find it particularly likes to be moved frequently, after which it flowers freely. *C. serotinus salzmannii* is a very strong grower with long pointed rosy-mauve petals whose colour matches that of its neighbour *Geranium sylvaticum* [wood cranesbill], a strong growing wildling which, with the equally robust *Papaver rupifragum* [Spanish poppy], has taken up its abode at the base of one of the stone vases where the geranium's flights of soft mauve complement the pale brick-red poppies for months on end.

Crocus sativus (Wikimedia Commons – KENPEI)

As early as the end of January hitherto undetected *Anemone blanda* [Balkan anemone] will often surprise us with its deep blue petals spread widely to every beam of sunshine, not to be outdone in colour or brilliance by the neatly packed spikes of various chionodoxas [glory of the snow] which spill out almost overnight. By this time, too, the winter aconites (*Eranthis hyemalis*) will have shaken out the Toby frills round their golden globes, and the earliest snowdrops, or fair maids of February (*Galanthus nivalis*) will have anticipated Candlemas Day.[3] Aconites are a little inclined to sulk for a while after they are first planted, but once firmly established they soon turn their attention to colonising by abundant seed.

Like so many other bulbous plants aconites prefer to be moved – should it be necessary – just as the flowers are fading and before their roots start work again for the next season. Snowdrops in particular are very fussy about this and in fact, one will often be met with disappointment if one plants dry bulbs at any other time of year as they may take several seasons to make any kind of show. This piece of knowledge proved very useful to us and we took good care to import plenty of flowering clumps which, when carefully divided and distributed, gave the immediate impression of an established garden and no hint of this apparently unorthodox treatment.[4]

The previous autumn a good collection of tried and trusty friends among the enormous possible selection of daffodils [*Narcissus*] had been packed into deep boxes and these too were set out in groups making a really worthwhile show where it was so badly needed. 'King Alfred' and 'Rembrandt', 'Carlton' and 'Fortune', 'Mary Copeland' and 'Cheerfulness', 'Mme. Krelage'[5] with primrose and snowy perianth, and 'Mrs. Backhouse',[6] the original pink daffodil, short trumpets and long, single and double, all types were represented, and have since multiplied unceasingly almost to become an embarrassment.

A few dozen chionodoxas [glory of the snow] both pink and blue, and an equal quantity of the deeper Russian blue squill (*Scilla bifolia* and *sibirica*)[7] on the top of the rock wall have increased to make a truly blue carpet in early spring, and another patch under the *Forsythia* in the shrub border have spread far and wide into an eye-catching splash of colour against the bare ground, though through no fault of its own the latter usually fails to complete the picture with its yellow bells.

Grape hyacinths (*Muscari*) were perhaps a slightly risky introduction for their reproduction rate is astronomical but who could resist the glorious azure spikes of *Muscari* 'Heavenly Blue' and even the darkest tones of the true species. If one is really ruthless their spread can be controlled, but it would be very convenient if they could keep their leaves tidily underground until flowering time, and not send them up in autumn to be battered by the elements.[8]

There are other species for which there can be nothing but praise and surprisingly we inherited one of these, the late flowering *M. neglectum* [common grape hyacinth] whose very dark bells have tiny frills of white and which smell deliciously of ripe plums. The tassel hyacinth (*M. comosum*) is a curiosity which sends up eighteen inch spikes of queer brownish flowers with an upright purple tassel of sterile blooms at the top from which it takes its name. This again has a very near relation known for obvious reasons as the feather hyacinth (*M. comosum* 'Plumosum') with its light bluish mauve petals finely shredded and curled in a most unusual and attractive manner.

The musk hyacinths (*M. moschatum macrocarpum* and *M. ambrosiacum*)[9] in shades of dull yellow and misty purple, smell entrancing, but do not take very kindly to our soil or climate and are really best planted in a cold greenhouse. The gem of them all, in our opinion, is the far from easy to grow, here at any rate, and no doubt more to be desired in consequence, is *M. paradoxum* (now *Bellevalia pycnantha*)[10] [paradoxical grape hyacinth], whose solid spikes are an unusual shade of greenish slate blue.[11]

Another genus to which we have always given particular attention is that of the so-called autumn crocus or *Colchicum*, which is not of course a crocus at all but belongs to the lily family,[12] with all its floral parts in sixes instead of threes. This too, accounts for the enormous leaves which follow the flowers and persist until the middle of the next summer, which means that almost inevitably they tend to be planted towards the back of any border or in rough grass. Mostly the flowers are very upstanding so that this is not quite the disadvantage it may seem. The native *C. autumnale* [meadow saffron] is generally the first to bloom in September with dainty tubes of palest mauve. Here this is usually closely followed by *C. x agrippinum* whose pointed lilac petals are thickly tessellated with darker purple. This charming plant increases rapidly and has less conspicuous leaves though unfortunately the long corolla tube makes them rather apt to fall over in rough weather – the flowers too are an epicurean delight for slugs!

October sees the appearance of the true *C. speciosum* and its very handsome hybrids. *C. speciosum* itself has spectacular stiffly stemmed purple goblets half-lined inside with cream. The hybrids vary considerably in size and depth of colour, but the choicest of all in purest dazzling white is *C. speciosum* 'Album'[13] which fortunately increases freely here, as in fact they all do. Last but not by any means least, and not usually venturing to show its less well richly chequered flowers until November, is the rather more uncommon *C. variegatum* which can be easily identified by the leaves, which not only have undulating margins but spread themselves flat on the ground.

Another bulb well established here when we arrived, and which could also become a nuisance were we not to keep a strict control on it, is the Star of Bethlehem (*Ornithogalum umbellatum*) though when it opens its branching inflorescence of green-striped white flowers in the spring sun one could forgive such an aptly named plant almost anything. One of the most enchanting of all bulbous flowers is, we think, another member of this genus,

Muscari comosum 'Plumosum' (Wikimedia Commons – Salicyna)

drooping Star of Bethlehem (*O. nutans*), whose tall spikes of nodding bells glisten with an almost pearly gleam of silvery whiteness. This too increases freely both by means of seed, and of the extraordinarily small bulbs which are in surprising contrast to the amount of growth above ground. This too, is one of the quickest plants to disappear when its life cycle is complete, it is literally here today and gone tomorrow, for at least another ten months.

There is another uncommon species of the same family hailing from the Pyrenees which has become naturalised in various parts of England and acquired the title of Bath asparagus[14] – *Ornithogalum pyrenaicum* – nearly as attractive in appearance with long spikes of greenish stars on eighteen inch stems.

Tulips? – well, many times we have planted them with enthusiasm but unless they are taken up after flowering – just when one's at one's busiest – they tend to disappear for ever, so except for the odd few which have established themselves we tend to turn a blind eye to the inevitable temptation. *Tulipa tarda*, *T. batalinii* and *T. linifolia* have proved more faithful friends than most. *T. sprengeri* surprised us by opening its buff-backed scarlet petals to the sun one day in late May – one of the last to flower – as neither of us remember ever acquiring the bulbs.

Notes

1. Now called *Crocus augustifolius*.
2. Now called *Crocus kotschyanus*.
3. Candlemas Day occurs 40 days after Christmas Day and relates to the Presentation of Jesus at the temple in Jerusalem.
4. Many plant sellers now offer snowdrops "in the green", and this is by far the best way to buy them.
5. Not listed in *RHS Plant Finder 2023*, but listed on the Internet as 'Mrs. Ernst H. Krelage'.
6. Not listed in *RHS Plant Finder 2023*, but listed on the Internet as 'Mrs. R. O. Backhouse'.
7. *Scilla bifolia* is more commonly known as the Alpine squill. *S. sibirica* is known as the Siberian squill.
8. I would echo Katie's warning about introducing grape hyacinths into borders, as they spread at an amazing rate and are very hard to eradicate. They are best planted in containers, and flower heads need to be removed before seeds form.
9. *Muscari moschatum* and *M. ambrosiacum* are both now known as *M. muscarimi*. *M. macrocarpum* is a distinct species, and not a subspecies of *M. moschatum*.
10. Now called *Bellevallia paradoxa*.
11. *Muscari* 'Valerie Finnis' (pale blue) and *M.* 'Pink Sunrise' (pink) are two superb cultivars, perhaps not available in Katie's day.
12. Although *Colchicum* resides within the order Liliales, the family name is *Colchicaceae*.
13. This plant name indicates a cultivar; not a hybrid.
14. More commonly known as spiked Star of Bethlehem.

Chapter 10
PROPAGATION

During the war years everything remained more or less static, except for the gradual emergence of the basic plan of the garden into a recognisable whole with shrubs maturing rapidly and a well established lawn. True, many of the smaller plants had disappeared, but those that were left no longer showed the unmistakable prim outlines which are the almost unavoidable evidence of recent planting.

But the very first catalogue which dropped through the letterbox, when such things became possible, had an almost immediate effect on the scene for the insatiable appetite for new plants, which doubtless to some extent satisfies the spirit of adventure, had been sharpened almost to breaking point by the long deprivation. What is that indefinable something which attracts one person to a particular plant while leaving another quite unmoved? Is it form, or colour, or scent? Who knows! but then who knows why some collectors are drawn to antiques or philately!

There is no doubt that as a result of considerable botanical study in the field I find immense interest in growing plants without any particularly obvious charm which tends to make our friends raise their eyebrows – but then sometimes their choice leaves me as cold as any flower could do! My luck in getting the most coveted seeds from the distribution lists is probably directly attributable to this fact that I fancy what most of the others disregard.

At one time there were a good many wild flowers growing here from seed personally collected during extensive travels in Britain in search of them. Even now the dainty pink flowers of hairy mallow[1] (*Althaea hirsuta*) from

Kent, wood vetch (*Vicia sylvatica*) from Gloucestershire, the true *Potentilla fruticosa* [shrubby cinquefoil] from Teesdale, the fine leaved umbellifer,[2] *Meum athamanticum* from Scotland and a host of others linger to carry my memory back to the years between the wars when they were collected, to fit quite comfortably into the garden scene.

Indeed, what better way is there of indulging one's acquisitive passion for plants than raising seed? The thrill of new seedlings breaking through the soil is almost as great as that of a parcel of hitherto unknown plants. The infinite variety of seeds themselves and indeed of the fruits which contain them, is a study all of its own. The only equipment available in those days was a cold frame, a dark potting shed, and an endless supply of pots, but we flatter ourselves that we achieved quite a good measure of success. Actually, the percentage is still much the same in spite of improved conditions as except when raising one's own seed it is often not available in the first flush of viability.

A source of considerable pride are flourishing clumps of several species of *Fritillaria* raised in this way. Certainly with most bulbous plants it does mean a wait of three or four years for the first batch to come to maturity, but after that there are always new ones coming along so that one does not notice the time lag. A glance at a present day trade catalogue shows that these clumps are quite literally worth their weight in silver, if nothing more valuable, the average price of a single bulb being around seven shillings and sixpence,[3] and some, of course, are not obtainable except by means of seed.

A large clump of the beautiful yellow hardy *Arum creticum* [Cretan arum] bears similar witness to the virtues of patience, as, among others, do goodly patches of *Cyclamen europaeum*[4] [purple cyclamen], *C. repandum* [spring sowbread], and *C. cilicium* [Cilicean cyclamen] besides several of the larger, rarer, and very decorative alliums such as the rose-coloured *Allium schubertii* [ornamental onion] and the deep violet *A. giganteum* [giant onion].

The story of the original *A. albopilosum*[5] [Persian onion] has often caused amusement. Browsing, many years ago, round the horticultural section of an agricultural show, I saw for the first time this plant on display and determined that by hook or by crook I had to buy that bunch at the end of the show sale. This was successfully accomplished and the bunch was put into a large vase where the flowers lasted for some weeks. Just as we were about to throw them out we noticed that the earlier flowers had matured into

Meum athamanticum (Wikimedia Commons – Jean-Claude Calais)

capsules of gleaming black seeds. These were duly sown and from these came our original stock. They are now beginning to sow themselves about quite discreetly, but in any case few people could have anything but admiration for the large globes of star-shaped silvery-blue flowers. The white-whiskered leaves which give the species its name are quite unobtrusive, and once the flowers are over, if the shapely heads are not needed for indoor decoration, they quickly dry up and disappear.

Apart from bulbs there are endless desirable plants in the way of herbaceous plants as well as shrubs which could easily be raised from seed – irises and paeonias are particularly rewarding. Brooms, both species and hybrids, need very little attention and with berberis and mahonia make a grand contribution to the garden scene – the rest are legion.

And we must not forget the bewildering array of annual flowers with which so many empty spaces in a new garden can be filled. During the first few years after the war we tried almost every one of the rarer hardy and half-hardy annuals we could lay our hands on, as well as many of the better known species. Biennials too came in for their share of attention, but were rather too much bother on the whole as they do not take quite so kindly to being planted where they are to grow. Besides, annuals have an engaging habit of re-sowing themselves, so that one can enjoy their offspring for several seasons without further effort – a boon to the busy gardener.

Particular favourites we would not like to be without are *Crepis rubra* [red hawksbeard] with enchanting rose-pink miniature dandelions on silvery stems, *Anagallis linifolia* 'Phillipsii'[6] [blue pimpernel], a deep gentian blue large-flowered version of the familiar scarlet pimpernel, which flowers for weeks on end, *Hibiscus trionum* [flower of an hour], whose white and yellow cups are centred with purplish-brown, and are followed by the most attractive seed pods. This plant used to be known as "Goodnight at Noon" but the modern improved version manages to keep awake all day. *Felicia bergeriana* – the African kingfisher daisy, with its brilliant blue petals, and its fellow countrymen *Dimorphotheca*[7] [star of the veldt], *Arctotis* [Africa daisy] and *Ursinia* [parachute daisy] in shades of salmon, orange and

Crepis rubra (Wikimedia Commons – Krzysztof Ziamek, Kenraiz)

pearly grey are indispensable. *Gilia rubra*[8] [standing cypress] – a biennial with ferny leaves and flowers of the most unusual red is rarely seen. And a most enchanting pair of miniatures for a trough garden or the like are violet cress [diamond flower] (*Ionopsidium acaule*) whose almost invisible foliage is smothered in a myriad of flowers whose four white petals are strikingly tipped with purple, and a grass *Mibora minima* [early sandgrass] – native to Anglesey[9] – whose grey-green tufts are barely an inch high. Once started these two will be a perpetual delight.

Cuttings, too, present an irresistible challenge, and certainly the number of shrubs here which have been grown from cuttings far outweighs that of the bought ones, in any case watching their gradual development is half the fun. Once again the equipment was of the simplest, a cold frame or, for summer cuttings a large sand-filled box covered with a pane of glass. In this mild area hardwood cuttings put into the open ground in October or early November yield a surprisingly high return of success. On one occasion when the frame needed new glass we dug out a square hole about eighteen inches deep – inserted the cuttings at the bottom and laid a piece of glass over the top not entirely excluding the air; the net result was quite satisfactory.

No doubt a higher percentage of cuttings, especially the more difficult ones – will root better if small slips are inserted into a closed glass-covered box of pure sand or other sterile material, and the whole thing then put into a small frame, which gives the effect of double glazing. This is probably the next best thing to the mist propagation which most nurseries

now use. A common fault to be guarded against is the insertion of too large cuttings in a vain attempt to get a larger plant more quickly – it is seldom successful, tempting as it is.

Although converted to plastic pots for most purposes in view of their lesser weight, lesser need of water and much less time and energy for washing, we have a decided preference for clay pots as cutting containers. It is probably only long habit dying hard, but their very thickness seems to give confidence as to the result – apart from the fact that it has to be very strong plastic not to need two hands for lifting when full of damp earth, in spite of claims that they are unbreakable.[10]

Fortunately my gardening friends are all very sympathetic to this irresistible urge to try to propagate any new plant that comes my way. Even if it does not capture my fancy sufficiently for it to become a permanent resident – or it seems as if it may become too large – I still want to live with it for a while to get to know it before it passes on elsewhere. Some species which look as though they will be very amenable refuse utterly to have anything to do with us, while others with which one would expect difficulty go ahead in a surprisingly short time. Of course, a lot depends on getting the right type of cutting at the right season, but we have learnt never to refuse an offer at any season as miracles do still happen.

Buddleias – except those with felted stems and leaves such as *Buddleja crispa* [Himalayan butterfly bush], are almost certainties, but most of the spireas which are such good shrubs on alkaline soils are, for me, very disobliging, as are potentillas such as *Potentilla fruticosa* [shrubby cinquefoil], *P. fruticosa* 'Manchu' and *P. fruticosa* var. *veitchii*. We read recently that spirea cuttings should be taken in December by which time we reckon to be having our winter's rest! Evergreens in the open ground and conifers in pots nearly give at least fifty percent of success, and it is a fetish of mine always, if possible, to insert six cuttings of each species to allow for waste. Clematis such as *Clematis montana*, *C. campaniflora* and *C. orientalis* have given excellent results but *C. flammula* is inclined to be uncooperative. Years ago I was told that *Mahonia* cuttings would only root in water and this has been so successful that we have never tried any other way, though a friend tells me he roots them in the open ground.

Linked with cuttings of course there is sometimes the bonus of a rooted side-shoot which can be detached (this has been our only success with spireas), or a drooping branch which can be layered quite easily – forsythias will usually do this for themselves, as will most honeysuckle species. The handsome [Japanese] wineberry (*Rubus phoenicolasius*) with its crimson-bristled stems will send up a new plant wherever it touches the ground as indeed will most of the family. *Berberis x stenophylla* [golden barberry] suckers freely but these do not always seem to care about being transplanted.

Herbaceous and a good many alpine plants can, of course, be divided and reproduced *ad infinitum* – in fact it is often imperative to do so to keep them within bounds, so that it becomes more of a chore than a challenge. A trick worth knowing with some of the more unwilling shrub cuttings is to tie them in bundles of a dozen or so and bury them almost completely in autumn – by the following autumn a surprising number will have rooted.

Roots cuttings, too, are rather fun but so far we have not been sufficiently ambitious with these though we intend to make further experiments with more interesting material.

Notes

1. More commonly known as the rough mallow.
2. More commonly known as spignel.
3. Converts to 38 new pence.
4. Now called *Cyclamen purpurascens*.
5. Now called *Allium cristophii*.
6. *Anagallis linifolia* is not listed in *RHS Plant Finder 2023*, but is listed on the Internet. *RHS Plant Finder 2023* does however list *Anagallis monelli linifolia*. *Anagallis monelli* is listed on the Internet as *Lysimachia monelli*. All a bit confusing!
7. Although perennial plants of this genus are now called *Osteospermum*, my understanding is that annuals have retained the name *Dimorphotheca*.
8. Now called *Ipomopsis rubra*.
9. Also found on the sand dunes of Merseyside.
10. Current thinking is that clay pots allow better movement of water and air, which benefits root growth.

Chapter 11

THE ANIMALS (1)

A few years after the war the fact of having a completely enclosed garden enabled us to achieve the long-term ambition of keeping a tortoise, which simple fact in itself led to a very long chain of events. Actually, our interest had been further stimulated by the finding on the roadside of a baby hedgehog which we brought home wrapped in a handkerchief (before the days of tissues!) and established in an old chicken coop and run. The nightly saucer of bread and milk[1] became a ritual and many a pleasant hour was spent in the deepening dusk awaiting the faint rustle which heralded his appearance. He spent his first winter comfortably buried in a pile of hay, and as soon as we were sure he was thoroughly awake in the spring we took him to a spot known to be a favourite haunt of hedgehogs and released him.

So not only Charles, but also Jane [tortoises] came to take up residence in the back garden, and made us the recipients of a good many gloomy prognostications as to the awful things they would do to our plants, till even we had a few qualms.[2] But they soon showed us that with very few exceptions they were definitely not interested in our type of plant, much preferring the white clover which had by this time appeared on the lawn and the convolvulus which no amount of hard work would ever eliminate from this soil.

It was obviously no longer going to be possible to grow lettuce, garden peas or sweet peas in this area, and that campanulas of any kind, or in fact most blue flowers, were going to be ruthlessly pruned at short intervals. Nice juicy plants such as *Sedum spectabile* [ice plant] which in early autumn has the flat pink cushions so beloved of butterflies are very acceptable, as are columbine leaves, and of course bright yellow flowers like buttercups and dandelions. Tortoises seem to have an uncanny instinct for recognising lily stems and quietly bulldozing them downwards until they can reach the titbit at the top. But over the years and the gradual expansion of our tortoise population into what might almost be termed a "flock",[3] we have no reason to regret their introduction for the interest they have brought far outweighs any negligible damage. A good many of them have come from people who can no longer keep them for one reason or another.

Here again the urge to collect made itself felt and since then we have acquired specimens of several species, some of them tropical, who spend their winters happily under an electric lamp bulb, while the hardier types sleep away the dark days in the frost proof cellar. It is no uncommon thing on a summer afternoon to find our chairs surrounded by a bevy of eager tortoises begging for a handout of banana or cucumber. They must have a very strong sense of smell, for even if one is feeding to start with it will only be a matter of minutes before all the others converge upon us. One is apt to look on a tortoise as a dim-wit of the animal world, but a more extensive acquaintance with them soon proves that not only are their memories excellent, but that there is more intelligence packed into those small skulls than one would ever have given them credit for. Year after year each one goes back to its favourite haunt directly it is let out in the spring just as if the five month's hibernation had never been.

Bella (*Kinixys belliana*)[4] who hails from the African forest country,[5] has an absolute genius for getting into trouble though after fourteen years residence there is nothing she does not know about her home indoors or out. If she does not approve of the weather on a summer day she thinks nothing of coming into the house and parking herself neatly in the warmest corner. On one occasion she was found in the nick of time floating on the top of a pool which has ever since been fenced with narrow wire netting.

Another time she somehow climbed up and fell over the dividing fence where it passes behind a shed and we had to import a small boy to be lifted over to extricate her from that predicament. Once she caught her shell on a bamboo spike and after thirty-six hours or so was in a very sorry state when she was at last discovered, though she soon recovered. Her worst escapade was to walk out one August afternoon when the gate to the Vicarage garden blew open in a gale, and spent a month on the Downs before she was found in a harvest field nearly two miles away. Our great worry was, of course, the fact that she knew nothing about hibernation and would certainly have perished in the winter if she had not been found. We have never ceased to marvel at the difficulties her short legs must have overcome in the way of large fields of standing corn, and the very thick downland grass which is the result of grazing cattle instead of sheep.

The next addition to the community – which incidentally originally consisted of two dogs, Meg, a Border Collie and Caburn Coral, a blue merle Shetland Collie [see photo in Introduction], who quickly learned to take all newcomers under their protection – were of a totally unexpected and unlikely character. We had been assured that a near relative of the tortoise, a terrapin or water tortoise would do a great deal towards lessening our slug and snail population. So we set out to procure one or two but it proved to be the wrong end of the season and our quest was unsuccessful. However, having fallen victims to the wiles of an astute saleswoman, who had realised that as far as animals were concerned we were, in the language of the day "pushovers", we did not return empty handed.

She had introduced us to two species hitherto entirely unknown to us – green lizards (*Lacerta viridis*)[6] and golden salamanders[7] (*Salamandra salamandra*) – both natives of Europe. Such were her persuasive powers that she had made their housing and care seem to be fairly well within our powers, so that we soon found ourselves *en route* for home with two cardboard boxes, one containing a pair of the lizards and the other a pair of salamanders. It seemed a momentous step at the time but how glad we have always been that we took it.

Green lizards are, as their name implies, beautiful creatures fifteen inches or so in length, whose streamlined bodies are clothed in grassy-green scales except for waistcoats of gleaming yellow. Some of the females have black and white stripes, and sometimes the green is a lovely olive shade, and both sexes develop a flush of brilliant blue on their throats during the breeding season. The salamanders on the other hand favour black and yellow for their livery, these colours being a built-in warning to predators that their method of defence is to exude poison from their pores. Salamanders are amphibians delighting in damp cool spots where they can hide under rocks and emerge at dusk to feed. They look rather like large newts with flattened bodies whose colour pattern is sometimes striped and sometimes in lozenge shapes.

The advent of these creatures led to the first of the consequences for which the tortoises were primarily responsible, because after reading all the information we could find about them we realised that we could not bear to keep them in cages, however palatial, and that if we were going to embark upon keeping reptiles at all we had got to provide them with a home which gave them the illusion of complete freedom.

So while they were spending their first winter in large aquarium tanks, we had constructed on the weedy piece of ground near the west wall, formerly occupied by gooseberry bushes, a large enclosure nine feet by six feet whose walls are about three feet high and – the most important thing of all – fitted with a ledge of zinc jutting out on the inside from under the top bricks, to prevent these inveterate escapees from climbing out.[8] This enclosure was furnished with a roomy square brick box to be filled with peat as a hibernating chamber, and a pool in the shadiest corner, and was then planted with tough plants such as lily of the valley [*Convallaria majalis*], dwarf ivies and ferns for shade and shelter, and flowering plants to attract bees and other insects as a ready-made buffet.

On the outside, between the south wall and the lawn another small pool was made with a sloping ramp with a view to the comfort of wild birds and the tortoises, but although it is immensely popular with the birds it has never, as far as we know, been used by the tortoises.

The arrival of weather warm enough for it to be safe to re-introduce these denizens of slightly warmer climes to outdoor life seemed extra long in coming when we were so anxious for them to be in direct contact again with Mother Earth. Incidentally green lizards cannot live indefinitely away from natural sunlight as other lizards can – it is apparently essential to their

Lacerta viridis (Wikimedia Commons – Uoaei1)

metabolism.[9] But finally the great day arrived in May, and after they had explored every nook and cranny, and selected the hiding places to which they could rush at the slightest alarm, the accommodation appeared to be greatly to their liking.

All this was exciting enough, but yet another event was to turn this into a red-letter day. All through the winter one of the salamanders known as Spots – to distinguish her from Goldie and Stripes[10] – such original names! – whose appetite seemed no larger than that of the others, grew steadily more matronly in outline. Just as I was about to release this one in the reptiliary – the grand name by which such a construction is usually known – something we had read prompted us to keep her under observation for a while longer, and to put her where a considerable depth of water was available. This happened to be a tank previously prepared for newts, with both land and water. To our great delight she almost immediately took up the prescribed position for imminent birth, sitting at the edge of the pond, so we left her alone for several hours.

When we finally decided that it was safe to return we found her taking no further interest in the water, and obviously looking for a convenient spot to conceal herself until nightfall, so we re-united her with her relations. A close inspection of the tank, which was full of thick weed, failed to reveal anything of interest for quite a time, until suddenly an ethereal miniature crossed a clear space, and we were able to congratulate ourselves that we had indeed had the beginner's luck of doing the right thing at the right time. We subsequently found that she had produced at least thirty babies, the tale of whose subsequent life has been told elsewhere.[11] Contrary to the usual amphibian procedure of laying spawn salamanders produce tiny replicas of themselves.

At about this time the long awaited terrapins began again to make their appearance in pet shops. Terrapins closely resemble tortoises but with flatter bodies and generally much longer, thinner tails and are above all aquatic in their habits, spending their nights and cooler days in the water and even hibernating there, if the pond is sufficiently deep. A depth of about three feet of which the bottom third is thick mud seems to be adequate here in the south, but after the most recent notably hard winter[12] cracked even our sheltered pond, and all but killed the inmates, we see to it that by Christmas they are safely installed in a large old-fashioned baby's bath in the cellar, which has a constant temperature of about 40° F [4.4° C].[13]

Salamandra salamandra (Wikimedia Commons – Didier Descouens)

Two species of terrapin are normally available of which one, the European pond tortoise (*Emys orbicularis*) is shown by fossils to have been at one time a native of Britain. These have a very dark coloured shell, almost black in some lights, dotted and streaked with yellow to match the colour of their lower shell or plastron. The other species, the Spanish terrapin (*Clemmys leprosa*) inhabits the waters of most Mediterranean countries, and is generally smaller and as one may expect not quite so hardy.[14] Their greenish-grey shells may easily be mistaken for damp stones when they are basking, and the tiny green and grey stripes on their necks remind one irresistibly of polo-collared sweaters.

So now there was always something to see in the reptiliary whether it was the flashing colours of the lizards darting from place to place, or the terrapins lazing in the sun on the edges of the little pool, or at dusk the gleaming bodies of the salamanders on the prowl, or the ring of expectant toads gathered round the feeding dish.

We were to find that although the terrapins were only too happy to clear up any amount of water snails, it was the salamanders who were worth their weight in the proverbial gold by reducing the slug population. Many a warm moist evening just after the lawn had been mown sees us with a haul of some two or three hundred slugs – secured with a flashlight, a spoon and a tin – and thrown into the reptiliary as an easily secured amd never failing food. A not unpleasant chore which has a noticeably good effect on the neighbouring plant life. Lizards too, will accept slugs, but do not really appreciate the sticky discharge on their faces, which they most meticulously wipe clean on the herbage after a meal.

Notes

1. It is now known that hedgehogs are lactose intolerant, so a diet of bread and milk is totally unsuitable. Hedgehogs should be fed on wet cat food or wet dog food, or on special hedgehog food, with Brambles brand being highly rated.
2. Readers of gardening books may be unfamiliar with tortoises, so some background information may not come amiss. Reptiles with shells are collectively called chelonia (family *Cheloniidae*). In the UK we call the terrestrial members tortoises, the freshwater members terrapins, and the saltwater members turtles. In the USA all chelonia are generally referred to as turtles. As far as keeping is concerned, tortoises can simplistically be divided into Mediterranean species, which hibernate, and tropical species, which don't. After World War Two vast numbers of Mediterranean tortoises were imported into the UK and other northern European countries. Many died or were injured in transit, and the majority were dead within a year due to poor understanding of their needs. These imports were banned in 1984, which led to the import of tropical species which are, in general, unsuitable for life in the UK. Today, it is possible to buy juvenile Mediterranean tortoises which have been bred from those imported prior to 1984. However, these cost in the region of £200 each, which is quite a contrast with the two shillings and sixpence (converts to 13 new pence) cost of a tortoise imported before the ban. Another disadvantage with these juveniles is that they must be kept in a heated vivarium for the first three to four years of their lives. All tortoises are quite challenging to keep, and are not suitable childrens' pets. If you must have a tortoise, buy from a private

breeder rather than a pet shop, and choose the hardiest species – Hermann's tortoise (*Testudo hermanni*). Feed on garden weeds such as dandelion and clover rather than commercial products such as lettuce, which have little or no nutritional value. Katie is uncharacteristically unhelpful regarding which of the three main Mediterranean species she was keeping.

3. The collective noun for tortoises is creep.
4. This is Bell's hinge-back tortoise; one of eight in the genus. All *Kinixys* possess a curious-looking hinge towards the rear of the carapace (the upper shell) which allows them to close the carapace to protect their hind feet and tail against predators. Unlike Mediterranean tortoise species they are omnivores; consuming invertebrates as well as vegetation.
5. This species has a large range across central Africa which includes a number of habitats, including savannah.
6. It is now recognised that the animal that was known as *Lacerta viridis* actually consists of two species – the eastern green lizard (*Lacerta viridis*) and the western green lizard (*Lacerta bilineata*). It is the western green lizard that is encountered in the Channel Islands, France and Italy, but I don't know which species was most commonly imported into the UK. There is also the Balkan green lizard (*Lacerta trilineata*) found in Greece and adjacent areas and Schreiber's green lizard (*Lacerta schreiberi*) found on the Iberian Peninsula.
7. More commonly known as the fire salamander.
8. Katie describes in her book *Living with Reptiles* (see Appendix A) how many of the green lizards introduced into this enclosure escaped (although many of them subsequently returned). People were quite relaxed in those days about non-native animals escaping into the wild, and some even deliberately introduced them. We now have numerous breeding populations of the non-native wall lizard (*Podarcis muralis*) living on the south coast, and at least one breeding population of the green lizard in Bournemouth. The problem with such introductions is that they may displace native species. It is now an offence under Section 14 of the Wildlife and Countryside Act 1981 to release, or allow to escape, any non-native species into the wild. It is therefore imperative that outdoor enclosures are 100% escape-proof, and for green lizards this would require a four foot wall lined with something completely smooth such as sheet steel. It should be noted that import of green lizards, and other European reptiles and amphibians, to the UK ceased many years ago, and there are now only a handful of people breeding such animals. They are therefore quite difficult to acquire.

9. Many reptiles use the UV-B component of sunlight to synthesise vitamin D3, which is required to absorb dietary calcium efficiently; calcium being crucial for skeletal health and overall well-being. UV-B lamps are now available, which means that green lizards and similar reptiles can be kept healthily indoors.
10. The pair of salamanders have somehow become a trio!
11. In Katie's 1961 book *Living with Reptiles* (see Appendizx A).
12. Possibly the winter of 1962/63 when much of the UK was covered in snow and the average temperature remained below zero for over two months. In nearby Kent there were eight foot snow drifts, and the sea froze out to a distance of one mile.
13. Some individuals choose to hibernate on land under leaf litter or something similar.
14. It is now known that there are two, not one, other European species besides *Emys orbicularis*. There is the Spanish terrapin (*Mauremys leprosa*) which lives on the Iberian peninsula, and the Balkan terrapin (*M. rivulata*) which lives in Greece and adjacent countries. These two species were previously assigned to the Caspian terrapin (*M. caspica*) which lives in Turkey and the Middle East. At the time when Katie was writing there were no significant imports of American terrapins. Subsequently, vast numbers of juvenile red-eared sliders (*Trachemys scripta elegans*) were imported from the USA, particularly after the release of the 2014 motion picture *Teenage Mutant Ninja Turtles*. Most of these cute, colourful one inch juveniles quickly died, but those that didn't grew into dull, one foot monsters that became unmanageable and were released into the wild. Here they are thankfully unable to reproduce (because their eggs need prolonged high temperatures to incubate), but during their thirty year lifespan they prey on native animals, including amphibians.

Chapter 12

THE ANIMALS (2)

One summer's experience proved to us that although all these creatures lived together amicably enough there was a grave danger of overcrowding if we indulged too freely in this new collecting craze, besides which, if as we hoped amphibians were to breed, no tadpoles would ever survive in the same small pond as the terrapins. It also appeared likely that the salamanders would be happier in a more shady situation. A likely site presented itself among the plum trees near the original sanctuary – as the reptiliary came to be known – though to avoid disturbing existing trees it would have to be longer and narrower.

By this time "do it yourself" had become the order of the day, so armed with the requisite number of breeze blocks and plenty of the necessary ingredients for cement, we set up as amateur bricklayers, digging out the foundations and levelling them in great style. Unfortunately, nobody mentioned until too late that we ought to have built our corners first so there is a slight discrepancy in the joining of the first course, but this is now mercifully hidden by vegetation. It is an almost exact copy of the original building on the outside, but inside the hibernating chamber is below ground with suitable drainage holes and a shallow pond occupies the whole of the southern end.

Here candelabra primulas [*Primula prolifera*] and the glorious marsh marigold (*Caltha palustris* 'Flore Pleno') have found a position much to their liking. The rest of the space is mostly occupied by three other lovers of cool conditions, a charming lady's smock (*Cardamine asarifolia*)[1] whose dark green persistent leaves are a splendid foil to the china-white flower clusters which appear in February, and make an excellent substitute for the better-known *C. trifolia* [trefoil cress] which will not grow for us. The space is also occupied by the very handsome ostrich plume fern (*Matteuccia struthiopteris*) which has tried to take complete possession and whose deep brown fertile fronds make the most entrancing winter decoration, and by the black, green and silvery foliage sprays of the variegated yellow deadnettle or archangel (*Lamium galeobdolon* 'Variegatum') which is one of the finest ground cover plants now so much in demand – not only because it will grow anywhere, but because it is so easily controlled.

As soon as the residence was complete we transferred the salamanders, leaving the gradually increasing ranks of green lizards and terrapins to enjoy the sunshine. To prove that they found conditions agreeable both lizards and terrapins began to breed, and although we have never yet managed to induce any terrapin's eggs to hatch – no light undertaking! – we have been lucky enough to raise several batches of green lizards from the white parchment-covered eggs which are about the size of small kidney beans. The newly hatched dark brown babies are about two inches long and the thickness of a diary pencil, and are, incidentally, veritable Houdinis! Mostly both species cover their eggs so neatly that one does not detect their presence until too late, as in both cases they have to be hatched artificaially in this country as they need a steady temperature of approximately 80° F [26.6° C], which of course our summers do not often provide. This accounts for their failure to establish themselves in Britain.[2]

Now that more accommodation was available it could not, of course, be be let go to waste, and gradually several species of toads found their way into the old sanctuary and the new building, now designated as "Toad Hall". Common toads [*Bufo bufo*] make interesting pets but the other British toad, the natterjack (*Bufo calamita*)[3] – inhabitants of sand dunes[4] – are most attractive little chaps with a light stripe down the centre of their backs, and an almost mouse-like trot instead of a lumbering hop.[4] Larger versions of these are the green toads (*Bufo viridis*)[5] which come from southern Europe,[6] and have almost identical greenish skins and really beautiful grey-green eyes. It would astonish many people to learn how quickly these apparently dull-witted animals find out where and when regular food supplies appear, and to see as many as eight of them at a time sitting round a a flat tin patiently awaiting their supper.

Bufo viridis/Bufotes viridis (Wikimedia Commons – NobbiP)

One of the favourite foods for most of the hardier reptiles and amphibians is mealworms, the larvae of the species of click beetle [*Tenebrio molitor*] which used to be common in the debris of corn mills. With the aid of these – one's natural antipathy for handling them is soon overcome! – and a large amount of patience it is possible to train most of these little people to feed from one's hand, though, strict individualists as they are, there are always one or two who refuse to be drawn into the circle. But the first time a green lizard gains sufficient confidence to climb into one's hand, and sit there enjoying the feast, gives one a great feeling of humility. Toads are relatively easy to tame, but a conquest which was one of our greatest surprises came when a batch of edible frogs [*Pelophylax kl. esculentus*][7] raised from our original pair, would come out of the pond with prodigious leaps when they saw the buffet was open, and take mealworms from our fingers quite fearlessly. Fortunately, we have a cine record of this almost incredible performance, frogs on the whole, being rather allergic to humans.

Three years ago we had the great misfortune to have a rat invade the sanctuary in the late autumn, so that when spring came the only survivors were the green lizards, one edible frog and one small toad, which meant that we had lost at least three dozen animals – all our original stock and their progeny – and that our records of longevity were spoilt.[8] The lifespan of a salamander has been known to reach twenty five years and that of a frog even longer. We have had considerable difficulty in renewing our stock, as like most other living things except man, their numbers in the wild are decreasing, and they are not so readily available. One of the saddest aspects of the tragedy from our point of view is that all these were hand tamed after approximately twelve years, and now we have to start all over again. We hope the salamanders' poison upset the rat's digestion! At first we thought the intruder was a field mouse and it was not until spring that we realised the truth.

One of the happiest results of the introduction of mealworms into our sphere is the attention consequently bestowed upon us by generations of robins, any one of whom will veritably sell his soul for such delectable fare. We like to regard the whole domain as a sanctuary for any wildlife which we can persuade to make use of it – except rats of course – and particularly for birds of which at least fifteen species show their appreciation by nesting on the premises, but the robins certainly top the poll.

Bullfinches are fortunately still comparatively scarce in this neighbourhood,[9] though last year their unmistakable calls and whistles indicated a breeding pair in the immediate vicinity. Greenfinches, goldfinches and a reduced number of chaffinches are permanent residents but we wish wagtails and flycatchers would move in – we had hoped that the addition of water would attract them. Every year house martins inspect the premises but are unable to attach their nests to the plaster, and although we tried artificial nests the sparrows finally ejected them. It is a pity that the lifespan of a robin is so short, the longest we have been able to keep track of one is four years, and he fell victim to a cat one day when we were out. Piqued no doubt by finding the door shut, Sweety Pie must have gone to the neighbours, and probably being too trusting as well as getting on in years, he was not sufficiently alert to escape capture. He was absolutely fearless of us and the dogs and would perch on one's knee or books without any hesitation – his going left a sorrowful gap in our lives.

Previously we had had another robin literally living with us. Attracted as they are by the mealworms we noticed one day that there was something wrong with his foot but were powerless to do anything about it. It looked as if he had got a piece of horsehair or its equivalent – as these are now a rarity – wound around the ankle joint, but it meant that he finally lost his foot at this point. Then he lost two toes on the other foot by being caught in an unprotected trap set for mice in a neighbouring garden. However, this too healed successfully but in October he decided that life would be much easier for him if he moved in with us.

We have a room which is almost entirely devoted to pets, where the tropical reptiles live, and dogs sleep, and here "Bobbie" made himself quite at home. He slept on the fold of a curtain over the cellar door so that there was no tiresome perching to bother about – he bathed in the lizards' water pan and dried himself on the fender, and sang lustily on the wireless. On really bad days he refused to leave the house and followed us from room to room. Every night for eight months we had to leave the back door open after till it was almost dark until Bobbie was safely in – (they are almost the last birds to go to roost). Then one night in May he sat on the gate, obviously hesitating about breaking the routine, but finally disappeared into the trees across the road and we never saw him again. Evidently love had the greater pull but how we missed him!

After we had finished building Toad Hall there was still a goodly pile of cement-making material left, and our zest for growing more water plants not zest being satisfied, we finally decided that another little pool would make a very pleasant oasis in what can be rather an arid spot in full summer. A site was cleared approximately in the middle at the north side of the lawn and excavation were begun. We expected to find solid chalk before we got down very far, but to our surprise we were able to dig out three and a half feet of soil without any trouble at all, and is probably one of the reasons why some of the plants which are less rabid in their dislike of lime, will grow for us.

The general shape was long and narrow, but we tried to avoid making it look like a disused bathtub by curving the edges slightly. All round we made a shallow trough of varying depth to accommodate the plants. This was the pool in which Bella, the tortoise, so nearly drowned herself. It has fulfilled its purpose admirably, and it is very pleasant on a hot afternoon to sit in the shade and look out on the clumps of astilbes in various shades which follow the primulas, globe flowers [*Trollius* spp.] and irises of early summer, and we no longer need to envy the possessors of natural pools though of course it will never be large enough!

Needless to say this pool gave us an excuse for adding another species to the existing crowd, and a few tadpoles of the edible frog (*Rana esculenta*)[10] whose legs are a gastronomic delicacy on the continent, laid the foundation of a colony which still persists. This choice was taken because once these

The Pet Room in 1961. *Living with Reptiles* Plate 31. From top to bottom – *Pogona vitticeps, Iguana iguana, Tiliqua rugosa* (*Brighton Argus* – with permission)

frogs accept a piece of water as their home base they usually remain without confinement. They are rather larger than British [native] frogs, with longer and more pointed heads, and much brighter green backs. Although the sound of their croaking can carry for some distance we usually try to limit the number of males to three or less for the sake of the neighbours, though to our ears it has a quality of laziness and serenity entirely in keeping with a summer day.

Coral, the Sheltie and her daughter Cassia are growing all too rapidly but have recently been joined by a bundle of mischief Raua, who finds, among other things, plastic pots, and worst of all, plant labels absolutely irresistible.

The net result of all this is that our visitors usually spend as much or more time with the animals as they do with us or the plants.[11]

Notes

1. Now called *Pachyphragma macrophyllum* (large-leaved pachyphragma). The common name of lady's smock applies to *Cardamine pratensis*.
2. But see Note 8 in Chapter 11.
3. Now called *Epidalea calamita*.
4. Natterjack toads also occur on sandy inland heaths and in salt marshes. They are fully protected by the Wildlife and Countryside Act 1981, and it would now be an offence to keep them.
5. Now called *Bufotes viridis*.
6. This is an eastern and southern European species.
7. When Katie was keeping frogs the situation regarding taxonomy was quite simple, but incorrect. There were considered to be three species in the UK: the common frog (*Rana temporaria*), and two introduced species, i.e. the edible frog (*Rana esculenta*), and the marsh frog (*Rana ridibunda*). We now have a greater understanding of the situation, but it is quite complex. There is no change to the taxonomic status or name of the common frog. The marsh frog, introduced into Romney Marsh in the 1930s is now known as *Pelophylax ridibundus*. A new species of frog, the pool frog (*Pelophylax lessonae*) was identified living in Norfolk, where it became extinct in the 1990s. It has since been reintroduced. This relates to the northern race. Populations of the southern race are non-native and have been introduced at various places in the UK. The edible frog has been introduced to several sites in the UK; mainly in the south. It is now known to be a hybrid between the pool frog and the marsh frog, and is named *Pelophylax* kl. *esculentus* (kl. is an abbreviation of klepton; signifying that this animal requires input from another species to complete its reproductive cycle).
8. This illustrates the need to cover outdoor reptiliaries with wire mesh, as in addition to rats; cats and birds, particularly corvids, will prey upon the occupants.
9. Katie is presumably referring to the bullfinches liking for flower buds, which would make them highly undesirable in a garden like hers.

10. Now called *Pelophylax* kl. *esculentus*. See Note 7.
11. There are three indications in this chapter that it was written after Katie's book *Living with Reptiles*, which was published in 1961. The first is the successful breeding of green lizards, which is not mentioned in the 1961 book. The second is the loss of livestock due to an attack by a rat. This is stated to have happened three years ago, and as it was not mentioned in *Living with Reptiles*, it dates the chapter to 1964 or later. The final indicator is the mention of two dogs (Cassia and Raua) which don't appear in the 1961 book.

Chapter 13

THE SINK GARDENS

When we first came here our enthusiasm for rock plants was further stimulated by the fact that we had collected a dozen stone sinks – the real kind which are now rarely available. Some of these were put in the shade at the front of the house, and some were alternated along the sides of the back lawn with some larger stone vases and some genuine "steddle-stones",[1] these being the stone pedestals with a flat overhanging mushroom cap at the top on which ricks were built to protect them from rats. In those good old days, when the hours seemed to be so much longer than they do now, one could give the time and attention which were needed to keep a wide range of smaller plants happy in their containers under the rather arid conditions of full sun for most of the day, which only the really tough ones such as silver saxifrages [*Saxifraga crustata* and cultivars], achilleas [yarrows], arabis [rock cress] and dwarf pinks [*Dianthus* spp.] really appreciated. A miniature version of the winged broom (*Genista sagittalis delphinensis*) with prostrate winged stems still survives all the other "dear departed".

For a while such treasures as globularias [globe daisies] with their enchanting little bluish-mauve powder puffs, *Aquilega ecalcarata*[2] whose elfin stems carry fairy red-purple lampshades, *Asperula suberosa*,[3] a woodruff with grey mats of fine foliage and shell pink flowers, and their confreres flourished quite happily but we could not keep pace with their demands. After a great deal of trial and error we finally compromised with a collection of houseleeks (*Sempervivum*) and sedums, which are decorative at all times of the year and just revel in such conditions, except when foraging birds are a little too attentive. The numbers of both families[4] are legion and the only way to buy them, at any rate the houseleeks, is to visit a good nursery and pick out the most distinctive. *Sempervivum ciliosum* [Tenerife houseleek] is one of our favourites with its light green hairy leaves. *S. octopodes* has small hairy, thread-like runners after the manner of a strawberry. The yellow flowered *S. heufelii*[5] [Job's beard] and its varieties have the unique habit of splitting the rosettes rather than offsets.

One of the cobweb houseleeks (*S. arachnoideum*) is a must with its woolly crowns, and *S. soboliferum*,[6] the waterlily houseleek, has a lovely incurved shape and forms masses of stemless rosettes which roll off to establish an ever increasing colony. *S. tectorum* [common houseleek], the one usually to be seen on old roofs, and said to be protection from lightening, makes enormous rosettes when well fed – its cultivar *S. tectorum* 'Glaucum'[7] is exquisite in sea-green, and the cultivar 'Commander Hay' can be even more magnificent in red and green.

All these produce starfish spikes of flowers in varying shades of pink, yellow and white, but it is their form and colour which have the greatest appeal. Some rosettes are almost entirely deep wine red, some have green leaves red-tipped, and some red leaves green-tipped, apart from the many shades of green itself – none of them to be despised, and the better they are treated the more spectacular they are.

Among the sedums there is much more variety in appearance, as well as the brilliance of their flowers, though most of them are mat-forming which makes them ideal for sinks or paving. Some species such as the common stonecrop[8] (*Sedum acre*) of our sea shores, are low growing plants whose stems erupt into a blaze of yellow in midsummer, and which thrive in the poorest of soil. Every leaf which drops from these members of the large tribe of succulents will form a new plant so they need to be planted with caution. *S. album* [white stonecrop] has a bad reputation for this but we have never found it unmanageable, and its variety *S. album* var. *murale* with mahogany leaves and stems is in telling contrast with some of the sempervivums. An indispensable trio for summer flowering with their flat heads of yellow flowers are the easily confused *S. middendorffianum* [Chinese mountain stonecrop], *S. hybridum* [Siberian stonecrop] and *S. floriferum*. Another pink flowered trio takes over in the early autumn, *S. ewersii* [pink Mongolian stonecrop],[9] most often seen in the miniature version, *S. ewersii* var. *homophyllum*,[10] *S. cauticola* [cliff stonecrop] with

Small barn supported by steddle stones (Wikimedia Commons – Peter Facey)

lovely slate-blue leaves and richer pink flowers, and the larger growing *S. spurium* [Caucasian stonecrop] whose cultivar *S. spurium* 'Schorbuser Blut' really lives up to its name with its deep red flowers.[11]

Several uncommon species deserve to be better known, such as *Sedum populifolium* [poplar-leaved stonecrop],[12] which grows like a foot high tree and whose pink-flushed flowers are faintly hawthorn scented. The native roseroot (*Sedum roseum*)[13] is hardly ever met with but sends up a cluster of solid leafy stems with a topknot of greenish yellow flowers, while the pink flowered *S. pulchellum* [Spanish stonecrop] has the idiosyncrasy of liking to grow in cool moist places. *S. amplexicaule* is particularly suited for trough gardens, for after the pale yellow flowers are over the whole plant dries up so that it looks like a handful of oats, until the autumn rains restore it to a more normal appearance.

In spite of the fact that we managed to keep *Primula edgeworthii*[14] [dwarf primrose] growing and flowering for several years in one of the shady sinks, after its demise their [the sinks'] upkeep was abandoned in despair. Apart from the fact that even when it rained they never seemed to retain any moisture, the sparrows adopted them as a kind of adventure playground and any form of protection such as wire netting made them look so horrible that they were distributed around the garden as bird baths, a very popular move.[15]

Primula edgeworthii/Primula nana (Wikimedia Commons – Karsten Heinrich)

Notes

1. Also known as staddle stones.
2. Now called *Semiaquilegia ecalcarata*.
3. Now called *Asperula arcadiensis*.
4. These are genera; not families.
5. Now called *Jovibarba heufelii*.
6. Now called *Jovibarba sobolifera*.
7. A plant name in this format is a cultivar; not a variety. Not listed in *RHS Plant Finder 2023*, but listed elsewhere, sometimes as *S. tectorum glaucum*.
8. Also known as biting stonecrop.
9. Now called *Hylotelephium ewersii*.
10. Now called *Hylotelephium ewersii* var. *homophyllum*.
11. Blut being German for blood.

12. Now called *Hylotelephium populifolium*.
13. Now called *Rhodiola rosea*.
14. Now called *Primula nana*.
15. Given that the sinks were not retaining moisture, does Katie mean dust baths?

Chapter 14

THE SCREES AND SAND BEDS

The next venture which caught our fancy was the making of one of the scree beds that were very much written about at that time. After considerable deliberation the best place seemed to be in the angle of the path at the extreme north of the back garden, behind the *Chamaecypris* [false cypress] 'Fletcheri', where the slight slope would give a little shade, and the trees protection without overhang. An excavation was made about eighteen inches deep and duly filled up in the prescribed manner with broken crocks for extra drainage, then a depth of good soil, covered with a four inch layer of granite chips, and top-dressed with a gritty alpine mixture. A few pieces of sandstone rock were introduced to break the level, and to give extra shade to the ledge below them.

This bed fulfilled our dearest wish for a number of years until there was a prolonged drought, when we found to our cost that on this type of soil it is unwise to provide extra drainage as by its very nature this is sharp enough. In the meantime we had unfortunately made a similar scree in front of the *Chamaecyparis* – virtually in full sun – but after our lesson had been learned we made haste to work as large an amount as possible of extra soil in among the chips, and with continual top dressing this made a very satisfactory home for certain plants. The first bed is now largely shaded by shrubs planted behind it for that purpose, providing the cool stony site which its present occupants clearly appreciate.

There has not been a great deal of change in the residents here since some of the earlier failures have been replaced. Blue-grey mauve-flowered clumps of *Linaria alpina* [alpine toadflax] appear freely from self-sown seedlings, as do the dark aromatic shrublets of a biennial *Satureia*[1] [savory]. Two other satureias are conspicuous in early autumn, *S. subspicata*[2] [winter savory] whose shapely mounds are covered with deep mauve spikes and another species of similar habit but clad in white. *Codonopsis clematidea* [bonnet bellflower] drapes its grey-blue bells through the white flowered branches of *Helianthemum rosmarinifolium*[3] [rock rose], and the dainty pink-flowered sprays of *Fuchsia microphylla* [small-leaved fuchsia]. *Scilla* 'Tubergeniana'[4] greets returning spring with azure spikes – not so easily distinguishable from those of *Puschkinia* which follow in March.

Primula marginata [silver-edged primrose] in silver and mauve and its near relation *Androsace lanuginosa* 'Leichtlinii' [woolly rock jasmine], both like these conditions of cool root run and heads in the sun, as do the microscopic stems of *Mentha requienii* [Corsican mint] whose presence is usually undetected until an unwary step releases its intense fragrance. Even the native *Saxifraga oppositifolia* [purple saxifrage] deigns to honour us with its presence even if it is, as usual, ungenerous with its flowers. Slow-growing *Salix apoda* [Caucasian willow] pushes up its superb pink and orange catkins in April – *Calceolaria biflora* [lady's purse] hangs out its tiny yellow slippers in midsummer, and, perhaps the choicest of all, a near relation of the hepaticas – *Jeffersonia dubia* [Asian twinleaf or rheumatism root] with plum-coloured leaves and truly mauve flowers remains unmoved by anything to which our climate has so far subjected it. *Hutchinsia alpina*[5] [Chamois cress] covers every available piece of rock with its dark foliage bespangled with clear white flower clusters, as does *Lippia repens*[6] [Turkey tangle frog foot] with its pale mauve mop heads. *Cyclamen neopolitanum*[7] [ivy-leaved cyclamen] in autumn and *C. coum* [common, or eastern sowbread] and *C. repandum* [spring sowbread] in spring also approve of their quarters and flower freely.

On the sunnier side of the tree a rather different type of plant is equally well satisfied, heath-like *Hypericum coris* [heath-leaved St. John's wort] from the Maritime Alps, *H. polyphyllum*[8] [Mount Olympus St. John's wort] with grey stems and substantial golden flowers, and even more fascinating *H. olympicum* 'Citrinum'[9] [Mount Olympus St. John's wort] with wide cups of an unusual luminous sulphur shade have made themselves completely at home. Shrubby aethionemas (wallflower cousins) [stonecress] make goodly

Linaria alpina (Wikimedia Commons – Robert Flogaus-Faust)

patches of pink, especially in the cultivar 'Warley Rose', or grey and white in *Aethionema iberideum* [iberis-like stonecress]. The prostrate artimisias make foaming mounds of gleaming silver echoed by the taller filigree of the choicer lavender cottons (*Santolina*), or offset by the deep green of *Santolina viridis*[10] [green lavender cotton]. A trustworthy member of the hawkweed tribe – *Hieracium bombycinum* [Spanish hawkweed] – with silvery silky foliage and soft yellow flowers – one of those trying plants which lead you to believe there is a vacant space only to find the plant has merely retired for the winter – is included here, as is *Anthyllis hermanniae* [yellow kidney vetch] – a much branched shrubby vetch smothered in yellow blooms for long periods and for which no dry spot can be too inhospitable.

An exciting new addition is *Carduncellus rhaponticoides*, a rosette plant with deep-purple stemless thistle flowers. Equally exciting, but in quite the wrong setting for a woodland plant, is the dawn poppy (*Eomecon chionantha*) whose subterranean secrecy prohibits its removal to better climes where it might more often delight us with its white blooms. Starry blue-eyed grasses (*Sisyrinchium*) in cream or pale blue scatter their miniature iris-like tuffets freely though the yellow version, *S. brachypus* [golden-eyed grass],[11] is very loath to stay with us.[12] The worst invader of all is the native hairy violet (*Viola hirta*) whose pale blue flowers win every heart in spring, but whose woody stems and thick clusters of foliage spell death to any weaker plant unfortunate to fall under its mantle.

Yet another experiment claiming our interest was to provide accommodation especially for the lime-haters which one invariably acquires however much one tries to steel one's heart against them – and it seemed that a bed of almost pure sand and leaf mould (materials readily to hand) might be the answer. At that time we had access to a sandpit which produced the most desirable fine, warm, pale sand that one could wish to have for the purpose – so a shallow bed of corresponding size was dug out to bring the remaining square at the end of the erstwhile herbaceous border into line with the two scree beds. A few crocks were put in the bottom and then the sandy mixture, rather in the shape of a ravine with sloping sides, and the whole covered with a thin layer of granite chips.

Over the years this has been so successful that there is very seldom a vacant space. In course of time a seedling of *Rosa rubrifolia*[13] [red-leaved rose] with the lovely plum-coloured foliage and spectacular clusters of hips, planted itself at the junction of the path and the lawn and made such a perfect corner-stone that it was allowed to stay. At one time the dainty golden *Oxalis chrysantha*[14] [sorrel] threatened to dominate the whole area but a timely frost snubbed it and it has never again been quite so avaricious. The picture it makes in late summer when the clear blue Himalayan pea (*Parochetus*[*communis*]) spreads amongst it is really enthralling. It seems that neither of these plants like lime as they never trespass beyond their boundary, and spend the winters quite happily under their coverlet of chips.

Celmisia bellidioides [New Zealand daisy] produces countless silvery daises, and the rare *Viola nuttallii* [Nuttall's violet] greets every spring with its yellow violets. *Helianthemum lunulatum* [shrubby rock rose] is indestructible with its little sulphur rock roses, and the Mount Atlas daisy (*Anacyclus depressus*)[15] reappears without fail to spread its prostrate stems of finely cut leaves tipped with large daisies whose snowy petals are backed with vivid crimson. *Leucojum autumnale*[16] [autumn snowflake] hangs out its dainty white lanterns which seem too fragile to weather the storms of early autumn.

Another very successful project was the siting half-way along the front lawn, and fully sheltered from all the "airts",[17] of a wooden tub filled with the same sandy mixture and topped with a sandstone ridge to give even more shelter from the coldest quarter. Here, until the tub disintegrated from sheer old age the shrubby *Lithospermum oleifolium*[18] [olive-leaved gromwell] opened its opaline bells every year, its cousin *Mertensia coventryana*[19] [a member of the borage family] matched them in deeper blue, and one of the greatest favourites, *Morisia monanthos* [morisia], which has rosettes of jagged leaves centred by stemless clusters of bright yellow four-petalled flowers all revelled in the situation. Gorgeous satin purple *Romulea bulbocodium* [crocus-leaved romulea] spreads its stars widely to every gleam of April sunshine, and *Leucojum roseum*[20] [rose snowflake] reserved its tiny rose-pink bells for early autumn. This last is one of the year's choicest gems of all bulbs and not difficult in such a situation.

Viola nuttallii (Wikimedia Commons – Sheri Hagwood)

Notes

1. Now spelled *Satureja*.
2. Now called *Satureja montana illyrica*.
3. Sometimes listed as *Crocanthemum rosmarinifolium*.
4. *Scilla mischtschkoana* 'Tubergeniana' has white flowers, so is Katie referring to *Scilla siehei* 'Tubergeniana' which has blue flowers? Its common name is glory of the snow.
5. Now called *Hornungia alpina*.
6. Now called *Phyla nodiflora*.
7. Now called *Cyclamen hederifolium*.
8. Now called *Hypericum olympicum* f. *minus* (f. being an abbreviation of forma, i.e. botanical form).
9. Listed in *RHS Plant Finder 2023* as *Hypericum olympicum* f. *uniflorum* 'Citrinum'.
10. Now called *Santolina rosemarinifolia*.
11. Now called *Sisyrinchium californicum*.
12. My experience, gardening on neutral to acid clay soil, is the opposite. I can't keep *Sisyrinchium* with blue flowers, but the yellow-flowered species spreads to plague proportions.
13. Now called *Rosa glauca*.
14. *Oxalis conorrhiza* appears to be a synonym.
15. Now called *Anacyclus pyrethrum* var. *depressus*.
16. Now called *Acis autumnalis*.
17. A Scottish word meaning points of the compass, particularly relating to wind.
18. Now called *Glandora oleifolia*.
19. *Decalepidanthus trollii* appears to be a synonym.
20. Now called *Acis rosea*.

Chapter 15

THE GREENHOUSE (1)

When we left the old home it was decided that the greenhouse was too elderly to take kindly to a move (it is still standing thirty years later) so we promised ourselves a new one later in the year. Unfortunately, Hitler put an end to that plan, and it was to be over twenty years before we could realise this dream. Looking back we often wonder however we managed without one, though the old cucumber frame with the heavy glass lights had stood us in good stead in spite of taking an enormous amount of space. It had stood in the lowest corner below the shrub bed.

The first problem was to find a suitable site for a greenhouse, which was quickly solved as it obviously had to be near the house if it were to be heated electrically, and of course it needed an open position. Down must come the now rather decrepit tool shed and coal sheds whose contents – as is usually the case – comprised a very great deal more than those for which they were originally intended, and here was the perfect position provided the important drains at either end were not disturbed.

The next problem was to find a greenhouse which would fit comfortably into the prescribed area and also serve the dual purpose for which we wanted it – that is as a refuge for humans in bad weather from the lawn where we spend every possible moment, and for an ever-increasing collection of tender plants. Tudor houses are notably dark and cool even in the hottest weather – and this looked like being a happy compromise.

Endless catalogues were consulted and almost immediately a Dutch light house of exactly the right dimensions, thirteen feet by ten feet, presented itself which, moreover, could be raised on two courses of breeze blocks to give us the extra headroom we wanted, and we have never regretted our choice. It was a pity no one warned us that by raising it we should not be able to reach the ridge without removing a light, but I do not suppose we should have listened and it has very seldom been necessary. It was also a pity that when the wooden fence between it and house was replaced by a brick wall no one realised we should never be able to fit a new light if need be. So far we have been able to effect temporary repairs to one pane which was cracked right across by a climber over-enthusiastic to reach fresh air, and not spotted in time.

Actually, quite recently modern science has come to our aid in this dilemma – as indeed it has simplified many of the garden chores described here – and provided us with a sheet of fibreglass, which has the strength but not the rigidity of glass, and has no objection at all to the slight curving necessary for its insertion. Added virtues of this material are that not only are the sun's rays prevented from burning as they do through glass, but that it is very useful in giving partial obscurity from observation though it cannot, of course, be used where one wishes for a clear view.[1]

The house was duly erected, provided with a cement floor surrounded by a narrow border of earth, and we were all set. Contrary to the usual advice we had a door set at the northern end which is protected by other buildings, so that we very rarely get the wind blowing directly into it as it would otherwise have done. It is a little unfortunate that the neighbour's house prevents any sun reaching it until nearly noon in the winter, but in the summer the temperature skips up to 90 degrees [32° C] at the slightest provocation. Green wash takes care of the southern end and gives us extra privacy, while external blinds keep it cool on all but the hottest days. In the winter months – when there is no room for humans – there are electrically heated pipes to keep the temperature around 45 to 50 degrees [7 to 10° C].

By the middle of May everything was ready and very soon cuttings, seeds and plants were flooding in as gifts from kind friends. Naturally enough everything I have learned about greenhouse management had been forgotten in the interim period, and for a while I suffered badly from a sort of horticultural indigestion trying to provide such a mixture of plants with their basic requirements of watering, feeding and ventilation, but gradually things sorted themselves out. First of all we wanted to plant the borders, particularly the back one to mask the wall behind – there is a permanent bench only at the south end. After some deliberation the choice fell upon *Jasminum polyanthum* [Chinese scented jasmine] which has most of the necessary virtues for such a position. Long panicles of pink-flushed buds open into clear white stars generally in February, the evergreen foliage is decorative in itself besides providing light shade, and the delicate fragrance is so strong that when the door is open on warm days it can frequently be detected as far away as the front gate. More important still it attracts no insect pests and is easy to prune, though one must cut it hard back as it is a very willing grower.

Following it very closely in the merit poll and something I have always longed to grow is the glorious sky-blue *Plumbago capensis*[2] [Cape leadwort] which certainly does its best to fill the greenhouse, but the more it is cut back the more it flowers, until it is finally pruned right back to the old wood in autumn, when one often has to sacrifice belated blooms. Its one slight drawback is that the old leaves often remain hanging in dismal black shreds which are prone to encourage mildew, as will the fallen sticky calyces unless they are cleared meticulously. Should you be unlucky enough to have acquired such an unwelcome pest they also make ideal winter quarters for mealy bugs. Both these plants can be confined to large pots, but of course the effect is not so luxuriant.

Plumbago then took the centre position and we thought a *Pelargonium* would be fine in the other corner. We had often seen scarlet 'Gustav Emich' recommended for such a position, but this is always a strong grower and was up to the eaves in no time. True, it flowered magnificently, but finally it had to be banished because its softly hairy leaves grew so enormous that all the air was excluded from the ones nearer the glass, which were dispensing mildew spores in all directions before we could pick them off. Probably we should have done much better to have used one of the ivy-leaved geraniums, but before we could try, a chance seedling of a plant often grown as an annual but which is perennial in a greenhouse, took over, and grew and grew and grew.

Maurandya lophospermum [climbing foxglove] too has softly hairy leaves, but not so deadly as the geranium, and it flung long trails in all directions, festooned with large pink flowers very much like foxgloves. Here again its exuberance led to its undoing for we finally cut it back too hard, and it expired in sheer resentment.

Mingling happily with these was another lovely climber with shiny mould-repellent leaves, the Chilean jasmine or moonflower (*Mandevilla suaveolens*)[3] which is as notable for its extraordinary fruit as for its giant version of jasmine flowers. Like many greenhouse plants it is a member of the Asclepiad family,[4] many of which have originally shaped rather beak-like fruits opening to reveal rows of dark-coloured seeds nestling in the softest, silkiest pappus one could wish to see. This particular plant grows twin carpels two to three inches long and about the thickness of a pencil, and these are joined at the tips into an oval shape in which they remain for months before ripening. This plant has, however, a hidden vice – it attracts every greenfly that ever dares to set foot in the greenhouse, and they remain impervious to all forms of discouragement that we have tried, though to date it has not been cast out.

The front border too has had various occupants which have failed to reach the high standard required to make them worthy of inclusion. A white-flowered specimen of *Abutilon vitifolium*[5] [Chinese lantern] gave us a glimpse of fairy land when its silvery leaves were intermingled with its wide white salvers – to have cut it back would have made it hideous so this

Jasminum polyanthum (Wikimedia Commons – Didier Descouens)

had to go before it pushed the roof off. The yearning for a mimosa is still very strong but so far the temptation has been resisted, as all too surely the same fate would befall it. A cutting of the silver-leaved *Convolvulus cneorum* [silverbush] with its white trumpets pushed into the corner, has made a worthwhile bush such as it would never do under harsher conditions.

Two blue-flowered plants have been outstandingly successful and both were raised from seed. *Sollya heterophylla*,[6] the Australian harebell, has slender twining stems, narrow leaves and, as its name implies, bright blue campanulate flowers very freely produced. The other has starry flowers of an almost indescribable shade of pale luminous blue which deepens with age, and grey velvet leaves. This is *Oxypetalum* (*Tweedia*) *coerulea*[7] [blue milkweed]. Recently they were joined by the shrimp plant (*Beloperone guttata*) – now threatened with rechristening as *Drejerella*[8] – whose pinkish bracts make a good contrast, and which has quickly shown that this treatment is far preferable to being in a pot.

A small plant of *Ficus pumila* [creeping fig] was put in at the base of the jasmine to cover the breeze blocks with its tight curtain of heart-shaped leaves. After a slow start it has covered the whole wall and outlined in a most attractive way every pane of glass right to the roof on that side of the house.

Oxypetalum coerulea/*Tweedia coerulea* (Wikimedia Commons – Dick Culbert)

Conscience tells us we should remove it, but we tell ourselves that its sucker pads are doing no harm – anyway we are keeping a sharp eye on it – in spite of its tremendous growth it has so far defied all our attempts at propagation.

The old time gardener's delight for table decoration, smilax (*Myrsiphyllum asparagoides*)[9] set below the bench climbs up behind it, and spreads its shining foliage and dainty miniature lily flowers (which amply repay close examination) among the pots above while the commoner tradescantias ramp in all directions and help to preserve the humidity of the borders.

Notes

1. Now, of course, we would use clear or frosted plastic sheet.
2. Now called *Plumbago auriculata*.
3. Now called *Mandevilla laxa*.
4. The *Asclepiadoideae* was formerly designated as a full family, but is now regarded as a sub-family of the *Apocynaceae*.
5. Now called *Corynabutilon vitifolium*.
6. Now called *Billardiera heterophylla*.
7. *Tweedia coerulea* is correct. Also spelt *T. caerulea*.
8. Now called *Justicia brandageeana*.
9. Now called *Asparagus asparagoides*.

Chapter 16
THE GREENHOUSE (2)

So much for the more permanent furnishings – what were we going to grow in a myriad of pots and pans which could be distributed around the garden in summer and take refuge here in winter? After a while it became possible to see where one's tastes really lay, and quietly dispense with quite a few specimens for which good homes could always be found.

Pelargoniums with their gorgeous colourings and more or less imperturbable character were of course a "must", and it is hard to select one's favourites, though it seems as if those with variegated or scented leaves hold pride of place, with one or two dwarf varieties coming in a good third. *Pelargonium* 'Happy Thought' with cream-centred leaves, 'Distinction' with a narrow dark circle near the rim, 'Mrs Henry Cox' whose leaf colour includes cream, green, black and red, and choicest of all 'Miss Burdett Coutts' whose cream, red and green foliage is quite outstanding make a pleasant quartet. On the whole the scented varieties are rather more shrubby in growth and make handsome bushes, though less handsome in flower. Of such are peppermint-scented *P. tomentosum* with its velvet leaves, *P. fragrans* [scented pelargonium] redolent of nutmeg or pine as it takes you, and curly leaved *P. crispum* [crisped-leaf pelargonium], so sweet as one brushes by it. Far surpassing them all, and a useful substitute for lemon verbena (*Lippia*)[1] – in fact hardly distinguishable from it with one's eyes shut – is the recently introduced 'Mabel Grey'.

Among the dwarfs now becoming very popular as taking much less room and not so given to legginess, 'Friesdorf' is a worthy representative of the very dark foliaged section, 'Granny Hewitt' is generous with her tiny scarlet rosettes, 'Petit Pierre' with tiny leaves and pink clusters to match, and the very unusual salmon butterflies of 'The Boar' all find a welcome.

A very free growing plant of the ivy-leaved section is a charming and very floriferous pink-flowered plant known to me as 'Roi des Balcons',[2] and another not commonly seen is 'Mme. Margot' with clear pink flowers and cream-bordered foliage. Then of course there are the species, always close to a botanist's heart, but unfortunately rather difficult and expensive to get. *P. bicolor violaceum*[3] is a gorgeous plant with silver leaves and bi-coloured flowers of palest pink and deep maroon at the base. *P. gibbosum*, the gouty knee geranium, has very long shanks between its few-leaved swollen joints and eventually produces a few tiny greenish yellow flowers which emit the most piercing sweetness at dusk. A wedding between this and *P. triste* [night-scented geranium] has produced an almost identical plant *P. apiifolia*[4] with blossoms of a most unusual brownish purple shade outlined in cream. These and *P.* 'Miss Stapleton', all semi-succulent plants, have the alarming habit of casting their leaves and shamming dead during the late summer, after which the latter usually produces its most handsome flowers of deep bright pink. *P.* 'Schottii' is one of the most uncommon, but is rather unwilling to produce its lovely deep red blooms.

When geraniums are beginning to grow winter-weary a good many of the *Begonia* species are ready to take over. Even if their flowers are not particularly showy, they mostly make up for this by being foliage plants *par excellence* with infinite variety of form. On the whole they will stand an amazing amount of neglect should it be necessary, and are mostly so easy to manage that it is surprising how seldom one sees but a few of them. It is true that the cane-stemmed varieties such as *B.* 'President Carnot' have a nasty habit of growing tall and ungainly unless continually pinched, apart from the even nastier one of dropping their leaves one by one if their management displeases them. One of the great things to avoid is getting their leaves wet for any reason – *Begonia rex* [king begonia] in particular strongly resents this and many a beautiful leaf is spoilt in consequence.

The most successful types for a temperature of 45 to 50 degrees F [7 to 10° C] such as ours are the rhizomatous and fibrous-rooted species – the florists' winter-flowering pot plants need quite a bit more heat to keep them happy – *B. rex* belongs to the former section but there are quite a few more species available. *B. bowerae* [eyelash begonia] is a willing grower with creeping rhizomes which make it very suitable for hanging baskets, where its bright green leaves margined with dark brown and fringed with white hairs are very effective. The flowers are small and pearly white but stand up well on slender stems. The rather similar *B.* 'Maphil' – sometimes known as *B.* 'Cleopatra'[5] – has particularly handsome, rather ivy-shaped leaves.

B. feastii 'Helix' [pond lily begonia] whose rounded leaves spiral as does a snail shell, and *B.* 'Ricky Minter' whose truly enormous leaves have lightly goffered[6] edges showing the bright red reverse, both belong to the "beef steak" group, so called in reference to their overall shape and the violent colouring of the undersides of their leaves. *B.* 'Skeezar' has a very delicate appearance, the mostly silver-grey leaf centres being narrowly edged and veined with light yellowish green, and particularly charming *eau-de-nil*[7] buds and flowers to match. *B. daedalea* has long red-spotted stems and boldly splashed leaves to match.

The best known of the fibrous-rooted species is probably *B. haageana*[8] [elephant-ear begonia], with *B. metallica* [metallic leaf begonia] as a close second. Both will make fine plants up to fifteen inches, after which they should be stopped regularly. Both have quite large pink flowers whose petals are covered in fine hairs but the leaves of *B. haageana* are closely and finely pilose, while as may be suspected, those of *B. metallica* are sparsely hairy on an almost luminous base, and both are shaped like elephant's ears. Two miniature easy-going types seldom without a few clusters of their pearly or coral flowers respectively are *B. legia* [9] which has almost mahogany brown stems and leaves, and *B. schmidtiana* which is an even smaller non-stop bloomer, whose almost rusty green leaves are backed with red.

The great advantage about most of these plants is that they can be increased with the utmost ease. Having learned in my early days that fleshy plants such as *Impatiens* [busy Lizzie] will often root freely in plain water in a warm place the obvious thing for a busy – if not lazy! – greenhouse gardener to do was to see how far this policy could be extended, and it has proved so successful that we now do at least 90 percent of our greenhouse propagation in this way.

A collection of glass jars of various sizes is always on hand and it is really surprising what can be done. The cuttings are best stood under a bench out of reach of the sun, though the warmer the weather the faster they seem to root – the championship for rooting speed is so far held by a *Columnea* [flying goldfish plant] for three days flat. When they are finally potted up one must be sure to use a soil mixture with no rough material to harm these extra delicate roots, and be sure to keep them very moist until they have got over the shock of removal.

Begonias are particularly rewarding, in fact it is almost second nature now to put any broken pieces or prunings of any greenhouse plant in water straight away. It is exciting, too, to be able to see what is going on and saves much valuable time. We get on better this way with *Begonia rex* than we do with the orthodox methods – in fact a leaf of this species has been standing in water now for several months, and we have already taken two plants from the top and there are four or five more happily developing on the stem underwater. There are, of course, plants which refuse to submit to this method, although easy enough in the normal way.

From Begonias we go on to Fuchsias and here the species come into their own. These particularly need to be kept pinched back hard from the time they are quite small to keep young growth coming on, otherwise the stems become woody and the display of blooms will suffer. Fuchsias are

Begonia haageana/Begonia scharffii (Wikimedia Commons – Krzysztof Ziarnek, Kenraiz)

incredibly easy to root in water – in fact we never try them any other way, though of course the cuttings must be of new season's growth – a woody stem will have nothing to do with it.

The most breath-taking of all is *Fuchsia splendens* and I shall never forget my first sight of this plant, a well shaped bush thickly hung with bells, the upper part of which is brilliant red but which flare suddenly at the base into a frill of clear pale green to match the stamens. *F.* 'Speciosa' and *F. fulgens* [brilliant fuchsia] are very near this in relationship, but the flower tubes are much longer and an all over softer red – the blooms too come together on an ever-elongating drooping spike at the ends of the branches.

Tall growing *F. corymbosa*[10] has long softly hairy leaves and bunches of deep red flowers, while *F. serratifolia* [toothed fuchsia][11] with shiny foliage very obligingly produces its almost indescribable flowers of green, pink and orange red in December, to be followed here by the others in very early spring. For hanging baskets the little New Zealander – *F. procumbens* [creeping or trailing fuchsia] is very attractive with its dainty foliage and greenish yellow bells surmounted by brilliant blue anthers. This is supposed to be hardy but definitely does not like anything we can offer though in the greenhouse it very obligingly produces self-sown seedlings. A fuchsia cultivar which combines the virtues of small growth with unusual colouring is 'Chang' whose flowers are very freely produced.

Fuchsia fulgens (Wikimedia Commons – Diego Delso)

Notes

1. Now called *Aloysia citriodora*.
2. Now called *Pelargonium* 'Hederinum'.
3. I can find no listing for the sub-species *violaceum*.
4. Listed on the Internet as a distinct species, so cannot be a hybrid between *P. gibbosum* and *P. triste*.
5. *Begonia* 'Maphil' is not listed in *RHS Plant Finder 2023*, but is listed on the Internet. *B.* 'Cleopatra' is listed in *RHS Plant Finder 2023*.
6. Goffer or gauffer, meaning to pleat, crimp, or make wavy.
7. Meaning a pale greenish colour.
8. Now called *B. scharffii*.
9. Not listed in *RHS Plant Finder 2023*, nor on the Internet.
10. Not listed in *RHS Plant Finder 2023*, nor on the Internet. Katie possibly meant *F. corymbiflora*, which is now called *F. boliviana* [Bolivian fuchsia].
11. Now called *F. denticulata*.

Chapter 17

THE GREENHOUSE (3)

As soon as word went around that we had acquired a greenhouse we were the happy recipients of a good many cuttings from our friends in the succulent world – in fact they did their best to fill it, but I had always been somewhat of a heretic in these circles, and could not see myself growing pot after pot of cactus "pincushions" however rare and precious! True, they mostly produce very colourful flowers but these too lack much variety of shape – apart from the fact that we are slightly allergic to being pricked!

Anyway, all these treasures were duly potted up, and after considerable time we began to be able to recognise the distinguishing characteristics of the more popular genera, but the novice grower of succulents other than cacti is not particularly well endowed with literature on the subject – especially as they are rather looked upon as not being so worthy of attention.[1] Recent discoveries of new plant material is, to a certain extent, now modifying this attitude. In any case apart from the fact that the genera themselves merge into each other in a most confusing way, they are almost impossible to identify by description alone. For someone trained to appreciate accurate botanical nomenclature this can become rather trying.

Having lived with succulents for several years and the excitement of entering a new field having died down a little, we became aware of several salient facts. Firstly, that by some convenient miracle quite a few of them had failed to hold our affections, possibly because their constant presence lacks the thrill of seasonal changes of the non-succulent world – like the perpetual summer of sunnier climes. Secondly, that we must begin to specialise in some of the more unusual species, and so reduce our ever-expanding population – besides, pot-washing is not our favourite occupation!

Our catholic taste in plants of all kinds can become a nuisance, and we sometimes envy the single-minded devotee of one type or genus as he is always careful to leave enough space to display his specimens to their best advantage.

It is fun to make a series of winter pictures by grouping a few of the choicer species together, contrasting their enormous range of delicate colouring from mother-of-pearl to plain purple, from bright green to almost blue, as well as their architectural variety. Some of the indispensables for such a purpose are *Echeveria gibbiflora* 'Metallica' in deepest mauve, *E. hoveyi* var. *zahni* virtually variegated in pink and white, and *E. elegans* whose grey leaves have an almost grape-like bloom – all of these of rosette shape. Ranged among them could be the brownish-purple sprays of *Pachyphytum roseum*,[2] [pink moonstone] the roseate spikes of *E. rosea* closely emulated in colour by *Sedum guatemense* 'Aurora',[3] the blue spines of *Kleinia cylindrica*[4] [narrow-leaf chalk sticks] or *K. repens*[5] [blue chalk sticks], or perhaps the almost black saucers of *Aeonium arboreum* 'Atropurpureum' [dark purple houseleek tree], the brown-edged furry leaves of *Kalanchoe tomentosa* [panda plant], or the meal-covered mauve leaves of *K. pumila* [flower dust plant] which has charming pink flowers to match. Then again there are the donkey's tails of *Sedum morganianum* [also called burro's tail], and the creeping stem-rooting crassulas such as *Crassula sarmentosa* [trailing jade plant] or *C. spathulata* [spathula-leaf crassula], and the almost mahogany purple of *C. marginata*.[6] For larger pot plants we use what must be the best known of all succulents – the sturdy-stemmed shrubby elephants' ears (*Crassula argentea*)[7] with its glaucous grey leaves edged and dotted with brown, or *C. obliqua*[8] [jade plant] in plain green, or cream variegated.

When the moment came to reduce their numbers we found there were many succulents we could not do without – special favourites such as the rather temperamental *Pachyphytum oviferum* [moonstones] whose white leaves are supposed to resemble bird's eggs, and whose enchanting pink bells nestle in sea-green calyces, or *Crassula falcata*[9] [propeller plant] with its curious sickle-shaped leaves and sometimes strongly-scented bright red flowers, or *Agave americana* 'Mediopicta' [century plant] whose fearsomely toothed boldly white-centred green leaves are so strikingly handsome. If

Kalanchoe pumila (Wikimedia Commons – Stan Shebs)

only it would grow into a single crown instead of endless smaller ones. The enormous family of spurges (*Euphorbiaceae*) has almost more succulent members than otherwise, most of which are exceedingly attractive and often mimic the growth of real cacti. One of the best known is the shrub-like *Euphorbia milii* [crown of thorns] with stoutly spiny stems, small bright green leaves, amd clusters of small brilliant red flowers. A more formidable looking plant on the same lines is *E. hislopii*,[10] whose flowers are a similar shape but brick red in colour.

Kalanchoe manginii [beach bells] has discarded the usual upright family stance in favour of long, slender, fleshy-leaves sprays hung with large glowing red four-sided lanterns in early spring. A near relation *K. youngensis*[11] is even less easily recognised, having similar sprays of linear leaflets tipped with shallow bells of brightest yellow. Both very desirable plants to which, if it can be obtained, should be added *K. uniflora* [coral bells] which makes a prostrate mat of spathulate toothed leaves liberally sprinkled with small pale crimson urns.

Tucked away in winter under the benches are several of the large-leaved epiphyllums [orchid cacti] whose flowers are so gorgeous in colour, and sometimes giving a bonus of scent, as in the case of *Epiphyllum cooperi*,[12] whose creamy flowers open at sunset and flood the air with fragrance. Taking rather less room are some of the smaller hybrid cactus of similar type which literally smother themselves with blooms in shades of pink, magenta and scarlet. The very floriferous rat's tail cactus (*Aporocactus*) freely bedecks its trailing stems with deep pink blossoms in late spring, and looks well on a high shelf or in a hanging basket. Here, too, the mistletoe cactus (*Rhipsalis cassutha*)[13] and its kin find a happy home, judging by the freedom of growth and flower. These, too, are epiphytes, and a good many of them have the thin, drooping, pliable stems which gave them their generic name derived from the Greek 'Rhips' meaning wickerwork, and they have the great advantage of flowering in winter. After the delicate blooms have faded their place is taken by small rounded white, or sometimes coloured, fruits whose appearance led to the bestowal of the popular English name. Some species have winged stems and all are attractive.

Another fascinating genus are the ceropegias of which the best known example is probably *Ceropegia woodii*,[14] known variously as hearts entangled or sweetheart vine. Most available species are climbing or trailing plants which can be trained effectively over any trellised support, or left to fall down from the pot like a long curtain, though with stems reaching from six to seven feet in length this can be a mistake in the greenhouse, though invaluable in the house where they seem totally unaffected by the dry air.[15] Their flowers are quite unique, and although perhaps more curious than beautiful, can at least never be overlooked. At the base the corolla is tubular, then the lobes separate, sometimes to reunite to make a miniature cage, or they may spread into a kind of fringed umbrella, or twist into a corkscrew. *C. radicans* [string of hearts plant] is particularly attractive with three inch flowers of emerald green and brown, and so is *C. ampliata* [bushman's pipe] with miniature water bottles faintly striped with mauve. In fact there does not seem to be one not worth growing, and most of them are completely individual and bizarre in their variation of the floral structure.

Ceropegia ampliata (Wikimedia Commons – Engeser)

Notes

1. There are now many books about succulents, including, for example, *Succulent Plants of the World* (2011) by Fred Dortort, and nurseries specialising in the group.
2. The correct name may be *Pachyphytum oviferum* 'Roseum'.
3. Now called *Sedum* x *rubrotinctum* 'Aurora'.
4. Now called *Senecio talinoides cylindricus*.
5. Now called *Curio repens*.
6. Now called *Crassula pellucida marginalis*.
7. Now called *Crassula ovata*.
8. Now called *Crassula ovata* 'Obliqua'.

9. Possibly refers to *Crassula perfoliata* var. *falcata*.
10. Sometimes listed as *Euphorbia milii* var. *hislopii*.
11. Not listed in *RHS Plant Finder 2023*, nor on the Internet.
12. Sometimes listed as *Epiphyllum crenatus* var. *cooperi*.
13. Now called *Rhipsalis baccifera*.
14. Now called *Ceropegia linearis woodii*.
15. Note that Katie had a cold, draughty Tudor house, probably without central heating.

Chapter 18

THE GREENHOUSE (4)

So much for the particular, now for the general. Our primary intention was, of course, always to have something interesting to see, even if barren periods without actual flowers should occur. This we seem to have accomplished. Indeed, at the beginning of February there are often more than a dozen species in bloom, not counting individual begonias, fuchsias or pelargoniums. This year the first jasmine buds had just opened, as had the pendent crimson lanterns of *Abutilon megapotamicum* [flowering maple] with the boss of brown anthers peeping from below their yellow frills. The Brazilian spider plant, *Tibouchina semidecandra*[1] [also known as glory bush or princess flower] so called on account of the peculiar arrangement of its stamens, had several wide purple salvers; Christmas cacti still lingered, *Cyclamen libatonicum* [Lebanon cyclamen] and *C. persicum* [Persian cyclamen] – the true species not the greenhouse hybrids, – both with exquisite pink shuttlecocks, the brilliant yellow of the apparently indestructible *Primula* x *kewensis* with the mealy leaves, and the rusty orange of a special favourite, the South African lion's tail (*Leonotis leonurus*) made a cheerful medley. The large crimson fruits of *Clivia miniata* [Natal lily] too, gave added colour – of course they should have been removed for the benefit of the plant, but we just had to see what they looked like when they reached maturity, which took eighteen months.

Out of reach of the sun's rays at all times a number of ferns flourish under the main bench – indeed the maidenhair scatters its spores into other pots so that there is nearly always a new generation coming on. Rock brake [also known as button fern] (*Pellaea rotundifolia*) and two or three varieties of ladder fern (*Nephrolepis*) outgrow their quarters very quickly, and the latter provides endless offspring at the ends of their long characteristic stolons. Golden polypody [*Phlebodium aureum*] has very large handsome fronds of the same pattern as the hardy native [*Polypodium vulgare*], and the rhizomes of the very aptly named hare's foot (*Duvallia mariesii*) creep endlessly over the sides of the pans – this plant is almost hardy but we prefer to keep it under cover. The chain fern (*Woodwardia*) has the largest fronds of all,[2] which very obligingly provide youngsters on their frons in the same sort of way as does the well-known *Asplenium bulbiferum* [hen and chickens fern, or mother fern]. A minute stag's horn (*Platycerium*) still in a pot and not yet transferred to a piece of cork bark, is quietly gathering strength under these conditions.

Several bulbs and their allies find their place in the greenhouse. The African *Haemanthus albiflos* [paint brush plant] with curious club-shaped heads of conspicuous golden stamens cupped in purest white petals, and wide handsome leaves fringed with white hairs, invariably opens its buds in time for Christmas. There could not be an easier plant to grow than the absolutely indispensable African *Veltheimia capensis* [sand lily] which does not delay long after the new year and lasts a long time. Its current foliage has hardly died down before the crimped edges of the new leaves are visible again. The flower spikes are somewhat reminiscent of a red hot poker [*Kniphofia*] but the colour is purplish-pink tipped with green.

There are two or three little scillas with decorative foliage. *Scilla violacea*[3] [silver squill or leopard lily] has widish leaves thickly sprinkled with darker spots, *S. ovalifolia*[4] has similar leaves in two tones of green, and *S. adlamii*[5] [zebra quill] has narrow plantain-like leaves striped with brown. All three have delightful spikes of greenish pink bells. The ginger lily (*Hedychium gardnerianum*) prefers these quarters to the open air, and produces its spidery yellow flowers in late summer.

A few Cape cowslips (*Lachenalia*) have been grown from South African seed. The first of these in shrimp pink opens in early autumn, to be followed before Christmas by *L. pendula*[6] [bulb-bearing leopard lily] whose red bells are so welcome in midwinter. This in turn gives place to one of the more familiar yellow-flowered species, and to finish off the season *L. cyaneum*[7] of an ethereal blue with faint sweet scent to match. A very special plant which grew quite easily from seed and which we read recently has become

Phlebodium aureum (Wikimedia Commons- Derek Ramsey)

very difficult to obtain,[8] is *Tropaeolum tricolor* [tricolor nasturtium or Chilean nasturtium] whose blooms we have yet to see, and which has most exasperating habits. The stems, which usually appear when one is least expecting them, in December, are only threads of green, but should one have the misfortune to break one of these – which is fatally easy to do – the plant just sulks and refuses to send up another stem until the next growing period. At the moment it has got to the stage of showing buds about the size of a dress pin's head amongst the tiny leaves, and we are fervently hoping that another disaster will not occur. (It did! They just died off!).

A great excitement in the current year is the first flowering of a green version of the common arum lily (*Zantedeschia aethiopica*) grown from seed.[9] Its origin seems to be open to question – possibly the colouring may be caused by a virus infection – even so the net result is particularly pleasing – from a creamy centre the colour deepens to the same shade as the leaves at the edges of the petals. Needless to say they arouse cupidity in the eyes of any beholder addicted to flower arranging.

To our considerable surprise we have been rather successful in growing several varieties of *Columnea* [flying goldfish plants] for which we were assured we should need a much higher temperature than the 45° F [7° C] or just over at which the thermostat is set. Ever since we saw them in a municipal glasshouse we were filled with covetousness and then a plant of *C. allenii* came our way. At first we thought the pundits were right but finally optimism was justified and we have since added *C. schleffleriana*[10] and *C.* x *vedraiensis*. Mostly the conspicuous tiger-mouth flowers which are freely produced along the thickly falling stems are in varying shades of red or orange or both. Here again all root with greatest ease by the water method, at almost any season, and will even flower freely if not potted up.

The wax plant (*Hoya carnosa*) got tired of circling round the wire in its pot and sent a strong, unnoticed shoot right up into the jasmine, but to no avail for it lost its head along with the jasmine at pruning time. *Hoya* invariably finishes its first flush of flowers before our Horticultural Show in August and begins the second in September – very trying. Another plant which tried to overrun the whole greenhouse until it fell victim to an enormous array of greenfly which seemed to materialise overnight, is an African member of the groundsel and ragwort genus (*Senecio mikanoides*).[11] This filled the greenhouse with sunshine in mid-winter before its banishment when it was literally covered in clusters of brilliant yellow daisies almost hiding the shiny foliage which could be mistaken for that of ivy – hence the English name of German ivy [also called climbing groundsel]! Actually, it has survived

Columnea (Wikimedia Commons – Wildfeuer)

several nasty winters outside on the heap of spare soil, and climbed strongly into the tree above it, but as it is a winter flowerer in this climate its efforts are rather wasted. The variegated form is much less rampageous and a worthy acquisition.

The Australian kangaroo paw (*Anigozanthus manglesii*) expanded until it filled its pot and then when repotted and parted sulked for a long time until we thought we would lose it – however it finally relented but we shall have to probably wait a long time for its furry red and green flowers. A New Zealander is also trying our patience very hard after being raised from seed. The blueberry [also called ink plant or flax lily] (*Dianella intermedia*), a lily whose sprays of small whitish flowers are completely overshadowed by the beauty of the half inch blue berries. The long narrow leaves are dovetailed into each other in a rather unusual manner somewhat reminiscent of a palm frond. Last year it flowered but set no seed. This year it seems to be going to fulfil its destiny at long last.

Notes

1. Now called *Tibouchina urvilleana*.
2. The king fern (*Angiopteris evecta*) is reported to have the longest fronds, at 8 metres.
3. Now called *Ledebouria socialis*.
4. Now called *Ledebouria ovalifolia*.
5. Now called *Ledebouria cooperi*.
6. Now called *Lachenalia bulbifera*.
7. Not listed in *RHS Plant Finder 2023*, nor on the Internet. Katie is possibly referring to the blue trumpet flower (*Iochroma cyaneum*).
8. No longer difficult to obtain, as *RHS Plant Finder 2023* lists seven nurseries selling this plant.
9. There is a cultivar 'Green Goddess'.
10. Not listed in *RHS Plant Finder 2023*, nor on the Internet.
11. Now called *Deleairea odorata*.

Chapter 19

THE GREENHOUSE (5)

House plants, as such, have not really found a place here. They mostly outgrow their quarters and with a certain few exceptions do not really find our sitting rooms congenial. However, some bromeliads have certainly proved themselves able to resist very tough treatment. Among the commoner species Queen's tears (*Billbergia nutans*) is certainly one of the easiest, and equally certainly clad in a veritable Joseph's Coat. The stem is encased in shocking pink bracts of which tint there is also a faint hint on the sepals. The green petals are edged with Oxford blue, and the yellow anthers have long green filaments.

When some of the smaller starfish plants (*Cryptanthus*) decided that their group is becoming too big, they quietly detach a few rosettes and let them drop on to the bench, where they will go on growing and increasing happily for months on end as their root system is almost negligible. Almost indestructible too are the common peperomias [baby rubber plant], which can be overlooked and dried right out – and still come up smiling.

Every available *Tradescantia* finds its way here and they make handsome plants. Our favourite is one of the most recent introductions (*T. sillamontana*) [cobweb spiderwort], which dies back in winter, and whose shoots are covered in thick, white, silky tomentum amongst which the lilac pink flowers nestle in a charming manner. Even the humble *Aspidistra* [cast iron plant] finds its place and will, one day, be joined by the variegated version.

In early spring *Coronilla valentina* [scorpion vetch] tries to rival the jasmine with the scent of ripe plums – the circlets of small golden pea-flowers in lovely contrast to the blue-grey foliage. *Oxalis* is a genus which always arouses our cupidity and is well represented. An unusual species with a dreadful name is *O. ortgiesii* [fishtail oxalis] from the Andes, a tall-growing rarity with large handsome leaves, and clusters of yellow flowers, which, had they been larger, could have made this a first class plant. *O. siliquosa*[1] is an almost perfect imitation of the widespread garden pest *O. corniculata* [yellow oxalis], but in pots at any rate has no bad habits. It stays in a tidy clump, flowers profusely for months at a time, and never sets any seed.

Two very unusual plants which attract immediate attention for their foliage are *Hypoestes phyllostachya* from Madagascar, and *Strobilanthes metallica*.[2] The former is often known as the measles plant [also as polka dot plant], and its coppery green leaves are thickly sprinkled with bright pink spots. Like most labiates[3] it grows fast, and must be kept pinched back hard, has small lilac-pink flowers which are best removed, and can be propagated endlessly by cuttings. The other plant has the most beautiful long narrow leaves of deep purple, overlaid with a blue sheen, almost indescribable, but very striking. Here again the flowers are negligible. Unfortunately, it is not too easy to propagate, though of course young plants have the most effective colouring.

Hypocryta glabra,[4] which came on the market only recently, is an oddity in the way of flowers, but quite easy to manage. The orange blooms are shaped like small clogs, hence the popular name clog or sometimes goldfish plant. Its thick dark shiny leaves are decorative at all times. Another easy and worthwhile species is *Lantana camara* [yellow sage], a near relative of *Verbena*. These can be propagated endlessly in water – and make small shrubs of which every twig carries a long lasting flower cluster. There are several colour variants pink, purple, yellow and white, but by far the nicest, to our way of thinking, is the cultivar which opens yellow and turns slowly scarlet – though another whose mosaic of pink buds opening cream, and flushing though lavender to deep pink, comes a close second. Incidentally this species was introduced to Africa as an ornamental shrub, but its vigorous growth has made it a weed in its own right, and a menace to health as well, for the tsetse fly [*Glossina* spp.] finds shelter in its thickets.

Streptosolen jamesonii [marmalade bush] is actually a climber, but can be kept within limits by pinching the shoots. The clusters of brilliant

Lantana camara (Wikimedia Commons – Alvesgaspar)

orange petunia-shaped flowers appear at about midsummer. Vivid scarlet is the choice of *Salvia fulgens* [Mexican scarlet sage] for its large softly hairy blooms. This is almost hardy but cuttings should always be kept in reserve. *S. rutilans*[5] [pineapple sage] will also surprise one outside by breaking strongly from the base after a difficult winter. This produces its many spikes of smaller, bright crimson flowers very late in the season, but is chiefly notable for the very strong pineapple scent which the slightest touch will release.

How much we appreciate this temperate sanctuary in the bleak days of early spring! May it be snowing outside, but who cares when one is happily pottering among the scent and colour of this mixed assemblage, which appears to find communal life in these conditions quite acceptable. Of course, we very soon felt we had to share our good fortune with a few members of the animal world, as well as robins and blackbirds which are our constant companions. It is the ideal summer house for tree frogs [probably *Hyla arborea*] – provided one remembers to close the windows, which are not escape proof, by dusk – as this is the time when these little creatures leave their daytime haunts to catch their suppers, for which there is always an excellent selection of winged insects. The feet of these one and half inch shiny green frogs, which can change their colour from green to brown should they wish to escape detection, are fitted with sucker pads which enable them to climb glass, so that no insect is really safe. They quickly become tame, and can usually be easily detected on their favourite perches, to which they return with faithful regularity. They spend their winters indoors, as 45° F [7° C] is too warm for them to hibernate, but not warm enough for them to feed.[6]

There is also a little green lizard, sometimes known as the American chameleon [or green anole] (*Anolis carolinensis*), whose colouring is also variable according to the temperature – green for warm, dark brown for cold.[7] He starts the summer in the greenhouse, but soon finds his way on to an adjacent brick wall masked in the foliage of an *Akebia* [possibly the chocolate vine]. Here he stays until late October, by which time he seems to be quite ready to let us catch him, and take him to his winter quarters.[8]

We have had one or two interesting but uninvited guests. On one occasion I saw a strange bird in trouble among the pots, and only after I had caught it, realised that the bright russet plumage could belong to none other than a nightingale. Unfortunately, it was too late in the season for us to hear his serenade.

A very unwelcome visitor appeared one morning during our coffee break, but we could never fathom how he got there. Out of the corner of my

Anolis carolinensis (Wikimedia Commons – Sydney Dragon)

eye I caught a glimpse of quickly moving dark greyish fur which immediately suggested Mr. Mole, and sure enough he it was, rushing around close under the wall. Before I could move one or two pots out of the way he was out of sight under the soil, and it was only frantic efforts on my part, with the only immediately available, and very inadequate, weapon – a dessert spoon – which enabled me to keep up with his incredible speed and catch him before he disappeared under the floor. Grabbing him firmly by his velvet coat at the back of his head – remembering warnings as to the sharpness of his nails – he was quickly banished to the field on the other side of the road, with a wall between us – a narrow escape indeed from some real vandalism.

Notes

1. Possibly now called *Oxalis vulcanicola* 'Siliquosa'.
2. Not listed in *RHS Plant Finder 2023*, nor on the Internet.
3. This species is not in the labiate family (*Laminaceae*), but in the *Acanthaceae*.
4. Now seems to be called *Nematanthus strigillosus*.
5. Now called *Salvia elegans*.
6. I have recorded temperatures of around 50° C in my greenhouse, so would hesitate to keep animals there, particularly amphibians.
7. The green anole changes colour according to mood, stress level, activity level, and as a social signal. There is conflicting evidence of a link with temperature.
8. The comments in Note 8 of Chapter 11 regarding release of non-native animals apply here too. The European tree frog (*Hyla arborea*) is quite capable of breeding in the UK, and several viable populations have existed here, although the best known, at Birdbrooke in London and Beaulieu in the New Forest have died out, possibly due to collecting. There seems to be a possibility that this species is an extinct native, as it was written about by Norfolk farmer Sir Thomas Browne in 1646 (See 2006 article by Snell). The green anole (*Anolis carolinensis*) is incapable of sustaining a population in the UK, as temperatures of 26° to 29° C for an extended period are required to incubate its eggs.

Chapter 20

CHANGE IN THE HERBACEOUS BORDER

Now[1] after exactly thirty years it is time to review the major changes which have taken place in what might be called the personnel of the garden. A great many of the original plantings are still here, but sometimes nature has taken her toll by frost, or gale, or plain old age. Only last year our original sixpenny maple was mortally wounded by a twelve inch fall of snow in December while it was still in full leaf. It tried very feebly to break from the base, but so often when this happens it is only a last flare of vitality before the finale comes. Though one always misses an old friend there is the consolation that it will leave a valuable space for one of the newer acquaintances which are always waiting on the sidelines.

Most of the original inhabitants of the erstwhile herbaceous border to the north of the strip of grass – which hardly rates high enough to be called a lawn, to which status it had first been elevated – had finally been moved out to the vegetable garden where they quickly showed their appreciation of the less sun-baked conditions. A clump of delphiniums was retained at each end of the border and the oriental poppies refused to be evicted. Without any warning from the donor I once acquired a gorgeous double scarlet poppy, but so far we have been unable to curb its ruthless passion for extension of territory. Its saving grace is that, as do all these poppies, it disappears completely directly it has flowered. Lovely as it is *en masse* it should only be introduced if its exuberance can be confined. Painting the leaves with paraquat[2] when they first appear does seem to lessening its vigour a little but the underground runners are very persistent. How much easier the introduction of selective weedkillers has made a gardener's life! Actually, we prefer to introduce only the minimum of chemicals, but at times such as these the temptation is too great to be resisted.

Incidentally two other happenings of the last decade which have had a far-reaching influence on gardening are the growth of the flower arranging movement, and the increasing use of ground cover plants, or boscage, as it is sometimes called. The former has made by far the greater impact for many a flower arranger has become a gardener almost overnight, and her demand for unusual material to grow has brought to light again many a plant which had lapsed into obscurity – a demand to the benefit of all concerned. It has also sharpened many people's perception of the intrinsic beauty of the plants themselves, and of the art of placing in the garden, though the aesthetic effect has to be governed by the space available, and it is surprising how comparatively harmonious such a medley can become by virtue of nature's wiles.

The demand for carpeting has also brought to light many forgotten plants of a slightly different type, where the accent is rather more on a procumbent habit and abundant foliage than on flowers. The advantage is that provided the ground is thoroughly cleaned of weeds before planting takes place there will be none of the vacant ground which Nature abhors and immediately starts to colonise with her own selection for which invasion, competition should prove too strong. Apart from this aspect even in the driest spell the ground is kept shaded and comparatively moist under a leafy coverlet.

To return to the border after this digression one of the first shrubs to arrive on the scene was *Philadelphus microphyllus* [mock orange] a twiggy four foot *Syringa*[3] [lilac] which fills the garden with the scent of pineapple in June. This was quickly followed by the orange flowered *Chaenomeles maulei*[4] [Japanese quince] grown from a pip. The gracefully arching growth of *Escallonia* 'Donard Seedling', and the grey velvet of *Phlomis fruticosa* [Jerusalem sage], whose whorls of yellow flowers leave starry calyces which make enchanting Christmas decorations when whitened and touched with glitter.

Two more very handsome umbellifers joined the giant hogweed [*Heracleum mantegazzianum*] here – the biennial [garden] angelica [*Angelica archangelica*] whose flower heads, leaves and stems are all of the same delicate

Phlomis fruticosa (Wikimedia Commons – Robert Flogaus-Faust)

green (probably more familiar on cakes in crystallised form) and the native Cambridge milk parsley (*Selinum carvifolia*) whose leaves are modelled on finest filigree lace, and whose creamy umbels, carried stiffly rather like the spokes of an umbrella, instantly attract attention by their unique character. Not to be overlooked are two other outsize plants which favour this area. The three foot shrubby *Euphorbia characias wulfenii* [Mediterranean spurge] prefers to choose its own site and particularly approves of the warmth and shelter at the base of the elderly *Chamaecyparis* [false cypress], where it flaunts its eighteen inch spikes of shrill green for weeks in early summer, and the rather tender, almost shrubby *Geranium anemonaefolium* [confusingly called Canary Island cranesbill] from Madeira, which has so far kept itself going by seedlings, and makes a yard-wide mound of shining foliage and wide red-purple salvers on sticky stems in midsummer.

In the early days a *Malus* x *purpurea* 'Eleyi' [crab apple] with dark leaves and flowers had been put in as a seedling about a third of the way along, and although this is now covered in ivy (for the convenience of nesting birds) and has been badly pruned into a mushroom to keep it from throwing too much shade, it forms a welcome host for a large yellow rose whose identity is uncertain. Behind this and next to the original *Chamaecyparis lawsonia* 'Fletcheri' [Lawson's cypress] has arrived *Rubus* tridel,[5] a fairly recently introduced hybrid of the blackberry group, which sends out long arching wands wreathed in May with white blooms as large as dog roses. In desperate need of support for a flourishing plant of *Clematis orientalis* [Chinese clematis] whose yellow petals are usually likened to a stripe of orange peel, we stupidly planted it by the *Rubus* not knowing its rampant qualities, and forgetting it would be in full growth just when the *Rubus* should be pruned, so by the end of summer there is a veritable jungle growth in the corner. The *Clematis* has, however, now begun sending up suckers round its feet, and as soon as we can secure another specimen its parent will be removed to a more suitable spot. It may not survive, but I always remember the advice of an experienced gardener, "Never let a plant know you are afraid of it" and it is indeed surprising what plants will put up with if they are carefully treated.

At the centre back of the border we tried to persuade a *Buddleja alternifolia* [alternate-leaved butterfly bush] to grow as a standard, but it insisted on making a thicket of slender branches massed with lavender clusters, whose gracefully weeping growth was entirely lost in such a position so this too had to be banished, and its place has been usurped by the mock laburnum [more commonly called evergreen or Nepal laburnum] (*Piptanthus nepalensis*) with large golden tassels and dark, shining, evergreen foliage which it drops sometimes in bad winters, though the shrub itself is quite hardy. This is flanked on one side by the spectacular *Spiraea arborea* 'Arguta', a sheet of solid white in early May, and on the other by the here rather unsatisfactory Korean relation of the forsythias – *Abeliophyllum distichum* [white forsythia]. Even in the warmest corner of the garden, after two moves, it refuses to give us more than a few of its honey-scented blush-pink flowers every spring when they should be literally packed together – we suspect it prefers less lime with its diet.

Towards the western end two or three of the later flowering shrubby mallows or tree hollyhocks [or rose mallow] (*Althaea frutex*) go to the opposite extreme and show their approval of the fare provided by smothering their sturdy shoots with pompons of white, red and dull purple respectively. There are single cultivars but the doubles last much longer. In front of these again *Daphne tangutica* [Tangut daphne], grown from seed, has made a handsome bush, whose leathery green leaves clothe stout shoots tipped at intervals all though the summer with clear pink flowers – to be matched at the east end by a neat eighteen inch dome of *Daphne collina* [rock daphne],[6] covered in May with fragrant rosy pink clusters.

This side of the garden seems best to fulfil the needs of the old roses. *Rosa* 'William Lobb' in off-beat shades of mauves and purples is trying to out-rival the *Chamaecyparis* [Lawson cypress] in height, and the purple-flecked flowers of *R*. 'Honorine de Brabant' are produced in very satisfactory profusion. *R. pendulina pyrenaica* [Alpine rose] runs about among the other shrubs pushing up its twelve inch stems bearing one or two single deep pink flowers in April in succession to the willowy shoots of the dwarf almond [more commonly called Russian almond] (*Prunus tenella*) festooned with conspicuously bright pink flowers in April.

Rosa 'William Lobb' (Wikimedia Commons – Storye book)

The clump-forming *Potentilla fruticosa* 'Mandshurica'[7] [shrubby cinquefoil] and *P. fruticosa* 'Vilmoriniana' with cream and white flowers respectively are seldom out of flower the whole summer. An old-fashioned shrub that finds its place here is southernwood or lad's love (*Artemisia abrotanum*) with its grey-green aromatic foliage. *Forsythia ovata* [Korean forsythia] is rarely seen, but we find it very satisfactory and apparently not recognised by the predators which often strip the more spectacular species. It makes a fairly flat-topped bush of about four feet, and smothers itself with primrose flowers at a very early date.

Most of the smaller willows are irresistible where we are concerned, so when we were introduced to *Salix hastata* 'Wehrhahnii' [halberd willow] of the rather unfortunate name as a dwarf, a specimen was immediately planted at the eastern end of the centre pool. It is now nearly five feet square, but one could forgive it anything for the enchanting snow-white miniature powder puffs which bedeck its red-purple branches for weeks in early spring, before they finally change to gold almost overnight. It is sometimes called the goat's beard willow on account of its shaggy catkins when they are fully expanded, but this seems rather unfair to a willow which at other seasons is the epitome of neatness. A recent catalogue designates it much more aptly as "snow pussy".

We are sometimes given credit for architectural planning, but the effects are merely the results of "happy accidents". One of these occurred when at the opposite end of the pond we introduced the tall reed-like *Miscanthus sinensis* 'Zebrinus' [Chinese zebra grass], which not only gives shade and shelter to the pool, but also makes a wonderful foil for the large round leaves of its neighbour *Peltiphyllum peltatum* (formerly *Saxifraga*)[8] [umbrella plant], and finally sends up handsome plumes in October, which make splendid winter decorations for the house as well as the garden. The creeping gnarled rhizomes of the *Peltiphyllum* have now advanced right into the pond much to the delight of the frogs. The tall naked stems precede the leaves, and are crowned with umbels of pink.

A large clump of the miniature *Salix* x *gillotii* [Gillot's willow] also overhangs the pool but unfortunately, as so often happens, it is the female of the species, so that the numerous catkins are modestly and inconspicuously attired in grey-green. Another very pleasing plant which finds the boggy border very comfortable is an unusual loosestrife (*Lysimachia ciliata*) [fringed loosestrife] with pale yellow lantern-shaped flowers. Several

Salix hastata 'Wehrhahnii' (Wikimedia Commons – Simon Garbutt)

small sedges help to disguise the artificial nature of the structure. *Carex pseudocyperus* [cyperus sedge] with its dangling fruit spikes rather resembling green furry caterpillars, *C. japonica* [East Asian sedge] whose fine leaves are bordered with cream, a little oddity from Australia, *C. buchananii* [Buchanan's sedge], of which the whole plant is clad in the soft rusty brown so typical of that continent's vegetation, and *C. grayi* [Gray's sedge] which a facetious visitor christened the "Sputnik sedge".

The wide yellow suns of *Hypericum* 'Hidcote' [St. John's wort] – a genus second only to the potentillas [shrubby cinquefoils] in taking the palm for continuous flowering – are flanked on one side by the silver *Helichrysum alveolatum*[9] [everlasting flower, or Cape gold], and on the other by the aptly named *Veronica cupressoides* [cypress hebe] whose slender grey-green branches deceive many a visitor before they erupt at the tips into a mass of lavender blossom.

One of the most spectacular plants in the garden, and one which few people recognise, bush clover (*Lespedeza thunbergii formosa*) (formerly *L. penduliflorum*) flings its lengthy wands with abandon across other shrubs, and then right at the end of the summer in September produces drooping panicles of eighteen inches or more in length of gorgeous red-purple pea flowers. So far it has defeated our efforts at propagation – the seed pods never get a chance to ripen, and cutting material is almost non-existent though we read recently that if one can be brave enough – take root cuttings. One cutting did pretend to grow for a while but even the greatest care failed to get it through the winter, a not unusual happening we find, though we are desperately anxious to get more plants.

There are no actual carpeting plants in this bed though lady's mantle (*Alchemilla mollis*) and the taller soft grey-leaved [Greek] horehound (*Ballota acetabulosum*)[10] do their best. Both are flower arranger's dream plants. The *Ballota* is almost shrubby in character with long spikes ringed at close intervals with circlets of curiously shaped sepals which surround the insignificant flowers. These often gracefully curved spikes dry exceptionally well for winter decoration. In Greek Orthodox churches they are sometimes used as wicks for oil lamps.

Once people are introduced to lady's mantle they invariably feel their gardens are not complete without it – not only is it very decorative in itself but it makes a wonderful foil, particularly for blue flowers, and also spills out gracefully to soften the edge of a path or border. The round, frilled, softly hairy leaves have a priceless habit of holding glittering raindrops in their centres, and the tumbling froth of tiny greenish-yellow flowers reminds one of *Gypsophila* [baby's breath]. Old plants are apt to get woody-stemmed and unwieldy and are best taken out, but there are always seedlings ready to carry on. The genus is native to northern Britain but this larger charmer comes from Asia Minor. The filigree leaves of Alpine lady's mantle (*Alchemilla alpina*) have the brightest silver-shimmering reverse of any plant we know.

It is quite a good plan to plant a selection of grey-leaved plants such as these, or *Santolina* [lavender cotton], or the well-known lamb's ear (*Stachys lanata*)[11] beside a path, as the faint luminosity of their foliage will help to define the edge after dark. *Lychnis coronaria* 'Alba'[12] [rose campion] is particularly useful in this respect, its silvery clumps having the bonus of chalk-white flowers on foot high stems.

One does not often think of herbaceous clematis, but in the back row here are magnificent specimens of *Clematis recta* [bush clematis] whose handsome foliage is in this case glaucous green, and in the other, *C. recta* 'Purpurea', deep red-purple. Even on this poorest of poor soil they carry their wide, two foot long clusters of creamy flowers, very similar to those of old man's beard [or traveller's joy – *C. vitalba*], at the top of five foot stems – in fact they are the only plants in the garden which have to be staked.

Round the feet of the larger shrubs several "old fashioned" plants find congenial homes. *Lychnis chalcedonica*[13] with its scarlet Maltese crosses so effective in a bowl of white marguerites [*Argyranthemum frutescens*], has considerable sentimental value, as does the purple-blue spring vetch (*Orobus vernus*)[14] which, with its colour variations of pink and white, pale blue, and white is a real harbinger of coming summer. A would-be coloniser that is allowed a certain amount of liberty on account of its charm is the white version of rosebay willowherb (*Epilobium angustifolium* 'Album')[15] whose tall slender spires of purest white flowers make such a wonderful contrast with the "round heads".

There are fewer liliaceous plants here than elsewhere [in the garden] but those that are here make up in size for lesser numbers. Towards the back *Curtonus paniculatus*[16] – often facetiously known as 'Aunt Eliza' in reference to its erstwhile surname *Antholyza* – and its very near relation, *Chasmanthe vittigera*[17] [African corn flag], with their neatly ribbed leaves and their giant orange-red montbretia-like flowers – which are almost indistinguishable without close observation – lift their branching heads above the shrubs in late summer. The bulbs of *Crinum* x *powellii* in both pink and the unrivalled white form grow ever more gigantic in the slight shade of the *Prunus* and certainly show no sign of regret for their African home.

Another African which really closes the summer season, opening its buds only a few days before the first of the autumn crocuses appear – is the miniature red hot poker, *Kniphofia galpinii*,[18] whose dainty orange spears seem always to take us by surprise when they unfold among the fine grassy leaves.

Notes

1. The date of 1969 has been pencilled on the page at this point, but not as a correction; more as an observation. This reinforces the belief that Katie and parents moved into Harveys, and started gardening there, in 1939.
2. The use of paraquat has been banned in 58 countries, including the UK where it was banned in 2007. It was widely used in suicides because ingestion of very small quantities is fatal, and has been linked with the development of Parkinson's disease.
3. *Philadelphus* is in the *Philadelpheae* family, and not closely related to *Syringa* (lilac) in the *Oleaceae family.*
4. Now called *Chaenomeles japonica*.
5. This, of course, is not the correct format for describing a hybrid. Katie is referring to what is now called *Rubus bambusarum* 'Benenden' which is commonly called tridel berry.
6. Now called *Daphne sericea*.
7. Now called *Potentilla fruticosa* 'Manchu'.
8. Now changed again to *Darmera peltata*.
9. Now called *Helichrysum splendidum*.
10. Now called *Pseudodictamnus acetabulosus*.
11. Now called *Stachys byzantina*.
12. Now called *Silene coronaria*.
13. Now called *Silene chalcedonica*. Common names are Maltese cross and Jerusalem cross.
14. Now called *Lathyrus vernus*. An alternative common name is spring pea.
15. Now called *Chamaenerion angustifolium* 'Album'.
16. Now called *Crocosmia paniculata*.
17. Possibly now called *Chasmanthe aethiopica*.
18. Now called *Kniphofia triangularis* according to *RHS Plant Finder 2023*, but *K. galpinii* listed on RHS website!

Chapter 21

CHANGE IN THE SALAD BED

For several years after our arrival the piece of ground between the border and the boundary path was used as a salad bed, but firstly a piece was taken off for the scree bed, and Toad Hall later removed a sizable portion from the other end, so finally it turned into a very welcome annexe to the garden proper. It is of course the most sheltered part of the whole domain, especially from the gales which periodically cause such havoc – often in the late summer when everything is in full leaf. Here we planted one of the few larger evergreens, *Eucryphia* 'Nymansay' [leatherwood], that we have admitted since we became slightly more sensible in these matters, as we felt that its potential height would do no harm here. When it had reached about six feet it received a most unwelcome snub in the shape of the famous 1962-1963 winter[1] and although its original leader was ruined, it has slowly recovered and now has a double head which may possibly have the advantage of restricting its ultimate height. The snowy whiteness of the many-stamened saucers is a real pleasure in August against the feathery *Cupressus* behind it. This cultivar has the proven distinction, not shared by the species, of thriving on chalky soil.

The next addition was rather in the nature of a mistake as we had no idea that the innocent little seedling in a pot meant to emulate the *Eucryphia* in spite of ruthless pruning after it had flowered. The offender, a broom, *Genista tinctoria* var. *virgata*, hails from Madeira and has frosted foliage, and long slender stems weighed down by the profusion of flowers. An August gale is quite likely to put an end to its career one day, but its offspring are all ready for such an event. A very similar broom – *G. cinerea* [Spanish broom], almost indistinguishable in flower, but with rather darker and stiffer stems, looks like a glorious waterfall against its sombre background in the front garden a little earlier. Every time it snows we expect this to be unable to rise again from its almost prone position but its resilience is remarkable. A useful factor in identification is that while *G. tinctoria* var. *virgata* seeds freely, *G. cinerea* seldom does so, in this country at any rate.

Another all-purpose shrub of the same family for which the same evergreen backcloth has proved its undoing is *Cytisus battandieri* [Moroccan broom] (for which the name *Argyrocytisus* has now been proposed).[2] This is a strongly growing shrub whose sturdy shoots and trifoliate leaves are covered in silvery down. As the countryside is rapidly becoming denuded of cover for birds, our *Cupressus* become progressively a more favoured roosting place, particularly for sparrows, and in this garden at any rate, they cannot rest until they have stripped every grey-leaved plant of its foliage. It was some time before we realised what was happening to our promising young bush, and it had taken very severe punishment for which we were blaming the insect world. It has taken three seasons to make up its mind that life is really worthwhile, and now has to be disfigured with the spun nylon web during the whole of the nesting season, as incidentally, does *Salix hastata* 'Wehrhahnii' [halbeard willow], though here the effect of white catkins and white web is quite ethereal. The flowers of the *Cytisus* appear as large upward pointing golden clusters shaped rather like the fruit from which it possibly takes its name – pineapple broom, and are particularly generous with their fragrance. Like most brooms it is easily raised from seed and has no fads about soil. A shrub which was completely annihilated by the attentions of nesting birds was the tree purslane (*Atriplex halimus*) which has blue-grey leaves.

A bad winter robbed us of another outstanding, though doubtfully hardy, shrub which we had hoped might escape injury in this warm corner – a hybrid Australian daisy bush (*Olearia* x *scilloniensis*) raised in the Isles of Scilly. The grey-leaved five foot bush was literally sheeted with white for several weeks in early summer. Unfortunately, our last batch of cuttings failed – they never were easy.

Daphne 'Somerset' is happy here and so is an unusual relative of

Phygelius capensis (Wikimedia Commons – Stan Shebs)

Helichrysum [everlasting flower] – *Ozothamnus rosmarinifolius* [sea rosemary] with long shoots clothed with very thick narrow leaves, reminding one of a conifer, and exciting reddish-pink buds which open into flat heads of white flowers. *Erica terminalis* (formerly *E. stricta*) is a [tree] heath which really flourishes on a limey soil – growing three to four feet high. The rose-pink flowers appear at the end of the summer, and, fading to a warm bronze, are attractive even in midwinter. A rooted cutting of *Stephanandra incisa*[3] [lace shrub] – a relative of the spireas – is making a nice bush with conspicuous rusty stems and finely cut leaves which colour pleasantly in autumn.

Cape figwort [or Cape fuchsia] (*Phygelius capensis*) produces its elegant panicles of penstemon-like flowers with great freedom and has never seemed ruffled by anything our climate can do. *Hebe* 'Bowles's Hybrid'[4] is seldom without some of the charming pinkish-mauve flowers on its abundant branching stems, and creeping out from beneath the *Euchryphia* 'Nymansay' [leatherwood] opens a succession of milky-blue periwinkles (*Vinca difformis*) throughout the winter.

On the other side of Toad Hall, beyond the little path, a bush of *Daphne pontica* [twin-flowered daphne] has almost reached the proportions of a hedge, and is another of the plants to flood the April evening air with scent. It is a pity more plants are not free of their scent in this way, as are, for example, the sweet box [*Sarcococca confusa*] in January or the Spanish broom (*Spartium junceum*) in July and August. Violet leaves of the sweet briar [*Rosa rubiginosa*] are well known for their fragrance, particularly after rain, but the spicy odour of the curry plant (*Helichrysum angustifolium*) with its fine grey leaves, or even the slightly alcoholic tang of the pleasant little pink-flowered creeper *Phuopsis stylosa* [Caucasian crosswort], are far less familiar. It is a curious fact that blue flowers are mostly not scented, apparently relying on their colour for appeal, yet when we come to the next colour on the spectrum, violet – lavender and heliotrope go to the opposite extreme.

Everlasting peas (*Lathyrus latifolius*) seed themselves around, and the finest of them all, the pure white green-centred version often called 'The Pearl',[5] scrambles over *Daphne pontica* [twin-flowered daphne] giving it almost a second blooming. Another little-known member of this genus which flowers in early summer, and has ample clusters of an unusual shade of reddish-purple, is *Lathyrus undulatus* [wavy pea].

We felt that no garden would be complete without a *Garrya elliptica* [silk tassel bush], so one was duly installed under the east facing vicarage wall. Already we have had to move the path back twice to accommodate it, but it would be a terrible winter that did not see those wonderful six to eight inch grey-green almost frilled catkins beginning to lengthen before Christmas. It is now ten feet or more high in spite of hard picking, and its top leaves often get singed by wind or frost, but the tree as a whole remains unperturbed.

Ivies are another of our passions and the wall between the *Garrya* and the vicarage is now completely clothed with the grey-green and white of *Hedera helix* 'Silver Queen'. The walls of the first reptiliary support vigorous growths of *H. helix* 'Glacier' and *H. algeriensis* 'Gloire de Marengo' in strong contrast. Both are variegated, but while the former is a small leaved retiring plant, the latter is boldly handsome, with deep red stems and large leaves varying from deep green in the centre, through grey to creamy white margins. There is also a fine spread of a very narrowly lobed cultivar which we believe to be *H. helix* 'Digitata' [finger-leaved ivy]. Toad Hall, too, has its share of ivies of which the most interesting are two other variegated types, *H. helix* 'Minor Marmorata' whose deep green leaves are stippled and splashed with cream, and another which I am never certain I really like except as a captive pot plant, which is known as 'Jubilee' or sometimes 'Golden Heart'.[6] This again has deep green leaves but this time they are centred with gold, which we think gives a very spotty effect when viewed from a distance. So far we have never found any of the ivies sold as house plants anything but hardy in the open, though it must be admitted that the large leaves of 'Gloire de Marengo' do sometimes look rather dejected in the spring.

Still another of our enthusiasms to which we give full rein is a collection of grasses which, especially the larger species, do so much to unify the appearance of a plant community such as ours. Besides, it is a field capable

Garrya elliptica (Wikimedia Commons – Sean A. O'Hara)

of infinite expansion even in a limited area, for many of them can be tucked into very small corners. The drooping bottle brushes of *Pennisetum alopecuroides* [Chinese fountain grass] are particularly charming in late summer, long after the waving plumes of the feather grass (*Stipa pennata*) have corkscrewed their sharp pointed fruits into the ground by an in-built method similar to one of which a good many geraniums make use.

Planted with caution the handsome silvery-blue of the lyme grass (*Elymus arenarius*)[7] contrasts with the rather coppery green of *Spartina pectinata* 'Aureomarginata' [gold-edged prairie cord grass]. Bowles' golden grass (*Milium effusum* 'Aureum') sows its neat sulphury tufts in quite the most effective spots where they gleam all summer. Much brighter in colour is the golden foxtail (*Alopecurus pratensis* 'Aureus'), and this again is eclipsed in metallic lustre by another newcomer to the garden, *Hakonechloa macra* 'Variegata'[8] from the Far East which has considerable affinity with a miniature bamboo.

Silver variegated grasses are also much in evidence as in the case of cock's foot (*Dactylis glomerata* 'Variegata') or false oat (*Arrhenatherum* var. *bulbosum* 'Variegatum'), and one of the most striking of all which likes a damp spot, *Glyceria maxima* var. *variegata* [variegated reed sweet grass], whose inch wide cream and green striped leaves develop a strong mauve-pink flush when they appear in the spring and again before they die in autumn.

Notes

1. Snow started falling around Christmas 1962, and much of Britain was covered in snow for over two months. Drifts were 8 feet deep in Kent and 15 feet in the west. Temperatures remained below zero, and the sea froze at Kent out to a distance of one mile. It was the coldest winter since 1740.
2. The name has indeed changed to *Argyrocytisus battandieri*.
3. Now called *Neillia incisa*.
4. Now called *Veronica* 'Bowles's Hybrid'.
5. This culivar is not listed in *RHS Plant Finder 2023*, nor on the Internet. However, the following cultivars are listed: 'Red Pearl', 'Rosa Pearl' and 'White Pearl'.

6. These are two distinct cultivars, although 'Goldheart' (not 'Golden Heart') is now called *Hedera helix* 'Oro di Bogliasco'. It is this cultivar which matches Katie's description, with 'Jubilee' having green and silver or cream leaves.
7. Now called *Leymus arenarius*.
8. Now called *Hakonechloa macra* 'Alboaurea'.

Chapter 22
THE SHRUB BORDER (3)

Moving on now to the shrub border, the main outlines remain unchanged though time has swept away quite a few of the original occupants – ginkgo [*Ginkgo* biloba] and bird cherry [*Prunus padus*] have increased their stature very considerably and the former is definitely the winner in the contest for height. These have been joined in the back row by a vigorous specimen of that evergreen standby *Viburnum tinus* [laurustinus] in the centre, and *Prunus tomentosa* [Nanking cherry] at the east end, both beloved of the birds for nesting purposes. Thrushes and blackbirds prefer the former, while goldfinches and greenfinches find the latter's slender twigs ideal for their wonderfully woven cups, often perched right at the tips of the shoots, but frequently undetected until the leaves fall, though the hungry fledglings apprise us of their presence. The flat white clusters of the *Viburnum tinus* are very well known, but the fragile pink flowers of the *Prunus* festooning the stems in early spring before the plaited leaves appear are less familiar.

In an attempt to rectify our original mistake of not planting sufficient evergreens, two, so far very slow growing conifers and a holly have been added, but it seems likely that our successors will reap most of the benefit. *Chamaecyparis pisifera* 'Squarrosa' [Sawara cypress] has the loveliest soft glaucous blue foliage, and *Crytomeria japonica*, sometimes known as Japanese cedar in one of its forms, has very deep green, almost mossy, foliage. The holly (*Ilex aquifolium* 'Silver King')[1] has creamy white edges and is now beginning to make its contribution to the scene.

At the far end a particularly good form of *Elaeagnus macrophylla* [large-flowered oleaster], closely related to the olives – though larger than most of our shrubs – could not have proved to be more exactly the right shrub in the right place. The very young shoots clad in rusty bark, and bearing wide silvery green leaves, curve and fling themselves about in the most graceful way so that sometimes the side shoots seem to be pointing backwards. They need careful pruning to keep the bush in shape, but flower arrangers and florists are insatiable in their demands for any pieces that are available. This fills in the whole of the end of the shrub border in a way we certainly did not expect, but which is precisely what was needed to contribute to the element of mystery. To add to its virtues it produces daphne-shaped fragrant blooms of the same silvery colour in October and November though, unfortunately, usually too late for it to have a chance of setting the amber fruits.

A Japanese member of the same genus, *Elaeagnus multiflora* [cherry silverberry], is just coming to maturity at the other end of the border. This grows in a more normal manner but its small leaves are less prone to hide the more abundant flowers which open in midsummer, so that quite frequently the bush is absolutely laden in autumn with its large glistening orange edible berries. Sheltering beside it is another willow, *Salix bockii* [small-leaved willow?], a potential three foot bush with neat foliage, which distinguishes itself by producing catkins in October, which it does very freely, but unfortunately our specimen is the rather dowdy female for whom we have not yet managed to find a "better half".

A golden mottled *Aucuba japonica* [Japanese laurel] under the quince [*Chaenomeles japonica*] has finally made an impenetrable screen, augmented by a flourishing *Mahonia japonica* [Japanese mahonia] flanked by *Viburnum fragrans*[2] [Farrer viburnum]. Our mahonia grew gaunt and leggy and finally wind-rocked, but before it was replaced we read that if it was cut back carefully to one of the joints directly it had fruited it would keep its shape, and this has proved very successful, as it flowers abundantly often from December to March. The last *Cistus* has just succumbed to a tricky winter, so, we regret to see, have all the cuttings, and as we just cannot do without them to drop their tissue paper petals every evening, and open a fresh batch of single "roses" next morning, they will have to be replaced.

The lead plant (*Amorpha fruticosa*) we have seen only in one other garden whence our seedling was transferred. It leafs very late in the season, and its dense terminal spikes of flowers attract immediate attention because of their unusual shade of deep blue centred with conspicuous brilliant

Elaeagnus multiflora (Wikimedia Commons – KENPEI)

orange stamens. The butterfly bush (*Kolkwitzia amabilis*) is indeed an amiable member of the community with its long arching sprays of pale pink, yellow-throated flowers followed by curious bristly fruits. *Bupleurum fruticosum* [shrubby hare's ear], brought as a seedling from Malvern where it is naturalised, is noteworthy as being a shrubby member of the enormous umbellifer family (the umbrella bearers). It has stiff sturdy stems, sea-green leaves and, over a very long period, flat heads of yellow flowers, which are excellent for cutting. It will grow anywhere, even in shade, but is more compact in the open.

The so-called poet's laurel [or Alexandrian laurel] (*Danae racemosa*) revels in shade, and sends up graceful shoots of shining green leaves, making, in time, handsome clumps, but with us at least, very loath to be propagated. *Syringa* 'Bellicent' is a very amenable substitute for the larger lilacs, though the scent is not quite so attractive. *Spiraea* x *vanhouttei* upholds the family reputation for floriferousness in May, and a harbinger of spring which must not be omitted from mention is *Corylopsis pauciflora* [winter hazel], whose cowslip-scented, palest yellow drooping clusters never fail to open in March before the leaves come, which in their turn give a good display of colour in the autumn.

Although they do well in this soil deutzias fail to arouse our cupidity – it is nice to feel one has not lost all power to say "No" – so they do not come into the picture, but we are looking for a vacancy for the bodkin bush [or barbed wire bush] (*Colletia armata*)³ from South America with the formidable spines, and delightfully fragrant crowded pinkish flowers in early autumn, and also for *Osmanthus delavayi* [Delavay osmanthus], whose very dark green leaves make an admirable foil for the white scented flowers in April.

We can never resist any interesting shrub roses that come our way so the 'threepenny bit rose' (*Rosa farreri persetosa*)⁴ sends up tall bristly stems, and studs them in profusion with the tiniest imaginable single pink roses – a delightful sight especially in association with *Kolkwitzia* and *Syringa* 'Bellicent'. *Rosa* 'Celeste', whose buds are surely the loveliest of all in exquisite shell pink nestling among the grey foliage, and *Rosa* x *alba* 'Alba Maxima' with wide creamy blooms, seem to like the cool root run and *Rosa*

Bupleurum fruticosum (Wikimedia Commons – Lord Koxinga)

'[F.J.] Grootendorst', originally planted at the edge of the lawn to shade the sink, literally covers itself with clusters of double pink flowers fringed like miniature carnations, and frequently produces deeper blooms of the type from which this cultivar originally came. A rather particular favourite at the front of the border is an eighteen inch pink-flowered burnet [or Scotch] rose [*Rosa spinosissima*] collected in the Channel Islands.

Tree peonies find a place here – *Paeonia delavayi* [Delavay's tree peony] is never without several of its deep crimson saucers set off with golden anthers, and so far six foot *P. ludlowii* [Ludlow's tree peony] has not yet outrun its allocated space, and gives us a good show of butter yellow flowers. The least robust moonlight peony (*P. wittmanniana*)[5] once produced seventeen flowers at once but so far has not gathered sufficient strength to do it again. One or two interesting spurges flourish among the shrubs. *Euphorbia palustris* [marsh spurge] makes a three foot branching bush of soft green and yellow in spring, remains quite undistinguished throughout the summer, but greets the approach of autumn by turning lemon yellow for some weeks before the leaves fall again. *E. sikkimensis* [Sikkim spurge] is another tall grower which greets spring with a forest of ruby-red shoots which fade, in due course, to the regular family green.

Clumps of one or two of the choicer elephant's ear saxifrages now known as *Bergenia* are beginning to help with keeping down the weeds, assisted by the improved (Chinese?) form of the foetid iris (*Iris foetidissima lutea*)[6] with large straw-coloured flowers, and particularly handsome berries. The weeds of cultivation on chalky soils always seem so much more conspicuous than those elsewhere – a flourishing plant of groundsel [*Senecio vulgaris*] sticks out like a sore thumb, though no doubt the grower of sorrel [*Rumex acetosa*] on acid soils has the same feeling about that. We often long for a neighbouring oak tree, or even a beech, for the fallen coppery leaves scattered over the ground give a warm look in winter that nothing else can provide.

A good collection of epimediums [barrenworts] with their creeping root stocks, handsome leaves, and bold spikes of sulphur, bright yellow, red or rust, which often appear while the weather is still wintry, do their part nobly as ground cover, while *Tellima grandiflora* [fringe cups] with its spikes of fringed green bells seems to be planning to shoulder the entire job. *Podophyllum peltatum* [May apple] too, runs about underground pushing up its attractive palmate leaves, but never producing fruits. The latest addition to these dual purpose plants is the uncommon Chinese *Rubus tricolor* [Chinese bramble], whose thornless but bristly red, arching stems take giant strides and root at intervals, bearing heart-shaped leaves of deep shining green with white undersides. It is apparently this triple colour scheme which has led to its specific name. It has not yet obliged us with the large, edible red berries it is supposed to produce.

A plant one often sees recommended as a shade carpeter is *Pachysandra terminalis* [Japanese spurge], a dwarf white-flowered member of the box family, which has an attractive variegated counterpart, but neither of them will have anything to do with any part of this garden, so presumably they are allergic to lime. Actually, we could have a perfect natural ground cover of primroses [*Primula vulgaris*] in all colours, but our arch enemies the sparrows deny us this pleasure, and as the enormous woody root stocks take so much goodness out of the ground they are ruthlessly weeded out. Our only hope of growing polyanthus [*Primula* x *polyantha*] is in a well cottoned[7] formal bed, which is rather out of place here.

Fortunately auriculas [*Primula auricula*] appear to be immune to the sparrows' attentions. Their round, often mealy, bear's ear leaves have considerable architectural value, and there is a wide selection of colours, but one must go round them very carefully in spring, pulling the clumps apart for replanting, as they invariably try to pull themselves out of the ground in winter.

Notes

1. Now called *Ilex aquifolium* 'Silver Queen'.
2. Now called *Viburnum farreri*.
3. Now called *Colletia hystrix*.
4. Now called *Rosa elegantula* 'Persetosa'.
5. Now called *Paeonia daurica*. Is this a tree peony?
6. This is not a recognised subspecies. Perhaps Katie is referring to *Iris foetidissima* var. *lutescens*.
7. I believe Katie is referring to the need to criss-cross the bed with strands of cotton to prevent damage by sparrows or other birds.

Chapter 23

THE "BANTAM" BORDER

As outside help in the garden became increasingly difficult to obtain, we came to the conclusion that it would save a great deal of work to buy eggs, and so with a certain amount of regret the bantams were handed over to a friend, and our planting area was happily extended. Before this we had installed a *Hydrangea aspera* 'Macrophylla', which likes a modicum of shade, under the wall opposite the *Elaeagnus* [*multiflora* or *macrophylla*?]. This has now reached its maximum height of about eight feet, and in late summer makes a magnificent show of its flat heads of pale blue florets, surrounded by lilac-pink bracts. The leaves are long and tough, and the cinnamon bark flakes away in autumn.

Three ivies were quickly introduced to clothe the rather bare wall – the strong growing parsley-leaved ivy (*Hedera helix* 'Crispus')[1] with the finely ruffled leaf margins, which is much appreciated as a nesting site by the resident robins. The large-leaved green and cream Persian ivy (*H. colchica* 'Variegata')[2] which prefers to grow along the base of the wall and display its remarkably handsome foliage to better advantage than when climbing, and finally, a specimen of the apparently normal type ivy, the shoots of which turn a lovely soft yellow where the sun reaches them.

The violet willow (*Salix daphnoides*) whose purplish shoots acquire a downy bloom in winter, was planted right in the corner of the boundary and has so far been kept in check by vigorous pruning at catkin time but the day is certainly not far off when it will have to be cut off to start again – that is – pollarded. By the New Year the silvery catkins are clearly visible, peeping out of their sheltering buds. Another sturdy but very slow-growing willow took its place here too, *Salix magnifica* [foot-catkin willow] from China, whose rather large laurel-like leaves open from brilliant red buds.

Actinidia kolomikta [kolomikta vine] sends out long twining stems on which, in a sunny summer, it produces leaves which are green at the base changing abruptly to white flushed with pink for the rest. Unfortunately, it usually needs more sun, and more space, than it has here but it is too big to move. Next to it is another Chinese plant which always excites attention – *Itea ilicifolia* [holly-leaved sweet spire], which has evergreen holly-like leaves. In late summer every branch is laden with nine to twelve drooping spikes of small white flowers which are often mistaken for catkins. Unlike a good many evergreens it is quite easy to raise from cuttings.

A bad mistake we made in spite of the direst warnings – so we have no one to blame but ourselves – was the introduction of dwarf bamboo (*Pleioblastus pumilus*) round the feet of the violet willow, for which we are now paying rather heavily, though the three foot *P. variegatus* 'Fortunei' is always welcome, with its long white-striped leaves which, in common with those of other members of the genus, strongly object to snow falling on them. In direct contrast is the appearance of the next shrub which found its way into this bed. A native of Sikkim,[3] *Coriaria terminalis* var. *xanthocarpa*, as its name suggests, produces its rounded spikes of small currant-like yellow fruits at the end of the almost horizontal branches, on which the leaves are so regularly arranged and lie so flat as almost to suggest a fern frond.

Here, too, is a plant to which I will never forget my first introduction. At intervals down the full length of a long shady border appeared this tall eye-catching plant with long deep pink spikes in a way vaguely reminiscent of a small species lilac at first sight. Enquiry showed it to be the Indian ink plant (*Phytolacca clavigera*),[4] so-called because these flowers give place to soft fruits full of brilliant red-purple juice, only too ready to stain hands or clothes. It makes an enormous tuberous root when it is happy, in not too dry a place, and sends up stout, freely branching stems each supporting a flower spike shaped rather like a corn cob, and making a display for two or three months in late summer. It usually produces a few seedlings in spite of the birds, which can be removed to strategic positions. There is a greenish white species – *P. americana* [American pokeweed], which is not nearly so desirable.

Rosa 'Belle de Crecy' pops up here and there in the bed and x *Fatshedera*

Phytolacca clavigera/*Phytolacca polyandra* (Wikimedia Commons – Karelj)

lizei[5] [tree ivy or aralia ivy] – the unique result of crossing the two genera *Fatsia* (aralia) and *Hedera* (ivy) – instead of merely two species – fills in the dark corner behind the willow with its large and lustrous leaves. The variegated form of this hybrid is often sold as an attractive house plant.

Hostas of every form we can lay our hands on approve of this situation, and have to be parted roughly every three years, even though it takes a strong man to part them, or they would make an impenetrable jungle. Their naming is in a very fluid state at the moment but our favourites are two that we know as *Hosta fortunei aurea* [Fortune plantain lily], whose spring foliage is almost primrose yellow, darkening with age, and *H. undulata* [wavy plantain lily] in which the cream-centred leaf is edged with bands of green. The one least often seen in other people's gardens is the late flowering *H. plantaginea* [fragrant plantain lily] whose variety *grandiflora*[6] has, curiously enough, the smaller flowers of the three. The leaves are not particularly distinct, but it waits until early autumn to open its pure white, scented trumpets.

The pink flowered version of the lily of the valley (*Convallaria majalis* var. *rosea*) apparently does not appreciate lime, and does not emulate its rampant relative, though possibly it prefers to choose its own quarters. The beautiful and all too fleeting snow-white St. Bernard's lily (*Paradisea liliago*)[7] of the alpine pastures seems quite happy. So too does that comparative newcomer to our garden – *Crocosmia masoniorum* [giant montbretia] which is akin to the montbretias – a [sub] family whose mostly flame-coloured flowers are almost luminous in the dusk – with handsome fan-shaped foliage and tall branching sprays of brilliant orange flowers in August.[8] Luckily our search for the warmest, dampest spot led us to put it in the light shade of the willow, for its intense colour makes it a little difficult to please, but here, where at this season it has the field to itself, except for the mauve and violet spires of the hostas, it is particularly arresting.

Crocosmia masoniorum (Wikimedia Commons – Dick Culbert)

Two especial treasures which often halt visitors in their tracks and have obviously found congenial homes are *Arum creticum* [Cretan arum] raised from our own seed which put up eight buttercup yellow spathes last year, and the autumn snowdrop [also known as Queen Olga's snowdrop] – *Galanthus octobreasis (reginae-olgae)*,[9] which usually opens its flowers punctually for the first day of the month for which it is named. It certainly does look a wee bit out of place, and one cannot really make up one's mind whether it is the first or the last snowdrop of the season.

[What follows may not be related to the "Bantam" Border. It seems to have been originally designated as a new chapter, but the chapter number has been deleted, and no chapter title provided. In addition, some of the paragraphs have a diagonal line drawn through them, indicating that they were to be omitted, but I have included them because I believe they have some merit.]

Looking for still further means of reducing labour a few years later we came to the conclusion that the disadvantages of our tenancy of the Vicarage garden out-weighed the advantages in the endless struggle against ever encroaching weeds from the flanking hedges and long neglected grassy banks, not to mention the constant pruning of ancient apple trees so – not without pangs of regret – we transferred our vegetables, cutting beds and miniature nursery to the not too distant allotments. There, where everything is planted in straight rows, weed control is reasonably easy and if a plant on trial becomes too large for us to manage, or behaves badly in any other way, help can be imported without the ever-present fear of a heavy foot on a special treasure.

There too, the soil is a little heavier and curiously enough in that open situation plants often survive the winter quite happily which kills them here – in the current season all cistuses were wiped out here but there, less than a quarter of a mile away, they are unhurt. This has always made it possible to keep one or two specimens which stray from the category of large shrubs into that of small trees, such as the cherished native whitebeam (*Pyrus aria*),[10] *Prunus pissardii*[11] [cherry plum], *Berberis* x *stenophylla* [golden barberry] and *Sorbaria aitchisonii*[12] [Kashmir false spirea], not to mention other such outsize plants as red hot pokers (*Kniphofia*), the globe thistles (*Echinops*) and for that matter globe artichokes, including the cardoon (*Cynara cardunculus*) for their leaves and dried seed heads which are always in demand for winter decoration.

Another advantage is that we have at last been able to realise our ambition for an adequate compost heap, though even the best of helpers never seem able to resist putting on those bits of sticks which multiply into a barbed wire entanglement when one wants to use the finished article! Unfortunately, we suffer too much from the attentions of wandering rats ever to venture on a heap of any kind near the house.

Needless to say, with such a large amount of vegetation to support, the ground needs all the assistance it can get in addition to the compost and bonfire ash which are in any case mostly ear-marked for vegetables. We can sometimes get organic manure from a neighbouring cowstall, but it brings with it such enormous crops of weeds that its use has been prohinited in the home garden. Mulching with lawn mowings has also been suggested but apart from the fact that grass grows exceedingly quickly from leaf cuttings, our mowings are always full of *Veronica filiformis* [slender speedwell] – the blue-eyed charmer from Asia Minor which has found the climate of Britain so much to its liking that it has spread far and wide, and has so far proved resistant to any known weedkiller, and the Welsh poppy (*Meconopsis cambrica*)[13] whose yellow and orange fairy lanterns illuminate most of the shady corners in May. Had it never been introduced to the garden our weeding time would have been reduced by at least three quarters. So, we have to fall back on a certain amount of chemical fertiliser augmented by generous waterings – when there is not a drought – of "sheep tea". After a long absence sheep have come back to this part of the South Downs so that a short walk with a basket will provide the wherewithal for many gallons of tonic water if a small sackful is kept in a convenient tank. This solution is, of course, weed free and therefore the more to be recommended. An occasional dose of the same concoction is very much welcomed in the greenhouse.

Notes

1. Does Katie mean *Hedera helix* 'Cristata', which is now called *Hedera helix* 'Parsley Crested'?
2. Now called *Hedera colchica* 'Dentata Variegata'.
3. A state in north east India.

4. Now called *Phytolacca polyandra*. Other common names are pokeweed and poke root.
5. The hybrid symbol x in front of the name indicates that this is an inter-generic hybrid. The contributing species are *Fatsia japonica* (Japanese aralia) and *Hedera helix* (common ivy).
6. Now called *Hosta plantaginea* var. *japonica*.
7. The correct name is *Anthericum liliago*.
8. According to Wikipedia the term "montbetia" is commonly used in the British Isles for orange-flowered *Crocosmia* x *crocosmiiflora* cultivars that have naturalised, while "crocosmia" is reserved for less aggressive red-flowered cultivars.
9. *Galanthus reginae-olgae* is correct. I can find no listing for *G. octobreasis* in RHS Plant Finder 2023, nor on the Internet.
10. Rose's *Wild Flower Key* and *RHS Plant Finder 2023* give *Sorbus aria* as the correct name for the common whitebeam, but Wikipedia gives *Aria edulis*.
11. Now called *Prunus cerasifera* 'Pissardii'.
12. Now called *Sorbaria tomentosa* var. *angustifolia*.
13. Now called *Papaver cambricum*.

Chapter 24

THE BULBS (2)

It will be fairly obvious that the names of more and more plants of the type usually known, rather inaccurately perhaps, as bulbous, are creeping into the story. Not only has our predilection for these increased, but they have so many advantages, apart from the fact that they are virtually labour-free, which as the years fly by becomes even more important. They certainly need dividing and replanting at intervals, but they do not have to be kept going by cuttings – or pruned – or have any other of the many attentions which herbaceous plants in particular are always needing.

Once one's fancy has been caught by miniature daffodils it seems as if these fit more naturally into a garden such as this than do their larger kin, which are more at home in grassy places and woodland gardens. Actually, our choice among the species is somewhat limited as the moisture lovers such as *Narcissus cyclamineus* [cyclamen-flowered daffodil], and to a lesser degree *N. triandrus* [angel's tears daffodil] will have nothing to do with us, except in pans, and even the hoop petticoats (*N. bulbocodium*) need quite a lot of fussing, though *N. bulbocodium romieuxii*[1] very obligingly opens its cream flowers in the greenhouse for Christmas most years.

The dwarf trumpet daffodils however increase and flourish very freely and what a delight their first opening bud. *N. asturiensis* [pygmy daffodil], the smallest of all at three inches, in pure yellow usually leads the way, to be followed by *N. pseudo-narcissus* [wild daffodil] itself, of which the outer petals are typically creamy yellow, with a deeper yellow tube, and by *N. minor* [lesser daffodil], again in pure deep yellow. When it condescends to flower *N. caniculatus*[2] is the perfect miniature of the well-known *N. tazetta* [tazetta daffodil], but though it increases steadily, it is niggardly of bloom, except after a hot summer.

The golden yellow rush-leaved jonquils should be in every garden – they never fail to fill the air around them with their powerful fragrance – and the more delicate species make wonderful plants for pans where, though perfectly hardy, they are safe from the various hazards of open air life. *N. watieri*[3] [watier cliff narcissus] in shimmering white, and *N. rupicola* [rock daffodil] in creamy yellow, are a pure delight in cold house or frame.

There are cultivars in plenty including those with *N. cyclamineus* [cyclamen-flowered daffodil] and *N. triandrus* [angel's tears daffodil] in their pedigree, which are not as fussy as their parents, and which allow an increasingly wide choice to suit every garden. *N.* 'Thalia' has several creamy-white flowers on each stem, *N.* 'Hesla' in creamy-white and *N.* 'Orange Queen' in real orange-yellow, again with three or four flowers to a stem, are some of our favourites, even if not the newest kinds.

N. x *gracilis* with several pale, scented blooms to each scape is almost always the last to flower, often waiting till early May. The neatly doubled *N. pseudo-narcissus*, whose origin is a mystery but which is often known as Queen Anne's daffodil,[4] increases fast here, but unfortunately the original bulb was planted too close to some singles of identical colouring which we have not so far managed to remove entirely, so it does not always get the acclaim it deserves.

As often happens in the wild, so here it is now almost impossible to put a trowel into the ground without exhuming some sort of bulb. Particularly prone to decapitation are the slender twiggy rhizomes of the wood anemones which are always hard to detect, but which seem to take no exception to this form of propagation provided they are quickly covered with soil. Several of these windflowers, whose appearance means that spring has come to stay, are indispensable and really have no vices. The single white *Anemone nemorosa* has a double version of which the flower centre has developed into a perfect rosette. There is also a cultivar known as *A. nemorosa* 'Allenii' whose lavender petals are backed with rosy purple. Another cultivar, *A. nemorosa* 'Robinsoniana' is deeper lavender, while *A. nemorosa* 'Royal Blue' vies with the later leathery-leaved *A. hepatica*[5] in colour. *A. apennina* [blue anemone] has the most enchanting sky blue flowers and will even thrive in competition with grass.

A. ranunculoides [yellow wood anemone] makes wide clumps of small upturned buttercups, which in the cultivar *A. ranunculoides* 'Seehiana'[6] increase in size and turn to sulphur in colour. *A. blanda* [Balkan anemone or winter windflower] with a more corm-like root is the first to flower and has seeded itself far and wide in the sun. All these and the various colour forms of the Grecian peacock anemone (*A. pavonina*) in shades of scarlet, magenta or purple are scattered among the shrubs in all parts of the garden and flutter in a joyous dance in the vernal breezes.

Arisarum proboscideum [mouse plant] is a delight to children, for the long brown tip of the spathe looks all the world like a mouse's tail disappearing into the clumps of shining leaves. The closely related *Arisaema candidissimum* [Chinese cobra lily] is quite a late riser, often showing no sign of its presence until in June its handsome leaves, rather too large in the end to be altogether welcome, push up rapidly and unfold to reveal the very decorative pink and green striped spathe. A particularly appealing version of our common native soldiers and sailors (*Arum maculatum*) [more commonly known now as lords-and-ladies or cuckoo pint] is *A. italicum* 'Marmoratum' [Italian arum] on whose shining leaves all the veins are traced in milky white – (never leave a flower arranger alone with your plant!).

The dragon arum (*Dranunculus vulgaris*) will on the other hand be quite safe if it is in flower because as it is desirous of being pollinated by flies it chooses to call their attention to its presence by emitting the most appalling smell of fleshy decomposition. Without this its spotted stems and red-purple spathe would be much more in demand. A fascinating family this [*Araceae*], and we are always on the lookout for potential additions to our collection.

The bluebells are well represented apart from the native *Endymion scripta*[7] and the larger, but not more beautiful *E. hispanica*[8] [Spanish bluebell]. *Hyacinthus amethystinus*[9] [Spanish or amethyst hyacinth] presents its porcelain blue miniature version in May, and the large conical heads in shades of blue or white of *Scilla peruviana* [Portuguese squill], which in spite of its [Latin] name hails from the Mediterranean – follows them very closely. Some people find the near-magenta *Gladiolus byzantinus*[10] [eastern gladiolus or common corn-flag] unwelcome, and it certainly increases almost like a weed, but in our eyes it blends admirably with the fresh young green around it – especially in combination with newly forming honesty [*Lunaria annua*] pods. For years we have tried to grow the pure white version, which should be well worth while, but it resolutely refuses to do more than send up a few weakly leaves no matter what we do. Every year without fail *Gladiolus tristis* [marsh Afrikaner] begins to send up its slender stems in the early New Year, and they seem completely unperturbed by anything our climate can do between their appearance and the final production of their sweetly perfumed greyish-ivory spikes in late April.

The reticulate section of irises is almost always ready to greet the opening days of March with its varying shades from the pale blue of *Iris* 'Cantab', through the gamut of blues of 'Clairette' and 'Joyce', to the deep mauve of the type and the reddish purple of 'J.S. Dijt', and as these bulbs increase freely we can expect annually increasing pools of welcome colour. Unfortunately though, they too have become popular titbits for the birds, but an expedient we have recently found effective, and not too distracting, is to inflate a small polythene bag and tie it to a short stick. It will move with every breath of wind, and is certainly not popular with the marauders.

Incidentally, labelling, particularly among the bulbs has always been a headache – if the birds do not pull them up puppies do – not to mention

Arisaema candidissimum (Wikimedia Commons – Peter Coxhead)

the frost displacing them. Finally, we decided that our list of acquisitions should be embellished with little plans showing the newcomer among its established permanent neighbours, and this seems to work well.

Snowdrops have come in for particular attention and do very well scattered around the shrubs. Fortunately, snowdrops are relatively immune from the attention of pests, feathered or furred, their bulbs being armed with minute sharp crystals called steroids, which even hungry mice will not tackle.

It is hard for any but a connoisseur to detect the differences between some of the named cultivars, but at least the representatives of the three main sections of the genus are easily recognisable, and we have been lucky enough to amass a good collection. Constant division has filled the garden to overflowing with both the single and the longer-lasting double form of common snowdrop (*Galanthus nivalis*) – ribbons of them outline the borders of the grass verges outside the walls, and even now they are pushing themselves out of the ground again in a plea for attention.

Preceding these by a month and representing the broad-leaved section comes the larger *G. elwesii* with conspicuous glaucous foliage, and long stems. There are several cultivars of these of which one of ours begins to flower in early December. The next to appear is the vigorous and handsome G. 'Atkinsii' which should be in every garden. Rather later, but close to it in merit, comes two other cultivars G. 'Magnet' which is easily recognised by the long slender pedicels of the flowers, and G. 'Viridapice' which comes quite late in the season, and ornaments its very large outer petals with green tips to match the inner ones, looking almost as if they had been dipped in green ink.

A quaint little snowdrop which does not take life too easily is G. 'Scharlockii', whose buds often open while still facing upwards, and whose twin spathes are lengthened and separated so that they have been likened to asses' ears. *G. ikariae* is a smaller plant with distinctive bright green, shining foliage in complete contrast to all the others, while *G. plicatus*, though quite one of the most robust, is immediately recognisable by its habit of folding back the edges of its wide glaucous leaves. So much for the snowdrops, of which one could surely never have too many.

The next place in our affections has almost certainly been given to the fritillaries, particularly as so many of them have been obtained only as seed. The largest of all – the crown imperials [*Fritillaria imperialis*] – came with us when we moved in, but although there are a goodly number of bulbs we seldom get many of their handsome candelabras. For this we cannot lay the blame either on the soil, or its moisture content, for those that grow the tallest and flower magnificently every year without fail, have been gradually overgrown by the lower branches of the *Chamaecyparis* [false cypress] 'Fletcheri', so that the soil is not only very poor but also very dry – in fact we are wondering if we have inadvertently hit on an answer to the universal problem of their non-flowering, and have replanted a good many bulbs in as nearly similar sites as possible in an effort to obtain proof – it surely cannot be entirely coincidence that the first spring of the experiment showed more buds than usual. We used to have both the orange as well as the yellow, and are always hoping to see the former reappear, as their replacement is an expensive business these days.[11] We like their foxy odour which floats across the garden on a warm spring day but it is anathema to some people.

The well known native *Fritillaria meleagris* [fritillary] finds our soil uncongenial and only just manages to exist, though their chequered maroon to white lanterns are most desirable. *F. pyrenaica* [Pyrenean fritillary] on the other hand, is making itself quite at home and seeding itself about. This has campanulate bells, on eighteen inch stems, in varying mixtures of mahogany-purple, chequered with crimson and yellow, hard to describe but lovely to look at. *F. gracilis*[12] is rather similar but there is more greenish brown in the pigmentation of its slender bells. *F. pontica* [Pontic fritillary] is also proving amenable, and here the bells have even more green in their composition and are not chequered, but are easily recognisable by the black nectaries which are tucked in round the stem at the base of the bell.

F. acmopetala [pointed-petal fritillary] has jade green bells with green nectaries and the tips of the petals have little brownish upturned ruffles. This, too, seems as if it is going to settle down. The *piece de resistance*, judging by current catalogue prices is *F. pallidiflora* [Siberian fritillary]. As its name suggests it generally has several greenish waxy white bells on a two foot stem and the leaves are wider than is usual. *F. persica* [Persian lily] has quite a different appearance, pushing up a stout stem hung with twenty or more small wide open bells of dull purple with a grey sheen – a most distinguished plant showing its appreciation of our placing by sending up more fat "noses" every year. There were several pots of flourishing seedlings coming along to augment the collection, but an "ill wind" certainly did them no good when it shifted their stand a few inches and threw them all on the floor in a most unholy conglomeration! Most of them were recaptured, but we shall have to wait many more moons for them to flower before we can return the labels to the correct pans!

There are a few true lilies among the shrubs, but on the whole, except for orange *Lilium henryi* [Henry's lily or orange tiger lily] and the old favourite Madonna lily (*L. candidum*), they are not happy in spite of our ministrations. We have always wanted to try *L. chalcedonicum* [scarlet martagon lily] but its astronomical price makes us think twice![13] We were always advised to put a handful of sand under bulbs when planting, but this has been discontinued as we found it only served to attract ants to the spot, and this may have something to do with our lack of success. In any case lilies are rather hard to fit into such a garden as this without being too conspicuous, so we are not inconsolable.

Fritillaria pyrenaica (Wikimedia Commons – Roger Culos)

A group of *Galtonia* (*Hyacinthus*) *candicans*[14] [summer hyacinth] with their branching spires of white bells make a worthy substitute in August, especially when they have for neighbours clumps of the hardy *Agapanthus* Headbourne hybrids in their varying shades of blue, as well as a particularly fine clump of a white cultivar. An even choicer plant – especially in the eyes of the flower arrangers – is *Galtonia princeps* [summer hyacinth] with the same graceful habit but whose bells are softly green.

Camassias – dark blue, light blue and cream, single and double, precede them with their two foot starry spikes – the cream being far too willing to colonise – and the asphodels of similar appearance and stature whose outer petals bear a rusty stripe, all bring a welcome contrast of form to a mixed border.

The other genus which brings a great variety of colour enhanced by their consistently spherical inflorescences great and small, are the alliums or ornamental onions, garlics if you like, but some visitors seem to lose interest directly it is mentioned. Contrary to expectations they do not pervade the air with the family odour, unless the foliage is bruised, or the bulb disturbed. An offshoot of flower arrangement is the drying of flowers for winter decoration, and these alliums make excellent subjects for the purpose, keeping their colour for months on end if picked fresh and allowed to dry gradually.

Allium siculum [Sicilian honey garlic] is a tall grower with branching umbels of almost square straw-coloured bells stained with red on the outer surface. After they have bloomed these have the unique and curious habit of lifting their flowers and pointing them skywards, reminding one irresistibly of a cluster of space rockets. *A. giganteum* [giant onion] has large, slightly over-rated purple heads. *A. pulchellum*[15] [keeled or witch's garlic] has abundant and particularly welcome reddish-violet flowers in August, some of which point upwards and some down. *A. moly* [yellow garlic], which can be used for cooking, has bright yellow star-like flowers in large loose heads making a striking display. A comparative newcomer, *A. obliquum* [lop-sided or twisted leaf onion] with pale yellow globes on stiff slender stems will almost certainly be hailed with delight by flower arrangers. Going to the other extreme are some species with hair-like leaves fit for the choicest rock garden – such is *A. callimischon* whose pearly flowers suddenly and unexpectedly erupt from the side of a stiff stem which has been in evidence for months.

Notes

1. Now called *Narcissus romieuxii*.
2. Now called *Narcissus tazetta lacticolor*, although it is possible that Katie is referring to *Narcissus* 'Caniculatus'.
3. Now called *Narcissus rupicola watieri*.
4. Other double daffodils are also given this common name, including *Narcissus x odorus* 'Plenus'.
5. Now called *Hepatica nobilis*.
6. Not listed in *RHS Plant Finder 2023*, nor on the Internet.
7. Now called *Hyacinthoides non-scripta*.
8. Now called *Hyacinthoides hispanica*.
9. Now called *Brimeura amethystina*.
10. Now called *Gladiolus communis byzantinus*.
11. These are still relatively expensive bulbs, typically costing around £13 for three bulbs in February 2025.
12. Not listed in *RHS Plant Finder 2023*, nor on the Intranet, but listed on the latter is *Fritillaria messanensis gracilis*.
13. Things haven't changed. Current price (February 2025) for one bulb is £43!
14. *Galtonia candicans* is the correct name.
15. Now called *Allium carinatum pulchellum*.

Chapter 25

THE SMALL GREENHOUSE

The joys of a warm greenhouse led us to appreciate how much more easily we could tend the plants which like a little winter protection if we, too, could get under the glass instead of having to reach into a very cumbersome cold frame, so as might be expected at last the inevitable happened. At exactly the right moment an advertisement appeared for a do-it-yourself seven foot by six foot "greenhouse kit" at a very reasonable price, and we decided to "have a go". The detailed instructions could not possibly have been easier for two rank amateurs to follow, and only a screwdriver was needed. The obvious site was where the cold frame had stood for so many years, with its back to the shrub border and the door at the south end. Naturally there were one or two little mishaps such as setting the framework containing the door at the wrong end, but fortunately this was discovered before the cement used to anchor it to the foundations had dried! The great advantage was that it had a unique system of glazing requiring no putty, so that we were able to boast proudly of having completed the job entirely unaided.

And what a boon this little house has been – actually as the years fly by it is very tempting to grow more and more plants under glass (or an equally satisfactory plastic substitute) for our comfort as well as theirs. All sorts of treasures which for various reasons of size or doubtful hardiness are best not exposed to the rigours of the outside world, spend their winters here very happily, with the added comfort of a paraffin lamp on nights when frost is forecast. A few plants, particularly bulbs, dislike paraffin and lose no time in making this quite clear by drying off their foliage, but it does not appear to do the plants any lasting damage if they can be accommodated elsewhere in the future, though it will probably prohibit the season's flowering. Here again we have been able to carry out our aim of having something interesting to see at all seasons, but particularly in the winter months.

By the time the chrysanthemums are over, not to mention the brilliant blue *Aster pappei* from Africa and the shrubby musk[1] from California (*Diplacus glutinosus*)[2] with its shining, sticky foliage and brownish-orange flowers, the first buds are ready to open on the half-hardy *Genista fragrans*[3] [florists' genista or Canary broom] in the corner, which has grown quickly though its pot, and like the jasmine in the heated house invites all and sundry to enjoy its heavenly scent.

Two other small shrubs have anchored themselves into position under the single bench – *Coronilla glauca*[4] [glaucous scorpion-vetch] – which here never stops flowering in spite of its cramped conditions, and a rather unusual seaside shrub, moon trefoil [or tree medick] (*Medicago arborea*). This has typical grey-green clover leaves and clusters of small orange-yellow flowers followed by curved seed pods. Not perhaps a particularly exciting plant but one which evidently means to stay, as does *Salvia africana-lutea*[5] [golden sage] grown from South African seed, which has rounded leaves and one of the most curious odours to be found, even in this family [*Lamiaceae*] which rather specialises in them. So far this resolutely refuses to flower for reasons of its own but no doubt will relent one day and let us see its yellow-brown flowers.

Another pair of particularly interesting specimens have also found this a welcome winter retreat. Both make steadily increasing clumps of large rosettes of stiff, recurved, wickedly spiny leaves similar to those of the pineapple, to which both are akin, but while *Fascicularia bicolor* [crimson bromeliad] flushes its inner leaves with scarlet as a frame for the stemless centre cluster of blue flowers which appear in autumn – *Puya alpestris* [mountain puya] sends up a stout spike of really spectacular flowers whose lurid blue-green petals surrounding vivid orange anthers, and a brilliant green stigma, seem almost unreal. The quite large funnel-shaped flowers are borne at the bases of long, tapering spikes composed of sterile bracts which it provides for the hummingbird pollinators attracted by the abundant nectar.

Diplacus glutinosus/Mimulus aurantiacus (Wikimedia Commons – Takwish)

Pride of place under the bench goes to a large pot of *Cypripedium calceolus* [lady's-slipper orchid], which we have not yet been brave enough to try in the open ground. After it had sent up eleven flowering spikes we plucked up courage to repot and divide it, which does not seem to have bothered it at all. It is the only plant of ours which has ever appeared on an important show bench and how proud we were when we found a red card sitting in front of it! It was only luck that it was at the peak of perfection at the critical moment.[6]

The bench itself supports some very precious treasures in the way of rare bulbs. *Cyclamen cilicium* starts the ball rolling in September with delicate rose pink flowers and is followed by *C. graecum* [Greek cyclamen], whose lovely velvety leaves are marbled with white. Our largest corm has just recovered from being decapitated by a mouse when in full flower five years ago! *C. libanoticum* [Lebanon cyclamen] perhaps the most handsome of all, several *C. persicum* [Persian cyclamen] collected in their travels by friends, and *C. pseudibericum* [false Iberian cyclamen] are kept in the warm greenhouse since we lost a batch to an early frost!

By February *Iris danfordiae* [Danford iris] will be ready to open its green-spotted yellow flowers, beating its brethren in the race by a couple of weeks or so. This is a 'must' but is best bought fresh every year to make sure of getting a good display – it is still quite cheap to buy. *I. histrioides* [orchis iris] in deep blue makes an excellent foil. Now, too, the fritillaries will be pushing up their noses with *Fritillaria crassifolia* [broad-leaved fritillary] from the eastern Mediterranean usually the first to open its wide sea-green bells.

Unusual serrate leaves of glaucous-green centred with fawn herald the appearance of what is, surprisingly enough, a member of the berberis family [*Berberidaceae*] – *Bongardia*,[7] whose flower spikes are not unlike those of a yellow oxalis. This is not uncommon in Turkey and thereabouts. The lovely 'Wisley Blue' cultivar of *Ipheion* (*Triteleia*) *uniflorum* [spring starflower] takes up the tale and opens continuously its very attractive deep blue starry flowers – a great improvement on the milky blue of the type which is relegated to the great outdoors, where it flourishes in any sheltered corner. The two closely allied *Muscari moschatum*[8] [musk grape hyacinth] and *M. macrocarpum* [yellow grape hyacinth] in dull yellow and slatey blue usually bring up the rear, and add their musky quota to the pervading scents.

Between the western side of the greenhouse and the path we were able to build up the soil to make what appears to be quite an ideal bulb bed, sheltered from most of the winds and catching every gleam of sun. In these parts, of course, stone of any kind is at a premium, but some while ago when an old cottage was demolished, we were able to acquire a load of what is known as Sussex marble. This marble is a deposit of limestone, incorporating millions of shells of marshland snails, which is found in the Weald of Sussex – hence its name.[9] The unpolished blocks are rough and heavy, but are invaluable for use in this calcareous area for building up beds or edgings of all kinds of jobs where stone is required, as in the case of the bulb bed.

Still more seedling fritillaries are coming to maturity here – a miniature Star of Bethlehem (*Ornithogalum balansae*)[10] makes a sheet of almost stemless white flowers in April sunshine, as a contrast to the golden-centred satin-purple flowers of *Romulea bulbocodium* [crocus-leaved romulea]. A rare and interesting plant which has put in an appearance here, after obviously having been supplied in error, has been identified as *Colchicum*

Cypripedium calceolus (Wikimedia Commons – T. Larsson)

ancyrensis [golden bunch crocus], which starts to flower profusely in January with small pale mauve pointed petals surrounding the conspicuously dark anthers – a welcome stranger. Beside it grows the much sturdier, strongly mauve *Bulbocodium vernum*[11] [spring meadow saffron] which it may have impersonated.

A miniature pink *Allium* flowering in late summer, and various odds and ends too precious for the rough and tumble of community life, find a real sanctuary here. A particular delight in late summer is an accidental grouping of butter yellow *Oxalis valdiviensis* [Chilean wood sorrel], sky blue *Commelina coelestis*[12] [blue spiderwort] with three-petalled blooms like a *Tradescantia*, and the dainty pink blossoms of the only hardy begonia, *Begonia grandis evansiana* [hardy begonia].

Notes

1. More commonly known as the bush monkey flower.
2. Now called *Mimulus aurantiacus*.
3. Possibly now called *Genista canariensis*.
4. Now called *Coronilla valentina glauca*.
5. Now called *Salvia aurea*.
6. At the time Katie was writing this the lady's-slipper orchid was perhaps the rarest plant in the UK, with only one known specimen living in a secret location in Yorkshire. It has subsequently been propagated and planted in a number of sites in the north of England. Katie's specimen presumably originated from continental Europe. Christopher Lloyd, writing in his 1970 book *The Well-Tempered Garden*, mentions a Colonel J. A. Mars of Haslemere, Surrey, being able to supply this species. An American equivalent, the showy lady's-slipper orchid (*Cypripedium reginae*) is an equally impressive plant, and perhaps more readily obtainable. There's a good account of the lady's slipper orchid in Peter Marren's 1999 book *Britain's Rare Flowers*.
7. There are only two known species in this genus – *Bongardia chrysogonum* and *B. margalla*. They do not appear to have common names.
8. Now called *Muscari muscarimi*.
9. Sussex marble is not a true marble, as it has not undergone metamorphosis. In Westminster Abbey the tombs of Edward III and Richard II are made of this material, and the Archbishop's chair in Canterbury Cathedral is made of a single piece.
10. Now called *Ornithogalum oligophyllum*. This is a member of the *Asparagaceae* family, so not a fritillary, which belong in the *Liliaceae* family.
11. Now called *Colchicum bulbocodium*.
12. Now called *Commelina tuberosa* Coelestis Group.

Chapter 26

THE NURSERY AND THE ROSE BEDS

Now it is time to continue our tour towards the house from this winter retreat. A white rosemary [*Salvia*], and prostrate white *Dimorphotheca* – which is hardly ever without flower, and whose lengthy name means two types of seed – flank the door of the greenhouse on the west with their backs to the foundation wall, and two plants of *Sternbergia lutea* [autumn daffodil] bake in the suntrap on the east and usually reward us in autumn with their golden yellow crocus-like flowers among the dark foliage, when they are so welcome. If they like you – or rather if you can find a spot they like this will be your rich reward – if not…

Quite accidentally we seem to have stumbled on a way to persuade *Amaryllis belladonna* [Jersey lily] to flower more regularly. We had to remove the colony by the frame to erect the greenhouse but one or two were overlooked. One or two large slabs of stone were laid to make a path, and what was our astonishment one day the following October to see two flower spikes thrusting up strongly from beneath the slabs, a performance which they have since repeated annually. We have now buried all the rest as an experiment, their lovely pink white-lined trumpets on their stoutish stems being worth any amount of trouble. Many bulbs appreciate this sort of treatment – cyclamen in particular – but somehow we had not thought of it in connection with larger species.

Sharing the *Sternbergia* bed another very worthwhile and trouble-free plant, which not only multiplies at a satisfactory rate but flowers generously in September and October, is *Nerine bowdenii* [Guernsey lily], so exotic in appearance as to make it difficult to believe it is a hardy plant. On a two foot stem this carries a loose umbel of rather shrill pink flowers with wavy-edged petals which have a darker line down the centre. Some folks criticise the colour but anything which will produce flowers during what may loosely be termed the winter months is grist to our mill.

Between the greenhouse and the shrubby patch where the *Aegle* [*Citrus trifoliata* – trifoliate orange] grows is a square plot, quite the weediest in the garden for some unknown reason. Our patience being finally exhausted with the conference pear [a cultivar of *Pyrus communis*] it is now the host of the late flowering *Clematis viticella* [purple clematis] with almost squarely four-petalled purple blooms and the still later *C. flammula* [fragrant virgin's bower], a smaller, very sweetly scented replica of the wild old man's beard [or traveller's-joy – *C. vitalba*]. The ring of deep purple *Colchicum speciosum* [meadow saffron or naked lady] round the trunk steadily increases in size. This bed has quite a mixed population having started life as a nursery, but of course some of the shrubs were left too long and there they will now have to stay until they can be repropagated, although we think they are beginning to blend in a slightly more artistic manner.

One or two hydrangeas nestle against and hide the greenhouse foundations – it was raised on bricks to give more headroom as we are both tall. *Euonymus planipes* [flat-stalked spindle] will probably outgrow its quarters, meanwhile we enjoy its autumn colour and scarlet fruits from which the orange seeds dangle on threads. *Senecio monroi*[1] [Monro's ragwort] has very pleasant grey leaves with wavy edges, less vigorous than the *S. rotundifolium*[2] [called muttonbird scrub in its native New Zealand] usually seen, and making a good backcloth for *Hypericum hookerianum* [Hooker's St John's wort] which departs from the family tradition among the shrubbier species by having light yellow flowers. *Cytisus austriacus* is a valuable late-flowering broom with dark silvery leaves and almost orange-yellow flower clusters. *Cassinia fulvida* (golden heather) [or golden bush] from New Zealand brightens the winter scene.

A deep purplish-pink form of the burnet [or Scotch] rose (*Rosa spinosissima*) is making a most attractive thicket, and *Microglossa albescens*[3] [lilac Himalayan aster or shrubby starwort] produces its flat heads of pale lavender Michaelmas daisy flowers in August – not spectacular but quietly

Sternbergia lutea (Wikimedia Commons – Engeser)

charming. *Osmanthus ilicifolius*[4] [holly olive] whose olive green leaves really do look like holly, should in time produce white scented flowers in autumn. A collection of whipcord hebes [possibly *Veronica ochracea*] interplanted with plain and variegated lesser periwinkle (*Vinca minor*) clothe the little bank by the path at the bottom. Behind this mini hedge is a ribbon of dwarf [bearded] irises – *Iris pumila* in various shades of blue, cream or yellow, the larger *Iris* 'Green Spot' with ivory standards and greenish falls, and *Iris* 'Zia' with palest blue tissue paper flowers. If only irises did not need so much space! – we have always regretted the large bed we had to abandon.

The larger hebes fail to arouse our enthusiasm but a notable exception is *Hebe macrantha*[5] [large flowered hebe] with neat leaves and clear white flowers large than most others. It is quite hardy but would, we are sure, prefer less lime.

Climbing monkshood (*Aconitum volubile*)[6] hangs out its rather unexciting deep blue clusters here and there among the shrubs, and the climbing ragwort (*Senecio scandens*)[7] has yet to become rampant as the catalogues warn, but earns its place in the sun by continuing to produce its panicles of bright yellow flowers as late as November. An architectural plant which seems to have accepted us is the false hellebore (*Veratrum album*) with magnificent pleated leaves and a tall spike of greenish flowers, whose violently poisonous extract is used as an arrow poison.

The finest of the hardy geraniums recently introduced, *Geranium candidum*,[8] with large milk-white flowers, as its name suggests, flings its long stems nonchalantly and harmlessly across the shrubs, and flowers indefatigably. Last but not least the mandrake (*Mandragora officinarum*), which did not shriek when it was removed from an unsuitable spot! – opens its greenish-brown flowers in March and quickly hides them with very large leaves rather in the way of a giant primrose. So far the birds have not allowed us to see the ring of fruits which should lie around the plant.

Passing the shrubby barrier we come to the area dignified by the name of rose bed, which is a reasonably fair description, though squatters are creeping in. After all, even shrub roses cannot live for ever, and vacancies are always at a premium, but so far roses are in the majority, though most of them belong to the category of Old Roses. The strongly scented *Rosa* 'Maiden's Blush' runs about in the background, with *R. moyesii* [Moyes rose] towering above it, grown to quite twelve feet so that the evening sun shines through the almost blood-red single flowers, and the enormous scarlet bottle-shaped hips appear to the very best advantage, and one runs less risk of being caught on its wicked thorns. An un-named but very lovely *R.* x *centifolia* known to us as "mother's rose" – one of the old cabbage or Damask roses – has reached the same height where it has scrambled through the hardy orange tree [*Citrus trifoliata*], and both here, and wherever else it appears in our garden or the neighbour's, it is always loaded with deep pink intensely fragrant blooms.

R. 'Capitaine John Ingram' with small wine-purple blooms, and *R.* "Nuits de Young" whose petals are almost black purple, represent the Moss Roses, and *R.* 'Charles de Mills' and *R.* 'Tuscany', both in shades of velvety crimson, the Gallicas. *R.* 'Cecile Brunner' and *R.* 'Perle d'Or' are exquisite little China Roses, with miniature blooms of flesh pink and apricot shading to cream respectively. Quite a few of these, being on their own roots, and not grafted, have begun to run about and make quite a shrubbery of their own, to which the little old double white *R. spinosissima* [burnet or Scotch rose] makes quite a contribution. We have several times been promised the soft yellow variety of this but so far it has not materialised.

When we were very green and full of enthusiasm for rose species, we were given *R. altaica*,[9] without any warning as to its pernicious undercover habits. For years we have been trying to eradicate its creeping stems – lovely as are its single white blooms – but to date the result is a draw. On a happier note the rambling *R.* 'Alberic Barbier' throws a mantle of cream over the aged quince [*Cydonia oblonga*] in the years between prunings. This is too big an undertaking to be an annual event.

One of the original introductions to this corner was the golden-variegated *Euonymus japonicus* [Japanese euonymous] 'Aureopictus', whose evergreen foliage of deepest shining green centred with gold has made a handsome bush. To strengthen the illusion of a sunshine corner the very showy golden-variegated *Elaeagnus pungens* [silverthorn] 'Maculata' was imported to keep it company – and planted a little too closely. Both are invaluable for winter bouquets.

This bed was the scene of one of our most exciting happenings. At one time a bush of *Daphne mezereum* [mezereon, or February daphne] resided in the coolest corner, and both this and the native green-flowered *D. laureola* [spurge-laurel] seeded themselves about discreetly among the other shrubs. Suddenly we became aware that one of the seedlings looked extremely peculiar in that it had very large, rather purplish green leaves which could not make up their minds whether they were evergreen or not, and rather dark purplish flowers. It was several years before we discovered that we had been lucky enough to have the rare and spontaneous hybrid between the two natives, *Daphne* x *houtteana* occur in our garden; *D. mezereum* being the seed plant. It lived for a good many years and like most daphnes finally died of old age, though not before a professional friend had managed to raise cuttings – no easy task.

The orange-flowered bladder senna (*Colutea* x *media*) has seeded itself here and the Montpelier broom (*Cytisus monspessulanus*)[10] also keeps itself going by seedlings – this sometimes suffers in a gale as it has rather a rigid stem and refuses to bend in the wind. It has pleasant dark green trefoil leaves and bright yellow flower clusters.

Having read somewhere that the winter cherry (*Solanum capsicastrum*),[11] so prized at Christmas time, is really an all but hardy evergreen perennial which would survive in the open ground, we decided to give it a trial, and to our surprise we find it is a real glutton for punishment, having come cheerfully through sixteen degrees of frost [-9°C] several times – it is only about eighteen inches high but flowers and fruits quite happily and is now in its fifth season.

A very elderly lavender hedge crying out to be replaced by cuttings, which root easily, makes a low barrier between which and the path several treasures find a sheltered home. The first chionodoxas[12] [glory of the snow] open their blue eyes here, and here too, we look for the first little wild daffodil – the Tenby daffodil *Narcissus pseudonarcissus obvallaris* with bright yellow flowers on stiff stems. *Allium beesianum*[13] [dark blue garlic] hangs its drooping heads of silvery bells in late summer, and *A. polyanthem* [many-flowered garlic] has, as its name suggests, large clusters of red-purple stars on tall stems. A very old fashioned plant which we were glad to rescue from a cottage garden whence it has now vanished is *Lychnis dioica* 'Flore Pleno',[14] the double form of pink [or red] campion that often grows among the blue bells.

Another very rare plant which badly needs moving to sunnier quarters is the yellow-flowered *Tropaeolum polyphyllum* [wreath nasturtium], which has the exasperating habit of sending up its glaucous-leaved trailing shoots in various places without a clue to the location of the main tuber which has so far completely eluded our cautious search.

Sweet violets [*Viola*] in several shades, and forget-me-nots [*Myosotis*], do their best to provide adequate ground cover. Unless one hardens one's heart sufficiently to pull up the latter before they have really finished blooming they would make an impenetrable blanket, but there are always enough left to make an azure carpet in spring. The most prolific violet which spreads to every corner of the garden is a lovely reddish-purple, probably *Viola* 'Amiral Avellan' which, when it used to infiltrate into the frame, appreciated the extra warmth and produced fine long-stemmed flowers soon after Christmas. Then there is a very tough grower with slaty grey flowers [not named], the truly pink *V.* 'Coeur d'Alsace', and of course the wild white and purple violets [*Viola odorata*]. *V.* 'Sulfurea' is a late bloomer with buff coloured flowers, *V.* 'Alassio'[15] has white flowers stippled with mauve and *V.* 'St. Helena' is almost sky blue.

Viola blanda [sweet white violet] is a charming tufty little white-flowered plant from North America reproducing in miniature another very attractive British wilding which, though not normally found in chalk, does not seem to mind it. This is *V. riviniana* [common dog-violet] which I was taught to recognise as the "owl-faced" violet. There are also pink and white forms of this well worth acquisition. *V. labradorica*[16] introduces quite a new note of colour with its deep purple leaves and flowers to match.

Bringing up the rear quite late in the season are the types from the North American woodlands whose nomenclature is confusing but which make clumps of thick woody rootstocks – *Viola cucullata* [marsh blue violet] and *V. septentrionalis*[17] [common blue or Missouri violet] – as we know them, both with large solid white flowers and distinguished by the former having deep mauve lines as honey guides. Here at any rate, in spite of their native habits, they prefer to be in an open spot where sun can reach them. Last of all comes the tall growing *V. elatior*[18] [fen violet] with milky blue violets branching out from a twelve inch stem. All these keep themselves going

Viola cucullata (Wikimedia Commons – Ayotte, Gilles)

by seed and need only the removal of the worn out woody stems. We did have an outbreak of the nasty leaf rolling mite [*Prodiplosis violicola*?] which affected them quite badly for a time but seemed, in the end, to clear itself up.

Notes

1. Now called *Brachyglottis monroi*.
2. Now called *Brachyglottis rotundifolia*.
3. Now called *Aster albescens*.
4. Now called *Osmanthus heterophyllus*.
5. Now called *Veronica macrantha*.
6. Now called *Aconitum hemsleyanum*.
7. According to *RHS Plant Finder 2023* this is now called *Delairea odorata*. However, Wikipedia identifies these as two different plants; *Senecio scandens* from south-east Asia and the Indian subcontinent, and *Delairea odorata* from South Africa.
8. Listed on the Internet, as is *Geranium saxatile* var. *candidum*.
9. *Rosa altaica* does not now seem to be considered a valid name, with *R. spinosissima* 'Grandiflora' used in its place.
10. Sometimes spelt *Cytisus monspessulana*.
11. Now called *Solanum pseudocapsicum*. The more frequently used common names are Christmas cherry or Jerusalem cherry.
12. Now called *Scilla*.
13. Now called *Allium cyaneum*.
14. Now called *Silene dioica* 'Flore Pleno'.
15. Not listed in *RHS Plant Finder 2023*, nor on the Internet.
16. Now called *Viola riviniana* Purpurea Group.
17. Now called *Viola sororia*.
18. Named in *The Wild Flower Key* by Francis Rose as *Viola persicifolia*. Occurs in Asia, Europe, and very rare in the UK.

Chapter 27

FROM THE BAMBOO TO THE GARAGE

Leaving the rose bed by the path between the *Lonicera* [honeysuckle] hedge and the bamboo, we pass in the corner one of the two trees which owe their presence in the garden entirely to the influence of flower arranging. Some people admire – some detest them. After sitting on the fence for a while we have come down on the side of the admirers. The corkscrew willow (*Salix matsudana* 'Tortuosa') which is tucked in here, makes charming patterns against the winter sky. We have been rather unlucky with this in that a south westerly spring gale, laden with salt from the five mile distant sea, wiped out our first tree just as it was making a nice specimen of about ten feet – now we have just planted another.

The other tree is built on very similar lines and is supposed to have been found wild in a hedgerow by an observant gardener. This, the corkscrew hazel (*Corylus avellana* 'Contorta') is quite inconspicuous during the summer months when clothed with the wide oval leaves, but comes into its own in winter especially when wreathed in catkins. This is in the opposite corner of the garden screening the disused gate – and also screened from acquisitive fingers!

Passing the bamboo corner on our right we come to a square patch between it and the fence, and here we have tried to combine an evergreen bird sanctuary with a summer plunge bed for pots. An exceptionally good form of laurustinus [*Viburnum tinus*] with a lovely pink flush to the clustered buds, and an unusual New Zealander – a *Coprosma* [mirror bush] – guard the northern flanks. The *Coprosma* should produce conspicuous berries but unfortunately they are inclined to be dioecious, needing both male and female plants, though this particular species is not entirely adamant in the matter, as we usually get a few pearly berries in spite of having only one bush. Ours is very definitely of the feminine gender, being so thickly covered in spring with the diaphanous styles as to create quite an effect of mist over the small paddle-shaped olive green leaves.

Backed by the box trees [*Buxus sempervirens*] on the other side of the fence, an overgrown *Skimmia* has only recently acquired one of the lily of the valley scented males as a neighbour, and we are now hoping for a crop of the really spectacular sealing-wax red berries for which we have so far waited in vain. It may be noticed there is very little mention of berrying shrubs, but curiously neither of us care very much for them, especially the one which ripen in autumn, and even if we did, doubtless the birds would get the most enjoyment.

There have been very little changes in the area immediately outside the back door, except that the addition of guttering to the neighbouring cottage has turned this erstwhile shady and very useful damp spot into a desert, much to the dissatisfaction of the rarely seen hoary willow (*Salix eleagnos*)[1] whose long, narrow leaves on slender wand-like stems much resemble those of a rosemary [*Salvia rosmarinus*]. *Physocarpus opulifolius* [common ninebark] 'Luteus', a near relation of the spireas, is a little less lusty than before, but continues to send up its vigorous shoots whose foliage is of purest cream colour, which it retains for quite a while before donning the more sober green of high summer.

The very small space that could be spared for planting round the greenhouse has been put to good use. One of the best and most striking of the variegated shrubs fills the little corner opposite the kitchen window – *Diervilla* 'Florida Variegata'[2] with its cream-edged leaves making an effective frame for the masses of clear pink foxglove-shaped flowers. At the south end a myrtle (*Myrtus communis*) had a tough time for several years, but has so far come up smiling. This is flanked by *Coronilla glauca*[3] [glaucous scorpion-vetch] which, if kept hard pruned, normally blooms steadily all through the winter.

On the sunny western side the lovely Chilean potato tree (*Solanum crispum* 'Autumnale'),[4] the poroporo of New Zealand,[5] reappeared after the shed, over which it used to scramble, was removed, but it cannot now be allowed to go its own way and is kept back to manageable proportions, an operation which it does not in the least seem to resent, in fact it seems to prolong the flowering season. Large clusters of glorious bright purple, yellow-centred flowers, which are excellent for cutting, and which bring a welcome and rather unusual addition to the colour range, follow each other in succession for nearly three months. A really worthwhile shrub for any warm corner when grown in this way as a bush, but usually very hard to place as a climber as it then needs ample support.

Breeze blocks being not at all ornamental we decided to make a narrow border along the side of the greenhouse with more Sussex marble. As it was impossible to affix guttering to the greenhouse the first thing to do was to break up all the old crocked pots and dispose of them all very neatly as a drainage area next to the wall, and then arrange the marble to make a bed about one foot wide and nearly as high. It is not a place for really choice plants, and *Phlox subulata* 'Temiskaming' [moss phlox], with the brilliant carmine flowers, has done its best to take possession but a rather surprising opponent, *Dorycnium hirsutum*[6] [Canary clover] – a shrubby clover with silky leaves and palest pink flower clusters – is disputing the claim, evidently liking the extra moisture it cannot fail to receive. The miniature *Euonymus japonicus* [evergreen spindle] 'Microphyllus Variegatus'[7] has made a neat pygmy shrublet thickly set with silvery white-edged leaves.

Facing us now is what might almost be thought of as another major error, though we still do not know where else the chaste tree (*Vitex agnus-castus*) could have gone. Described as an aromatic European shrub needing a wall to induce it to produce its long spikes of violet verbena flowers often as late as October, a spot against the south wall of the garage seemed ideal, though now that it has reached ten foot or more it is certainly an out-sized shrub. It was badly shaken by the 1963 winter and failed to flower that year, but has now quite recovered. It has to be stopped from blocking the path which has led to some bad pruning, not so far remediable, so we are always glad when the hoary maple-like leaves bring concealment.

Next to this a seedling "granny's curls" or flowering nutmeg[8] (*Leycesteria formosa*) established itself in exactly the right place, sending up ten foot olive-green stems resembling bamboo canes, and loading them for weeks on end with pendulous clusters of white flowers enclosed in claret-coloured bracts, to be followed by juicy berries of the same shade filled with microscopic seeds packed into sticky mucilage, and much beloved of the blackbirds.

Competition for the next position was very close and has resulted in a tangle which would no doubt make proper gardeners frown. A deep red *Althaea* [marshmallow plant] has taken the back seat, with a glorious bush of the old Damask rose (*Rosa gallica*) at its feet, which is literally weighed down with its profusion of lilac-rose blooms, whose delicate scent must surely take the palm for pervasive sweetness. To the left is another excellent small variegated shrub, the golden-green *Symphoricarpos orbiculatus* 'Variegatus',[9] another "must" for the flower arranger. Sheltering under the wing of these stalwarts, *Iris japonica* 'Ledger' might well be mistaken for an orchid when it opens almost flat its frilly lilac petals with their orange beards in early summer. This iris increases rapidly here in any warm corner.

A handsome clump of *Libertia ixioides* [golden libertia] – a New Zealand iris – adds to its girth annually and gives a long succession of snow white, three-petalled flowers above its narrow rigid leaves. Around this is a carpet of *Asarum caudatum* [western wild ginger], a curiosity which hails from America, of which the doubtfully native English species, beloved of herbalists, is called asarabacca [*Asarum europaeum*]. The American species has upturned rusty brown cup-shaped flowers on which the tips of the petals are drawn out into long points, or tails, as its name indicates.[10]

The south western end of the garage would seem to be one of the choicest sites in the garden but it so often happens that one puts a special treasure in just such a place, and it entirely fails to show its appreciation, but push it in somewhere with scant ceremony and it will immediately change its tune. So far we have not dared to move *Lonicera sempervirens* [trumpet honeysuckle] which steadfastly refuses to show us its rusty orange trumpets, but we are only awaiting certainty that cuttings have struck before taking our courage in both hands.

A plant which, on the contrary, has made the most of this shelter from all the cold quarters is the Californian [tree] poppy (*Romneya coulteri*), which pays dividends from July to September, and after considerable activity has come up on the other side of the path to surround the large stone ball which originally formed the weight of a cheese press. With its tall ice-blue stems and leaves, and wide white crumpled tissue paper petals around the central boss of golden stamens, it cannot fail to attract attention.

In early May *Rosa sinica* 'Anemone' [pink Cherokee rose] makes a wonderful picture against the brownish black boards, with its enormous single rose-pink flowers among the shining foliage – with here and there

Phlox subulata 'Temiskaming' (Wikimedia Commons – ghislain118)

Romneya coulteri (Wikimedia Commons – Sheila Sund)

the creamy rosettes of the banksia rose [*R. banksiae*] peeping through. How often we bewail the fact that so few of our walls lend themselves to such purpose, just as the lie of the land and the height of the windows make it almost impossible to provide any room with a satisfying view of the garden, or even a little patch of winter cheer.

Notes

1. Sometimes spelt *Salix elaeagnos*.
2. Now called *Weigela* 'Florida Variegata'.
3. Now called *Coronilla valentina glauca*.
4. Now called *Solanum crispum* 'Glasnevin'.
5. *Solanum crispum*, as its common name suggests, is from Chile and Peru. The name "poroporo" is normally restricted to New Zealand species such as *S. aviculare*.
6. Now called *Lotus hirsutus*.
7. Now called *Euonymus japonicus* 'Microphyllus Albovariegatus'.
8. This is a plant with many common names, including Himalayan honeysuckle.
9. Now called *Symphoricarpos orbiculatus* 'Foliis Variegatis'.
10. Caudatum is Latin for tailed.

Chapter 28

THE UPPER LAWN (2)

It is interesting to note that the word "lawn" not only means a "smooth expanse of ground covered with grass generally beside a house", but also "an open space between trees, a glade", for this is what, without any apparent effort on our part, has developed on the strip alongside the house usually referred to as the front lawn. The gate in the hedge dividing the two gardens gives a surprisingly long vista between the shrubs, whose billowing growth has now effectively disguised the original straight lines. It would really be better if the flowering cherry [*Prunus* 'Kanzan'] were removed but I am afraid it is here to stay. The Judas tree (*Cercis siliquastrum*) threatened to become a casualty because of a mysterious fungus but the trouble seems to have been arrested. Much as we would mourn its loss, its enormous leaves cast a great deal of shade and are very untidy when they fall.

Besides the tumbling gold *Genista cinerea* [Spanish broom] in June the Mount Etna broom (*G. aetnensis*) has now grown tall enough to display its golden cascades against the sombre green of the thuyas [*Thuya plicata* – western red cedar] in late summer. For want of a better place a *Fatsia japonica* [false castor oil plant] was planted in dense shade under the *Gleditschia* [*triacanthos* – honey locust], but seems to have no objections and is steadily filling an ugly corner. The veteran *Daphne mezereum* [mezereon, or February daphne] in the same corner is struggling valiantly to put out a few blossoms but we fear that wind, snow and drought have each taken their toll, and it is likely to be its swansong. Unfortunately, it has never had any berries so although we have seedling daphnes they are of alien stock.

Viburnum davidii [David viburnum] is a low and slow growing bush with particularly attractive dark green deeply parallel-veined leathery leaves which will not regale us with its turquoise berries until we have acquired a female plant. So far all those we have examined in anyone's garden are brothers under the skin, but it is well worth its place without them. Another unusual shrub which has joined this community is *Sarcococca ruscifolia* [fragrant sweet box] whose foliage closely imitates that of butcher's broom [*Ruscus aculeatus*]. This is said to be the most tender sweet box, and is the only one to produce red berries. It has a near neighbour – the hermaphrodite form of butcher's broom – the curious shrubby lily whose rigid stems support what appear to be sharply spine-tipped leaves, but which are really modified branches looking exactly like leaves, and on which are produced the curious little flowers to be followed around Christmas time by an excellent crop of large brilliantly scarlet berries.

At first sight it seemed as if the gift of pampas grass might be an embarrassment, until we discovered it was the smaller cultivar *Cortaderia selloana* 'Pumila', whose plumes are no less imposing at four to five feet, so this was placed at the western end of the lawn, and has made a pleasant addition. At the eastern end, in strong contrast to the softly rounded curves of the pampas grass, was introduced New Zealand flax (*Phormium tenax*) with its rigid sword-like leaves from which an almost unbreakable fibre is produced. It was a toss up whether to give it shelter, or to put it where its spears would make a great decorative impact. In the end compassion prevailed, but really did not reap its just reward for the plant threw up not one but two flower spikes and promptly died, without a sign of a struggle. The only explanation seems to be that the previous winter's snow had damaged the base, causing it to rot below ground.

There have been only a few additions to the company in the bed at the top of the rock wall. *Tulipa saxatilis* [candia tulip] sends up masses of leaves in ever increasing circles, but never a flower, though in a neighbour's garden, where it is confined against the house walls, it produces its pink satin flowers [with yellow centres] quite satisfactorily. *Campanula sarmentosa*[1] is not often seen but it is quite one of our favourites, sending up fifteen inch well-flowered hoary spikes of pale silvery-blue bells, and is a plant which does not share the invasive tactics of so many members of this genus.

Polygonum vaccinifolium[2] [rock knotweed] emulates spikes of pink heather where it tumbles down the wall in late summer though we have a suspicion it would prefer a neutral soil, and *Tetragonolobus maritimus*[3] [dragon's teeth] throws up its small lemon butterflies above the silvery tufts for a good few months, following them with its square sided pods. An engaging plant, the American miniature *Forsythia* [golden bells] 'Bronxensis', at a height of about twelve inches, makes a good showing – and has so far escaped the attention of birds – as does *Spiraea* x *bumalda*[4] [Japanese spirea] with its pink pompoms at about six inches. *Cytisus* x *kewensis* [Kew broom] with flat sheets of cream flowers is another favourite, and shrubby alyssum (*Alyssum spinosum*)[5] makes attractive cushions of grey leaves and white, or sometimes pink, flowers.

One or two miniature roses have found their way here – *Rosa* 'Roulettii' in clear rose pink, *R.* 'Perla de Montserrat' in a more delicate shade, and a dark red rose whose name is lost in obscurity bloom on and off all through the summer with very little attention. *Micromeria corsica* [mountain thyme], a charming little grey-leaved shrublet with a pungent scent, has had to be banned as it is an irresistible magnet to every cat within a wide area – they flock to it sniffing and rolling on it and all its neighbours – in ecstasy.

Close at hand in delicate contrast of colour is the clear pale pink *Scorzonera rosea* seldom mentioned in catalogues these days. This is closely allied to the salsify [*Tragopogon porrifolius*] grown as a vegetable, whose delightful flowers are in a most uncommon shade of mauve. Neither this, nor the winter salading chicory (*Cichorium intybus*) whose similarly dandelion-shaped flowers are the most entrancing shade of blue, should be relegated to the vegetable garden – they are well worth introduction to the flower border.

Punctually every year within a day or two of June 18th the rock wall is lit with miniature greenish fairy lamps, in the shape of glow-worms [*Lampyris noctiluca*], rescued from precarious places in the road outside. Once comfortably established on a clump of rock phlox [*Phlox subulata*] or *Dianthus* [pinks, carnations, sweet Williams] they do not seem to move but patiently await their less conspicuous "better halves" and keeping their lights burning for three or four weeks.[6] Some must survive the winter as they usually reappear the next year in the same chosen spots. It was quite a while before we discovered that these rescue operations are much to our advantage as apparently the larvae eat the soft parts of snails. The very first arrival having been christened "Ermyntrude" it is now quite an event among our friends to come and greet the "Ermyntrudes". The shady stretch along the base of the boundary *Cupressus* [cypress] has been largely given over to geranium species and lungworts [*Pulmonaria*] which do a grand job of weed suppression as well as providing a sequence of colour. The first geranium to bloom is the well named dusky geranium (*Geranium phaeum*) in shades of mauve and purple, to be followed by white *G. rivulare* [white geranium], and bright rosy-mauve *G. sylvaticum* [wood cranesbill] which is a native of northern England. The pink chintz petals of *G*. 'Striatum', and the dull slaty blue of *G. ibericum* [Caucasian cranesbill], carry on until *G. psilostemon* [Armenian cranesbill] breaks out with its large, arresting black-eyed magenta blooms whose brilliance is welcome in this all-green setting. *G. pratense* [meadow cranesbill] closes the season in both its normal blue, and very attractive pure white form, as well as the occasional plant which has not made up its mind which colour it wants to be and produces bi-coloured petals.

The lungworts or Jerusalem cowslips (*Pulmonaria*) flourish mightily under these conditions and the red-flowered ones, in particular, often greet the New Year, with the pale blue and white ones to follow. The best of the bunch, apart from the lovely gentian-blue *P. angustifolia* [narrow-leaved lungwort], which does not care for lime, is *P. saccharata* [Bethlehem lungwort] whose leaves are often so splashed with silver that the green is

Geranium psilostemon (Wikimedia Commons – Frank Vincentz)

almost invisible, and they seem to shimmer in the spring sun. Two rather invasive plants which need a sharp eye – and spade – kept on them are *Symphytum orientale* [white comfrey] – a tall growing white-flowered comfrey, and *S. grandiflorum* [creeping comfrey] – a low growing plant with short croziers[7] of creamy crimson-tipped bells often out for Christmas – ground cover par excellence.

In deepest shade at the west end are two other harbingers of spring which also need frequent discouragement, but which we would not like to be without, are *Trachystemon orientalis* [early-flowering borage] with rough leaves a foot high and stems of pinky blue shooting stars and a coltsfoot [giant butterbur] (*Petasites japonicus*) whose large umbrella leaves are preceded by delightful snowballs of white florets at first just peeping through the ground. Running riot amongst them is the native moschatel (*Adoxa moschatellina*) – a little succulent herb, whose three inch flower stems carry miniature four-square green belfries in April, and then disappear for another ten months.

At the eastern end under the winter cherry [*Solanum pseudocapsicum*], *Helleborus orientalis* [hellebore, or Lenten rose], in almost every available shade from purest white to deepest purple, makes ever increasing clumps, which are a joy for at least three months. Amongst them, *Euphorbia robbiae*[8] [wood spurge], one of the best and earliest spurges to flower, throws up its neat dark green rosettes topped with a slender flower spike, and the frogspawn spurge [or Mediterranean spurge] (*E. characias*) nods above them all with the dark-eyed flowers which gave it its colloquial name. *Brunnera macrophylla* [Siberian bugloss] too, so much more aptly described when it was known as *Anchusa myosotidiflora* – does not mind these rather grim conditions of dryness and shade, and sends up airy sprays of its small but so brilliantly blue forget-me-nots.

In the central area *Campanula latifolia* var. *macrantha* [giant bellflower] (from seed collected in Teesdale) sends up graceful spires of imperial blue and milky white bells, and if not cut down directly the flowers are over, produces enough seed to fill the whole garden – though mercifully it is not wind-dispersed. Actually, these strong stems, which are almost impervious to the elements, make splendid camouflage for any unsightly area at the base of a shrub or hedge.

Campanula poscharskyana [Serbian bellflower] and yellow corydalis [or fumewort – *Corydalis lutea*] have taken complete possession of the base of the house walls, and a few plants of *Alchemilla mollis* [lady's mantle] have

Euphorbia characias (Wikimedia Commons – Isidre blanc)

been introduced to make a most charming picture. For years we have being, perhaps rather rashly, trying to establish red valerian [*Centranthus ruber*] among the paving stones, and at last it seems as if success may be within our grasp – it might well be said of this plant that it gives "either a feast or a famine".

Hydrangea petiolaris [climbing hydrangea] is at long last beginning to make its presence known, but nothing could have made a slower start. One or two branches are reaching out along the rather bare piece of wall which seems to need a very little softening growth to set off the Tudor bricks. *Parthenocissus* (*Vitis*) *henryana* [Chinese Virginia creeper] too, with its silvery-centred leaves has no objection to a northern exposure, and is beginning to scramble through the *Cotoneaster horizontalis* [wall cotoneaster] which hangs over the garden wall, to make a colourful autumn twosome. A disappointment in this little corner is *Salix gracilistyla* 'Kuro-me' ('Melanostachys')[9] [black willow] from Japan, whose large catkins are almost black in the bud, flushing to scarlet at the tips, and finally fading to silvery pink, but neither this willow nor the type will have anything to do with our soil. A dose of Sequestrene[10] cheered them for a while, but alas! they have finally turned their backs on us.

Outside the garden wall and between it and the road there is quite a wide strip of grass which has been enclosed with chains and stones against each of which a rose has been planted – but unfortunately they do not do nearly so well now that we have been provided with a smart curb to carry away the rain water which they so much appreciated. *Rosa* 'Frensham' at the bottom has made a very handsome bush, with *R.* 'New Dawn' and *R.* 'Golden Showers' above it. An earlier and unfortunate choice by the gate was *R.* 'Excelsa' whose colour is far from ideal to our way of thinking,[11] and who needs pruning at least twice a year, but who did such a good job of stopping a short cut over the grass that I imagine it is there for all time.

Above the gate a slender-growing white musk rose – *R.* 'Ruth' is linked by a rampant *Clematis montana* var. *rubens* [pink anemone clematis] to a charming but unknown yellow rose. Then comes a rather rare, but very strong growing musk rose – *Rosa* 'Aglaia', and finally, via *Clematis montana* 'Elizabeth' to *Rosa* 'Albertine' at the top. Under the wall *Cotoneaster horizontalis* [wall cotoneaster] has become immovably settled, and *Corydalis lutea* [fumewort or yellow corydalis] has acquired full rights to the base of it, when not outdone by a colony of foxgloves [*Digitalis purpurea*] which thrive here though not really chalk plants. An ever increasing quantity of spare snowdrops [*Galanthus*] have made a wide ribbon all the way along, which is much appreciated by passers-by.

Notes

1. A synonym may be *Campanula rigidipila*.
2. Now called *Bistorta vaccinifolia*.
3. Now called *Lotus maritimus*.
4. Now called *Spiraea japonica* 'Walluf'.
5. Now called *Hormathophylla spinosa*. An alternative common name is spiny madwort.

6. The glow-worm is a species of beetle. It is the female that glows to attract a male. They are now much less common than they were in the 1960's. There is also the lesser glow-worm (*Phosphaenus hemipterus*). John Tyler's booklet *The Glow-worm* (2002) provides a fascinating insight into these creatures.
7. See Botanical Glossary, although Katie is here extending its use to a flowering plant. The term is presumably derived from the hooked staff carried by a bishop as a symbol of office.
8. Now called *Euphorbia amygdaloides* var. *robbiae*.
9. The correct name is now *Salix gracilistyla* 'Melanostachys'.
10. See Note 9, Chapter 4.
11. I do not understand Katie's objection to *Rosa* 'Excelsa', which is dark red in colour.

Chapter 29

THE PEAT BED

Our very latest experiment has been the making of a peat bed to accommodate various plants which are merely malingering under the conditions we had to offer. The site was no trouble to find – a little bit of no-man's-land between the reptiliary and the path by the *Garrya elliptica* [silk tassel bush], which would provide cool shade for most of the day. This has been so successful that when time and energy permit we propose to annex another piece in a line with the pool and the sand patch, and make a similar bed in full sun, but it is surprising how much soil, which has to be disposed of, seems to come out of even the smallest excavation, and what an enormous amount of new soil is needed to fill it in again.

All we did was to dig down about eighteen to twenty four inches, and then apply some strong weedkiller in the vain hope of exterminating the very firmly established *Campanula rapunculus* [rampion] which makes our lives a misery. The two foot spikes of blue flowers are not unattractive if one can look at them without a jaundiced eye, but the carrot-like main root sends out white spaghetti-like runners, each of which in turn sends out several more shoots, so that it is almost impossible to dig it out and has so far proved impervious to weedkillers. It probably owes its presence here, and elsewhere, to the fact that it was formerly much in demand by herbalists.

A layer of thick polythene was then fitted into the hole, being held in place at the upper edges by fuel peat blocks, which have since given us a generous crop of male ferns [*Dryopteris filix-mas*]. A few pin holes were made in the polythene for adequate drainage, and the cavity filled with all the neutral soil we could lay our hands on – old leaf mould and bags of loam that had been cherished for years, and finally a fairly rich mixture of peat, loam and sand.[1] The chief drawback is that this type of soil attracts spores of moss and liverworts in no time, so that there is always a green film on the top which is hard to discourage.

But how the plants have appreciated the trouble we took! As this was really only an experiment, polythene seemed adequate for our purpose, and has in fact proved that it was, but if our other project is ever carried out we would use one of the newer, stronger materials to make it even more permanent.[2] What a boon plastics have proved to be! One surprising result of the clearance of our hoard of various soils was the reappearance in quantity of a long-lost plant – the lovely orange scarlet *Mimulus cardinalis* [scarlet monkey flower], whose seed must almost certainly have been preserved in the dry soil. This is a very showy plant for a cool corner which was welcomed joyfully.

The preparations were finished in time to allow a period for the soil to settle and then we were able to take a trug and go in search of the invalids, and other treasures which had been cherished in pots. *Potentilla alba* [white-flowered cinquefoil], a diminutive member of the clan with lovely clear white "roses" and dark trefoil leaves started to grow almost overnight – so to did *Schizostylis coccinea*[3] [kaffir lily] which is now trying to annex the whole area.

A trio of unspectacular but none the less interesting liliaceous woodlanders hailing from the Far East were quick to show their appreciation. *Liriope spicata* [spiked lilyturf], which is sometimes grown as a pot plant, has tufts of grassy leaves and spikes of deep blue flowers very like a belated grape hyacinth [*Muscari*]. *Ophiopogon* [lilyturf] has similar tufts of grassy leaves, but in this case the flowers are white. *Reineckea carnea* [ribbon grass] arranges its foliage in a very distinctive manner on either side of its creeping rhizomes, so that after we had acquired it – by permission! – from a derelict garden, we knew it for years as "the parted hair" plant. Its pink-flowered spikes appear in quite late autumn.

The European [or black] false hellebore (*Veratrum nigrum*) now four years old from seed is at last promising to show its wonderful spikes of deepest maroon, and steadily increases in girth. Two species of wake robins, or North American trilliums, are also taking their time. From the same continent *Vancouveria hexandra* [white inside-out flower], another quaint

Veratrum nigrum (Wikimedia Commons – Agnieszka Kwiecien, Nova)

berberid somewhat resembling an *Epimedium* [barrenwort], but with even more graceful foliage, bloomed well last year, as did the [large-flowered] bellwort (*Uvularia grandiflora*) with drooping yellow flowers to be followed by yellow fruits.

Another striking plant very much at home here is the May apple (*Podophyllum emodi*)[4] which sends up two large lobed, almost freckled leaves enclosing a solitary stem, which throws off its bristly green cap to reveal enchanting, but all too fleeting, apple blossom-pink buds. The large soft dangling fruits which follow turn brilliant red before splitting to release the many seeds.

A particularly handsome cultivar of the willow gentian (*Gentiana asclepiadea*), with large upturned bells lined with white, sends up two foot stems and flowers for weeks in lovely harmony with pink *Schizostylis*[5] [kaffir lily]. *Geranium wallichianum* [Wallich cranesbill] 'Buxton's Blue' produces an endless succession of white-eyed blue flowers and *Galax aphylla*[6] [beetleweed] of the beautifully rounded, varnished leaves is obviously happy. The dog's tooth violet (*Erythronium dens-canis*) named from the appearance of its tubers – never fails to produce its mottled leaves and dusky pink flowers.

A quaint little carpeting blackberry (*Rubus fockeanus*)[7] [creeping raspberry] with leathery crumpled leaves has had to be snubbed, but the dwarf rowan [or Chinese dwarf mountain ash] (*Sorbus reducta*) is still sulking after this, its third move. One or two of the smaller, rarer Solomon's Seal (*Polygonatum*) have been tucked in, more for safety than because they dislike chalk, but we were only just in time to save two ferns. The larger is the very handsome *Lomaria magellanica*[8] [Chilean hard fern] with large deep green leathery fronds, which is now popping up all over the place rather too freely, though it is no trouble to find new homes for these offsets.

Uvularia grandiflora (Wikimedia Commons – Kurt Stueber)

The other, *Aspidium laserpitium*,[9] is rare but apparently quite hardy and has filigree fronds.

The native lady's smock or cuckoo flower (*Cardamine pratensis*) is trying to invade in spite of strong discouragement, but we are not so adamant with the very charming double-flowered form which extends the season. Another native, encouraged to grow here for sentimental reasons, is the little golden saxifrage (*Saxifraga chrysosplenium*)[10] which often lines the Wealden streams with its leafy pads and starry flowers.

An appealing newcomer here is an American relation of the British *Persicaria* with a most unusual name – *Tovara virginiana* 'Variegata'[11] [variegated buckwheat or Virginia knotweed] – whose leaf colouration is almost identical with that of *Pelargonium* [geranium] 'Mrs H Cox' in light green and cream with a flash of red.

Notes

1. There were no concerns about destruction of peat bogs in the 1960's. Now we would use a peat alternative such as coir.
2. Butyl rubber, used for lining ponds, would be an ideal, but expensive, solution.
3. Now called *Hesperantha coccinea*.
4. Now called *Sinopodophyllum hexandrum* var. *emodi*.
5. Now called *Hesperantha*.
6. Now called *Galax urceolata*.
7. Now called *Rubus rolfei*.
8. Now called *Blechnum chilense*.
9. Not listed in *RHS Plant Finder 2023*, nor on the Internet. Katie is possibly referring to *Arachniodes standishii* (upside-down fern).
10. Not listed in *RHS Plant Finder 2023*, nor on the Internet. There is a subspecies called *Saxifraga rotundifolia chrysosplenifolia*, but it is not native to the UK. I believe Katie must be referring to either the opposite-leaved golden saxifrage (*Chrysosplenium oppositifolium*) or the alternate-leaved golden saxifrage (*Chrysosplenium alternifolium*).
11. Now called *Persicaria virginiana* 'Variegata'.

Chapter 30

L'ENVOI[1]

So much then for the last thirty years. In spite of the number of plants which have been discussed there are many others whose claims are not quite so strong. We hope that the overall blend of form and colour, flowers and foliage makes a satisfactory setting for the old house, though our own familiarity with every aspect makes it hard to judge this for ourselves.

Yet still there are seedlings waiting to be pricked out, and still a list of plants and shrubs with which we should like to be on growing terms before time runs out, for still the compulsive infection is very active in our veins.

At least it is always possible to pick a posy even if it is only a selection of coloured twigs or contrasting foliage, and it is fairly safe to say that only in the very worst weather would there not be a flower to add to it.

The greatest pleasure of a true gardener is said to be to share his hobby and we hope we have been able to do so in these pages.

Notes

1. French for concluding remarks.

L'ENVOI

An elderly Katie in the garden at Harveys (Andrew Lusted – with permission)

Appendix A

LIVING WITH REPTILES

Katie had one book published in her lifetime, called *Living with Reptiles*. The book is undated, but I have a copy, originally owned by a resident of Texas, containing a letter from the publisher, Thomas Nelson & Sons Ltd, which states that it was published on 5 October 1961. The book contains 222 pages, and thirty-six black and white photographs. Two of the photos were taken by the Brighton *Argus* newspaper, then known as the Brighton *Evening Argus*, and five were taken by *She*, a monthly magazine for women which ran from 1955 to 2011. The majority of photos, of reptile and amphibian species, were taken by a young Robert Bustard, and were not necessarily of the particular specimens owned by Katie. Robert went on to gain a doctorate, specialised in chelonians and crocodilians, and become President of the British Herpetological Society.

The book contains thirty-two chapters, and charts Katie's progress over five years as she starts with tortoises, moves on to hardy European lizards, terrapins and amphibians kept in outdoor enclosures, and finishes with some of the larger tropical lizards that require heated vivaria. Almost without exception the majority of books about keeping reptiles and amphibians take a standard approach, describing the care requirements for each group or species. Katie adopts a completely different approach, telling us about her life with these animals as she expands her collection and gains in experience. A unique feature is the way Katie interacts with, and tames, her animals. For example, most reptile keepers segregate their animals into individual vivaria, but Katie had a room dedicated to tropical species where I suspect she and her husband spent most evenings. Here, the doors of the vivaria were left open, and the occupants were free to visit other vivaria, roam around the room, and climb over their owners. We learn all about Stumpy the stump-tailed skink,[1] Ig the green iguana,[2] and Drag the bearded dragon, amongst others. This results in a book of great charm that is a joy to read and re-read. There is only one other book of a similar nature, and that is *My Family of Reptiles*, written by the well known archaeologist Audrey Noel Hume (1927-1993) in 1955. However, that is a much shorter book, and lacks the charm of *Living with Reptiles*.

Katie had a range of reptiles and amphibians available to her that is somewhat different to that available today. European reptiles and amphibians, including tortoises, were easily obtainable, but the variety of tropical species was limited. The situation today is that export of European species from the continent has quite rightly ceased, but a huge number of tropical species can be bought, including poison arrow frogs, day geckos, leopard geckos, chameleons and pygmy monitor lizards. One group of reptiles that Katie did not keep was snakes; not because they were of no interest, but because of the difficulties of feeding them. That has changed due to the ready availability of frozen rodents, and snakes are now the easiest reptiles to keep, although inactive and therefore rather interesting.

Knowledge about the care of reptiles and amphibians was rudimentary in the 1960's. There were few books available, and, for example, the role of the UV-B component of sunlight to synthesis vitamin D3, required to absorb dietary calcium efficiently, was not fully understood. Identification guides were also very basic, and it was not until 1978 that we had a comprehensive guide to the European species in the form of *A Field Guide to the Reptiles and Amphibians of Britain and* Europe by Arnold and Burton. The choice of live food was very limited, confined mostly to mealworms, which were sold in pet shops for feeding tropical aviary birds. Now a vast range of foods can be bought, including various species of crickets, cockroaches and locusts. Finally, the range of available equipment was poor. Most vivaria had to be home built, and there were no UV-B lamps, ceramic basking lamps, foggers, dedicated mineral supplements, etc. that are commonplace today. Katie did well to keep her animals alive and healthy.

It is sad to learn in Chapter 12 of *A Garden Grew* that many of the animals kept by Katie in an outdoor enclosure, and described in such detail in *Living with Reptiles*, died as a result of an attack by a rat. This must have been heart-breaking after spending so much time taming them.

Book cover (Richard Baker)

When Barbara Abbs provided me with the original typescript of *A Garden Grew* she also provided a typescript of *Living with Reptiles*. The paper used is A4-size, and of good quality. This is surprising, as I would have expected it to have been written on an old paper size such as the UK Quarto (10" x 8") used for *A Garden Grew*, which was written several years later. Also, there are few if any correction of errors in the script, and my belief is therefore that Katie retyped it around 1981 with a view to getting a revision of the book published. This supposition is supported by a contents page that lists an additional final chapter 33 titled "Recent Events", a dedication to her husband Frank, who had died in 1975, and a copy of a letter accompanying the typescript, proposing to Collins that the book be re-published. Katie confirms all this in the 1991 interview with Andrew Lusted. Unfortunately, the additional chapter in its entirety is missing, as are chapters 4 to 14. There are, however, a couple of pages of handwritten notes that appear to be additions to the original text, plus two pages of new typescript. These two new pages are likely to be extracts from the missing chapter 33, and impart some interesting updates. Bella – a Bell's hinge-back tortoise, who featured so prominently in the book, died of old age, and the green lizards in the outdoor enclosure survived the rat attack, including Gary, one of Katie's favourites, who lived for twelve years in all.[3]

For anyone wanting to read *Living with Reptiles*, used copies are still reasonably easy to find, and not too expensive. The website www.abebooks.com lists five copies currently available (February 2025) ranging in price from £15 to £21.

Notes

1. We learn in the December 1991 interview with Andrew Lusted that Stumpy had been acquired in 1955 and was 36 years old. A second lizard of the same species was subsequently obtained from an Andrew Thompson, and was named Stumpy Thompson. Both animals were males.
2. We have seen in the Introduction that Ig died in 1961, and was almost certainly replaced with another green iguana.
3. I believe the rat attack took place on "Toad Hall" – housing the amphibians, and not the original repiliary – housing the lizards and terrapins.

Appendix B

A DOWNLAND GARDENER

Well known gardening writer Barbara Abbs wrote an article for *My Garden* magazine in 1994 about Katie and her garden at Glynde. The article was titled *A Downland Gardener,* and consisted of a brief biography of Katie, followed by extracts from chapters 15 to 19 of *A Garden Grew*, which dealt with the greenhouse. What follows is the biography written by Barbara, to which I have added explanatory notes.

I first realised that Kathleen Pickard Smith wasn't an ordinary gardener in the very early days of our local NCCPG,[1] when we had an outing to the Chelsea Physic Garden. Katie took some salvias with her which were exchanged for cuttings given to her by one of the gardeners. The rest of us, who were all very keen, bought from Beth Chatto and grew tricky things from the RHS seed list, but this seemed to hint at quite a different level of knowledge and expertise.

It was only several years later and after many visits to her garden in the downland village of Glynde in Sussex, that I realised how special she is. At 91, Katie lives alone and manages a three quarters of an acre garden almost without assistance. The flower beds contain far too many treasures to let anyone else touch them, even if they promise to restrict themselves to removing only grass or creeping buttercups, so only a privileged few are allowed to cut the grass or carry plant debris to the compost heap or bonfire.

Eventually she told me that she had written a book about plants and her garden in 1959,[2] but it had never been published. Margery Fish's *We Made a Garden* had filled that publisher's niche, and the typescript remained in the Elizabethan house, among the brochures that Frank Kingdon Ward[3] sent out when he returned from his plant collecting, the bulb lists of a young Jim Archibald,[4] and copies of *The Proceedings of the Linnaean Society* and bulletins of the Wild Flower Society.

Her book contains tantalising references to unnamed eminent figures in the gardening world. I asked her who they were and why she hadn't named them and she told me she thought most people these days wouldn't have heard of them. Men like A. T. Johnson (for whom a wonderful ceanothus was named)[5] and Claridge Druce[6] belong to an unfashionable generation that has long gone, but is awaiting rediscovery. I always feel when talking to Katie that I touch a great web of gardeners and botanists stretching not only across the country but back through decades.

Kathleen Pickard was born in Glynde where her father, Tom, was Land Agent to the estate.

Having gained her LRAM[7] in 1918, she became a student teacher at a school of music in Brighton. But botany, and later gardening, had always been a serious passion as she describes:

'An introduction to the joys of gardening came suddenly and unexpectedly in my late teens… My interest in natural history and wild flowers in particular had always been strong and has been fostered by several eminent botanists whom I had the good fortune to meet, and I covered a good deal of Britain in search of them. This botanical training has always stood me in good stead, both in the unravelling of Latin names and family identification. Not one, but two dedicated gardeners came into my life during this period and played a considerable part in shaping my future, by giving me treasures such as I had never dreamed it was possible to grow in ones's garden.

'Capitulation eventually came when I went, in early May, to spend a weekend near a large nursery. Sheer chance, or was it fate led my steps along a path by alpine plunge beds and the temptations there offered were my final undoing, when I discovered that any of them could be mine for the trivial sum of 9d. *Gentiana acaulis*, with its wide trumpets of vivid blue was the first selection, then *Androsace sarmentosa* with its soft pink clusters, *Vitaliana primulifolia* (Douglasii) a grey mound covered with tiny yellow

Magazine cover (Richard Baker)

primroses, *Antennaria dioica*, that delicious native with bright pink flowers over silver carpets and *Arenaria balearica* which, if it likes you, will find a cool spot with softest green and star it with dainty white flowers.'[8]

One of the dedicated gardeners Katie recalls was the vicar of nearby Firle, the Reverend Arthur Gregor,[9] F.L.S.[10] She learned much from him, but was unimpressed by the way he planted:

'... there was no consideration at all for aesthetic values, everything was planted in straight rows beside the garden paths as if in an open air museum ...'.[11]

Another influential figure was George Claridge Druce, an Oxford pharmacist and author of several floras. He was particularly interested in British wild flowers and is remembered today by the *Geranium* x *oxonianum* 'Claridge Druce'.

As a member of the Wild Flower Society, Kathleen travelled round the British Isles recording native plants, accompanied by other enthusiasts;

Druce, Lady Davy,[12] John Watson,[13] and Mr Wilmott[14] and Miss Campbell from the Natural History Museum (later Miss 'Maybud' Campbell left England and moved to the French Riviera near Menton; her garden at the Villa Val Rahmeh is open to the public).[15]

Lt. Col. A.H. Wolley-Dod,[16] son of the Rev. Charles Wolley-Dod of 'Wolley-Dod's rose (*Rosa* 'Wolley-Dod') pays tribute to Kathleen in his *Flora of Sussex* which was published in 1937. Hardly a page of this 500 page tome can be turned without coming across a flower being recorded as being 'found by K.P. nr Glynde' and often much further afield.

Kathleen moved with her parents to 'Harveys' before the last war. A 15th Century house with leaning gables, beams and a 'Tudor Rose' at the base of the north wall, it was named after the local brewers, who owned it for many years thinking they might establish a public house in the village.

The Pickards lived at Home Farm[17] a short distance away and like all keen gardeners, prepared carefully for their move, with plants divided and cuttings taken, everything was carried in its pot across the intervening field to the new house.

The oblong garden runs from east to west and the house stands in the south eastern corner behind a low flint wall facing the village street. It contained a few scattered fruit trees, a well-used hen run complete with derelict wire netting, a tumble-down pigsty and rows of staggering Brussels sprouts. Shelter was provided by a sharp downland slope to the north, a twenty foot high hedge of *Chamaecyparis lawsoniana* and a boundary of old flint walls, seven feet high.

Making a garden was not so easy then as there were few nurseries in Sussex. However, there were other sources:

'Instead of the seeds for which today's RHS member is entitled to apply, one used to fill in a short questionnaire as to the type of plant which suited one's conditions and in due course an exciting parcel of plants and cuttings was received, many of them normally unobtainable by an amateur …'

'Another treasure on which it was wise to keep a watchful eye and for that matter still is, though without quite such notable results, was Woolworths. Many a rare, and now expensive shrub still growing happily here, was bought there between the wars for the noble sum of 6d, including our now tallest and most beautiful of trees *Gleditsia triacanthos*, the honey locust.'[18]

Many plants were grown from seed, including a large bird cherry *Prunus padus* which was collected in Scotland.

'At one time there were a good many wild flowers growing here from seed that I had collected during my extensive travels searching for them throughout Britain. Even now the dainty pink flowers of the hairy mallow *Althaea hirsuta* from Kent, wood vetch, *Vicia sylvatica,* from Gloucs., the true *Potentilla frutilosa* [sic] from Teesdale, the fine-leaved umbellifer *Meum athamanticum* from Scotland and a host of others, carry my memory back to the years between the wars.'[19]

There were other sources too: 'Browsing many years ago round the horticultural section of an agricultural show, I saw for the first time on display a bunch of cut flowers of *Allium albopilosum*[20] and determined that by hook or by crook I had to buy that bunch at the end of the show sale. This was successfully accomplished and the bunch was put into a large vase where the flowers lasted for weeks. Just as I was about to throw them out, I noticed that the earliest flowers had already matured into capsules of gleaming black seeds … from these came my original stock.'[21]

In 1939 the Second World War began and ornamental horticulture ceased; nurseries grew vegetables and new plants were unobtainable. It was not until six years later when the war was over did catalogues offering garden plants again drop through the letterbox. Only then could Katie's insatiable urge for new plants, 'sharpened almost to breaking point by long deprivation'[22] be satisfied. Soon her plant list reached a grand total of almost 2,000 species and cultivars, of which one sixth were bulbs, corms and tubers.

Kathleen married Frank Smith in 1952. He was the perfect gardener's husband. Unlike Margery Fish's Walter, he had no desire to plant large dahlias in rows but was an aider and abetter in all Kathleen's plans, and as she wrote in her book: 'After some training, he has become a useful asset, particularly where muscle is required.'[23]

I hope readers will be inspired by Katie's example and the excerpts from her book as much as I have been.

Notes

1. National Council for the Conservation of Plants and Gardens, now known as Plant Heritage.

2. Katie has supplied Barbara with an incorrect date. The draft of *A Garden Grew* was probably completed in 1969.
3. Frank Kingdon Ward (1885-1958) was an explorer and plant collector. He was the author of twenty-five books, published under the hyphenated name of Frank Kingdon-Ward, and was given an OBE in 1952.
4. Jim Archibald (c1942-2010) was a freelance plant hunter who travelled throughout Europe with his wife in a Volkswagen camper van, collecting plants and seeds which he sold through a mail order business.
5. Arthur Tysilio Johnson (1873-1956) lived near Bodnant in North Wales and wrote a number of books, including *A Garden in Wales* (1927), *A Woodland Garden* (1937) and *The Mill Garden* (1949). In addition to the ceanothus, he also has a geranium and mimulus named after him.
6. See Introduction, Note 19.
7. Licentiate of the Royal Academy of Music.
8. This quote comes from Chapter 3 – The Shrub Border (1).
9. See Chapter 3, Note 7.
10. Fellow of the Linnean Society – a society founded in 1788 devoted to the study of natural history.
11. This quote comes from Chapter 3 – The Shrub Border (1).
12. Joanna Charlotte Davy (1865-1955) was a plant collector and painter.
13. John Watson (1936-2024) was a botanist specialising in the flora of South America. He co-founded a nursery called Flores and Watson Seeds.
14. Alfred James Willmott (1888-1950) was a botanist and museum curator.
15. Maybud Sherwood Campbell (1903-1982) was an opera singer and amateur botanist who was Secretary of the Botanical Society of the British Isles. A species of eyebright, *Euphrasia campbelliae*, is named in her honour.
16. See Introduction, Note 20.
17. An article in the *Sussex Express* dated 22 April 1938 gives the Pickard's address as Caburnside. This would have been their last address before moving to Harveys.
18. This quote comes from Chapter 3 – The Shrub Border (1).
19. This quote comes from Chapter 10 – Propagation.
20. Now called *Allium cristophii*.
21. This quote comes from Chapter 10 – Propagation.
22. This quote comes from Chapter 10 – Propagation.
23. This quote comes from Chapter 3 – The Shrub Border (1).

Appendix C

KATHLEEN PICKARD-SMITH PAPERS, ETC. HELD BY EAST SUSSEX AND BRIGHTON AND HOVE RECORD OFFICE AT THE KEEP

A search using 'Kathleen Pickard-Smith' on The Keep website (www.thekeep.info) reveals the documents listed below. The documents are not available online, and must be viewed at The Keep. Due to time constraints on a brief visit to East Sussex in September 2024 not all the documents were viewed. The main purpose of the visit was to unearth a plan of the garden at Harveys, but this was unsuccessful. It would appear that no such plan exists, and perhaps was never created. I have added my comments in square brackets after each document. The list will be expanded in the future when documents, etc. used in the compilation of this book are transferred to The Keep.

Papers of Kathleen Pickard-Smith. ACC7854. c1930-1998.
[A collection of documents, including some listed below, and some in the Addendum below].

Photocopy of obituary of Kathleen Pickard-Smith by Barbara Abbs: the *Independent*. ACC7854/2. 11 Dec 1998.
[Not viewed, as previously seen online at www.independent.co.uk].

Notes on wild flowers by Kathleen Pickard-Smith; possibly the plan of a book. ACC7854/7. c1930.
[Definitely the plan of a book. Consists of 96 sheets of handwritten notes; mostly double-side. The title is difficult to discern, but may be 'Wild Flower Days'. The notes are arranged according to habitat, thus there are chapters on woodland, grassland, marshland, etc. The text is in the form of notes, rather than a finished script, and this, combined with Katie's hard-to-decipher handwriting, would prevent any thoughts of publication].

Typescript of *Living with Reptiles* by Kathleen Pickard-Smith. ACC 7854/9. c1961.
[The original typescript consisting of 255 pages].

Papers of Kathleen Pickard-Smith. PIC/ACC7871/16. c1960.
[see Addendum below].

The Alpine Garden Society newsletter; contains note concerning Kathleen Pickard-Smith submitted by Barbara Abbs. ACC7854/8. Sep 1998.
[Not viewed. Item already in my possession].

Kathleen Pickard-Smith, *Living with Reptiles*. PIC/ACC7793/3/50. c1961.
[Not viewed. Presumably a copy of the book, possibly even Katie's personal copy, published on 5 October 1961 – see Appendix A].

Archive of Thomas William Pickard and Kathleen Pickard-Smith, of Glynde. PIC/ACC7793. 1839-1955.
[Not viewed].

Article *Skink on the Hearth*, published in *She* magazine, concerning Kathleen Pickard-Smith's collection of animals. Feb 1961. Letter from *She* enclosing the article, Jan 1961. ACC7854/3. 1961.
[Not viewed, as obtained previously from Hearst Publishing, who hold the copyright for *She* magazine].

Mrs K Pickard-Smith, Glynde: papers of William, James, Elizabeth, Eugene, Thomas, Flora and Kathleen Pickard. PIC/ACC5767. 1726-1955.
[Not viewed].

Papers of Thomas Pickard of Glynde, land agent. PIC/ACC7871. 1799-c1960. The papers were formerly kept at Pickard's home at Harveys, Glynde, but became separated from other papers kept there after the death of his daughter, Kathleen, in 1998.
[Not viewed].

Records of Kathleen Nora Irene Pickard (-Smith). PIC/ACC5767/8. 1913-1935. K N I Pickard, the daughter of Thomas William Pickard, was born on 25 March 1902.
[Not viewed].

Tape recordings of oral history reminiscences of Glynde and Beddingham, recorded by Andrew Lusted. ACC8631/1/7. 1991. Kathleen Pickard-Smith, Harveys, Glynde, born at Seven Acres, Glynde, 25 Mar 1902 (daughter of Tom Pickard, land agent for the Glynde estate): memories of her early life, schooldays, Brighton Schoo…
[At the time of writing (February 2025) there was a technical problem regarding accessing the recording via The Keep website, but it can be heard on the following link: https://esccbhro.access.preservica.com/uncategorised/SO_2ed3c43e-0412-4757-ae15-48855273cf15/. It is in two parts. The first, ACC8631-2-7 01 runs for 47.08 minutes, and the second, ACC8631-2-7 02 runs for 24.23 minutes. The recording was not available during my visit in September 2024, but did become available in November 2024].

Archive of the Pickard family of Glynde. PIC.1726-1982. The archive contains documents relating to Thomas William Pickard, and agent of the Glynde Estates, his wife and children, his parents James and Elizabeth Pickard of Balcombe, Barcombe and Lewes a…
[Not viewed].

ADDENDUM

The following documents can be found within some of those listed above:

Catalogue of perennials in the garden of Harveys, Glynde. 1933-1941. ACC7854/4.

[Part of ACC7854. Consists of loose sheets of paper with plants listed in alphabetical order. Written with a fountain pen using mostly green ink. Also contains a receipt dated May 1945 for the services of a piano tuner for tuning a Bechstein Grand for Miss K. Pickard at 3 St. Peters Place, Brighton. Presumably this is a misfile].

Catalogue of alpines, bulbs, herbaceous plants, trees and shrubs in the garden of Harveys, Glynde. 1939. ACC7854/5.

[Part of ACC7854. A spiral-bound notebook with no title or date, listing plants alphabetically, i.e. alpines, bulbs, etc. beginning with 'A', alpines, bulbs, etc. beginning with 'B', and so on].

Catalogue of plants in the garden of Harveys, Glynde, with note of provenance and date of purchase. 1934-1993. ACC7854/6.

[Part of ACC7854. Contains lists of plants arranged in alphabetical order, with origin (often abbreviated) and date of acquisition. Loose leaf, and written in black biro with red biro additions].

Handbill concerning opening times for Harveys, Glynde. c1960. ACC7871/150.

[Part of PIC/ACC7871/16. See Introduction, and reproduced at Appendix E. Has the number 67 added in pencil, which may possibly refer to the date 1967].

Appendix D

QUEENWOOD LADIES' COLLEGE

Initial information about Katie's schooling was obtained from the December 1991 interview with Andrew Lusted. Katie gives the name of her school as Ladies' College in Eastbourne, and I interpret this to mean Queenwood Ladies' College.[1] A history of the school, and a flavour of life there, can be obtained from Dorothea Petrie Carew's 1967 book *Many Years, Many Girls.* In the book, the author refers constantly to the school as 'Queenwood', so why she and Katie summarise the school's name differently is strange, especially given that the two women were of a similar age, and attended the school over a similar period. Is it possible that Katie is is getting confused with the name of the Ladies' School of Gardening established at Ragged Lands, Glynde in 1905 by Frances Wolseley? Contrary to what you might expect, Katie had no involvement with this teaching facility for gardeners on her doorstep.

Katie gives the address of her school as Rusington Road, Eastbourne. However, as far as I can determine, there is no Rusington Road, or Rustington Road, in Eastbourne. The school moved location several times in Eastbourne (see below), but during Katie's schooling era its address was in Darley Road.

The following information is largely obtained from *Many Years, Many Girls*. The school was founded in 1862 by Emma Ogier Ward (1823-1903), who was an outstanding pianist, and was located first in Caen in Normandy

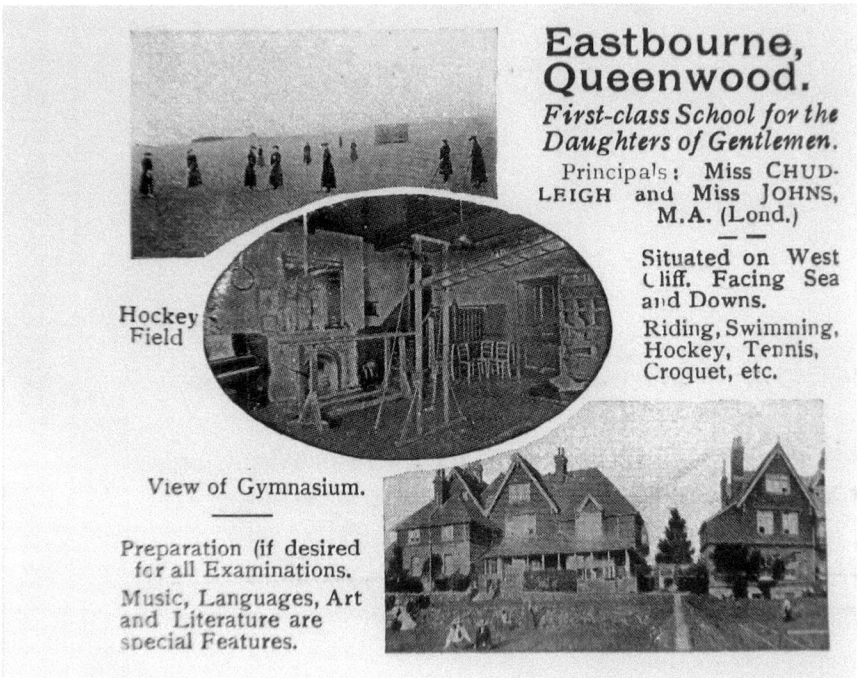

Advert for Queenwood at Staveley Road (1903 edition of *Country Life* magazine). The two buildings comprising the school were connected by a glassed corridor.

before moving to Germain-en-Laye near Paris. The Franco-Prussian War of 1870 prevented the school opening there, and when the war ended it moved to Eastbourne. Its first location, in 1871, was in Hyde Gardens, followed by a move to Wilmington Gardens in 1884. In 1890 Emma Ogier Ward's daughter, Annie Bowen Lawrance (1847-1904) took over as principal, and moved the school to Staveley Road. It was at this point that the school was named Queenwood Ladies' College, but the origin of the name is unknown. In 1899 Annie left Queenwood, having sold it to Lillie J. Chudleigh (1857-1939)[2] and Edith Lydia Johns (1867-1937). These ladies acted as joint principal during Katie's period at the school.[3] In 1906 they had a a new building erected in Darley Road, which overlooked the sea on the slopes of Beachy Head, and retained the Queenwood name. They continued the emphasis on music set by the school's founder, so it is no surprise that Katie developed an interest in music and made it her career. Botany was also taught at the school, which must have been a favourite with Katie, and she must have appreciated the sight and smell of the large rambling rose *Rosa* 'Seven Sisters' which framed the drawing room window.

As far as sports are concerned, these are listed as hockey, lacrosse, tennis, croquet and cricket, but there is no mention of netball, despite Katie stating in the December 1991 interview with Andrew Lusted that she was captain of the netball team. Horse riding was also available, side saddle of course, but presumably Katie's allergy to horses would have prevented her involvement, and swimming was popular, both in the local swimming baths and in the sea.

Queenwood was, by most accounts, a very happy school. The principal always took a personal interest in every girl, and one, in the period after Katie left, made a point of shaking the hand of each girl, and reciting their name, twice a day as they entered and left the dining room. There were over one hundred girls enrolled at this point! The food was good, and lessons do to seem to have been too onerous. Academic lessons were taught in the morning, followed by games or long walks in the afternoon. Evenings were spent singing, dancing, staging plays or operas such as *Yeomen of the Guard*, or engaging in needlework. In the 1991 interview with Andrew Lusted, Katie states that she boarded until 1916, then became a day girl. She

Advert for Queenwood at Darley Road (1912 edition of *Paton's List of Schools and Tutors*))

would therefore have missed these evening activities, and the reason for this change in arrangements is unknown. The round trip by train from Glynde to Eastbourne and return was approximately twenty five miles. The school does not appear to have encouraged the idea of day girls, and typically limited their number to around three, although this limit varied from year to year.

A number of principals followed Miss Chudleigh and Miss Johns after they left the school in 1920. The school was unaffected by World War One, but during World War Two, because of its vulnerable location on the south coast, it had a succession of moves to Wimborne, Malvern, and finally Harrogate. It closed in 1942, for reasons which Dorothea Petrie Carew doesn't explain. The closure is a bit odd, as many other private schools survived World War Two. The building in Darley Road known as Queenwood was sold to Eastbourne Corporation on 18 July 1949 and became a teachers' training college.

Famous attendees at the school include writers Dorothea Petrie Carew (1895-1968) and Annie Winifrid Ellerman (1894-1983), better known by her pen name of 'Bryher'. They were 7 or 8 years older than Katie, so she may not have met them, or if she did, did not know them very well. Despite the heavy emphasis placed on music by the school, it does not appear to have produced any famous musicians or singers.

Chapter VII of *Many Years, Many Girls* is composed of contributions from girls who attended Queenwood Ladies' College, but there is nothing from Katie, and she doesn't get a mention in the book, despite her becoming owner and principal of the Brighton School of Music, and being a published author.[4]

There is an interesting postscript to the Queenwood story. Grace Carola Lawrence (1873-1932) was the daughter of Annie Bowen Lawrance, who had been

Queenwood Ladies' College crest[5]
(Richard Baker)

the principal of Queenwood Ladies' College between 1890 and 1899. She in turn was the daughter of Queenwood's founder, Emma Ogier Ward. In 1902 Grace went to Australia, and in 1908 started a school at Toowoomba with her sister Margaret Lawrance, who had been on the staff at Queenwood. This school was later to be known as Glennie Memorial School. After a few years, Margaret left the school to become headmistress at another school, and in 1925 Grace left the school with senior mistress Beatrice Rennie (1893-1971) to open Queenwood School for Girls in the Mosman suburb of Sydney. Beatrice became principal in 1931, and the following year Grace died. In 1937 Violet Maude Medway (1909-1996) became a partner, and in 1942 co-principal. In 1961 she became full principal, with Beatrice taking a step backwards to run the school library. Violet retired in 1982.

Dorothea Petrie Carew writes in *Many Years, Many Girls* (1967) that she was expecting Beatrice to produce a book about the school, but this does not appear to have happened. It was left to Violet to write the book titled *Queenwood: The First Sixty Years, 1925-1985*, published in 1986. She followed this up with *Queenwood: The Next Ten Years, 1985-1995*, published in 1995. She died the following year.

After starting with only 4 students in 1925 the school has grown considerably, and has had several principals since Violet retired. It now has over 900 students spread over four campuses.

Notes

1. Not to be confused with Queenwood College, Stockbridge (1847-1896) or Queenswood School, Hatfield (1894-to present).
2. Lillie J. Chudleigh was born in Liskeard, Cornwall, which coincidently is only four miles from where I live. The current British Telecom Telephone Directory for Cornwall and the Isles of Scilly lists five persons named Chudleigh living in Liskeard and surrounding area, who may well be distant relatives.
3. In the 1991 interview with Andrew Lusted Katie states that she attended the school from the age of 11 and left around 1918. Her attendance at the school was therefore approximately from 1913 to 1918, and would have been at the Darley Road premises (the transfer from Staveley Road to Darley Road having taken place in 1906).

4. Dorothea Petrie Carew mentions in her book the existence of school magazines, and that she was loaned a complete set dating from 1910 to 1939 to assist with research for her book. It may well be that Katie features in one or more of these magazines. However, copies of these have proved impossible to obtain; even the East Sussex and Brighton and Hove Record Office at the Keep, which is the obvious place to look, does not appear to have them.
5. A possible translation of the motto is 'While I breathe, I aspire'.

Appendix E

ADVERT FOR THE BRIGHTON SCHOOL OF MUSIC C1936/37

From website www.jamesching.co.uk. Origin unknown. Note Katie's name at bottom of advert.

Patron: HER GRACE THE DUCHESS OF NORFOLK

The Brighton School of Music
(INSTITUTED 1883)
Director: JAMES CHING, M.A., B.Mus. Oxon., F.R.C.O.

Vice-Patrons:

THE RT. HON. LORD LECONFIELD
THE LADY OTTOLINE MORREL
THE EARL OF CHICHESTER
EARL DE LA WARR

THE HON. MRS. T. S. BRAND
THE BISHOP OF CHICHESTER
MAJOR SIR ROBERT E. W. GRIERSON, BART.
SIR GEORGE BOUGHEY, BART.

LADY DAVY
REAR ADMIRAL AND MRS. BEAMISH
MISS SPRENT KING
CHARLES H. ELLIS, ESQUIRE

The School and what it does

Situate in the most delightful position in Brighton, between St. Peter's Church and the Dome, and overlooking the gardens in Marlborough Place, the re-organized Brighton School of Music in its new building offers to residents of Sussex and district a complete training in every branch of music, as well as in elocution, dramatic art, stage and operatic technique and dancing. It offers them in fact all the facilities of London, with greater accessibility and considerably less expense.

Its Staff and Famous Past Pupils

Its visiting staff from London includes such eminent musicians as Topliss Green, Sydney Harrison, Dr. William Lovelock, Mme. Kate Menges, Mme. Palgrave Turner, Lionel Salter and Archy Rosenthal. Its long list of internationally famous past pupils includes: Evelyn Laye, Frank Bridge, Clive Carey, Hyam Greenbaum (the first Director of Music for the B.B.C. television services), de Groot and Helena Dysart.

History and Traditions

The School began in 1883 over a music-shop in Ship Street and was immediately successful. Since that time it has trained over five thousand students. Of these over one hundred have obtained academic honours in the form of degrees, diplomas and scholarships. At the present time no less than nine students are holding scholarships at the Royal Academy of Music and other institutions.

A Real Musical Background

The School prides itself on providing a real musical background for all its students, who may enrol at any stage of any term for any subject from private or group lessons in a single subject to a full professional course. And its teaching methods belong only to the present and the future. The School has also for its special consideration the welfare of those students who want music primarily for the pleasure it provides in leisure hours—for those who do not necessarily want to consider music from the professional point of view.

The Facilities of the School

The facilities of the School include two choirs, an orchestra, chamber music, Yorke Trotter musicianship, at least two public concerts a term in Brighton and one a year in London. All students who attain the necessary standards are eligible to perform at these concerts irrespective of the fees which they pay. There are also frequent informal concerts open to all students irrespective of their standard.

The Junior Department

The School accepts children from the age of four and upwards. The staff of the Junior Department is a specialised one and consists entirely of highly qualified teachers who have made the musical education of children their particular study. The children also have a room to themselves with appropriate furniture and decorations.

TUITION FEES

The fees of the School begin with those for group tuition which range from twelve shillings and sixpence to one guinea per term. The fees for private individual lessons in a single subject begin at two guineas per term.

Next Term begins 18th January, 1937

The new 16-page syllabus, giving full details of all the School's activities, will be sent on receipt of the usual postcard or phone call to:

The Secretary
5 Marlborough Place,
Brighton 1.
Telephone: BRIGHTON 6797

K. PICKARD

xiii

Appendix F

HANDBILL OF OPENING TIMES AT HARVEYS

Item ACC7871/150 (found within ACC7871/16) in East Sussex and Brighton and Hove Record Office at The Keep.

Harveys · Glynde
Nr. LEWES
SUSSEX

(by permission of MR. & MRS. PICKARD-SMITH)

Picturesque Tudor House

Garden of Botanical Interest

Collection of Hand-Tame Reptiles including Iguana and Bearded Dragon · Terrapins

Tortoises and Amphibians

**OPEN: Wednesdays and Saturdays
2.30–5.30 p.m.**

ADMISSION: Adults 2/-   Children under 14 1/-
Tea and Biscuits 6d.

TRANSPORT: Half-hourly trains from Brighton, Eastbourne and Lewes to Glynde Station (5 minutes)

FARNCOMBE & CO. (1928) LTD., *Printers*, LEWES

BIBLIOGRAPHY

Anon. *Glynde Place, Sussex: An Illustrated Guide.* Undated. 12pp.

Arnold, E. N., and Burton, J.A. *A Field Guide to the Reptiles and Amphibians of Britain and Europe.* 1978. Collins. 272pp (Revised in 2002 to include additional species, including those from Madeira and the Canary Islands).

Abbs, Barbara. *French Gardens: A Guide.* 1994. Gryphon Press. 173pp.

Abbs, Barbara. *The Conservatory Month-by-Month.* 1997. David & Charles. 143pp.

Abbs, Barbara. *Obituary: Kathleen Pickard-Smith.* 1998. *Independent online* website.

Abbs, Barbara. *Gardens of the Netherlands and Belgium.* 1999. Mitchell Beazley. 144pp.

Abbs, Barbara. *Choosing and Using Climbing Plants.* 2003. New Holland Publishers (UK) Ltd. 96pp.

Abbs, Barbara, and Pickard Smith, Katie. *A Downland Gardener.* 1994. *My Garden* magazine. pp. 42-53.

Carew, Dorothea Petrie. *Many Years, Many Girls.* 1967. Browne & Nolan Ltd, Dublin. 161pp.

Cubey, Janet (Ed.). *RHS Plant Finder 2023.* 2023. Royal Horticultural Society. 876pp.

Dortort, Fred. *Succulent Plants of the World.* 2011. Timber Press, Inc. 344pp.

Farrar, Reginald. *On the Eaves of the World.* 1917. Edward Arnold. Vol. 1, 311pp, Vol 2, 328pp.

Fish, Margery. *We Made a Garden.* 1956. W.H.& L. Collingridge Ltd. 182pp.
Hampden, Anthony. *A Glimpse of Glynde.* 1997. The Book Guild Ltd. 125pp.
Inns, Howard. *Britain's Reptiles and Amphibians.* 2009. WILDguides Ltd. 164pp.
Lang, David. *Wild Orchids of Sussex.* 2001. Pomegranate Press. 144pp.
Lloyd, Christopher. *The Well-Tempered Garden.* 1970. Collins. 479pp.
Loudon, John Claudius. *The Encyclopaedia of Plants.* 1829. Longman. 1157pp.
Lusted, Andrew. *A Guided Tour of Glynde Street.* 2008. Andrew Lusted and Philip McBrown. 40pp.
Lusted, Andrew. *Glynde.info* website.
Marren, Peter. *Britain's Rare Flowers.* 1999. T & A D Poyser Ltd. 334pp.
Massingham, Pam. *Skink on the Hearth.* February 1961. *She* magazine. pp. 54-55.
Medway, V.N. *Queenwood: The First Sixty Years, 1925-1985.* 1986. Macarthur Press, Sydney.
Medway, V. N. *Queenwood: The Next Ten Years, 1985-1995.* 1995. McPherson Printing Group.
Noel Hume, Audrey. *My Family of Reptiles.* 1955. Frederick Muller Ltd. 94pp.
Pickard-Smith, Kathleen. *Living with Reptiles.* 1961. Thomas Nelson and Sons Ltd. 222pp.
Rice, Graham, and Strangman, Elizabeth. *The Gardener's Guide to Growing Hellebores.* 1993. David & Charles. 160pp.
Rose, Francis. *The Wild Flower Key.* 2006 (revised edition). Frederick Warne. 576pp.
Snell, C. *Status of the Common Tree Frog in Britain.* 2006. *British Wildlife* magazine. Volume 17. Number 3. pp. 153-160.
Tyler, John. *The Glow-worm.* 2002. John Tyler. 75pp.
Wolley-Dod, Lt. Col. A.H. (Ed). *Flora of Sussex.* 1937. Kenneth Saville. 571pp.

BOTANICAL GLOSSARY

Anther – the part of the stamen that produces and contains pollen.
Bract – modified leaflike structure usually below a flower or inflorescense.
Calyx (plural calyces) – the outermost whorl of a flower that protects the petals.
Carpel – the female reproductive part of a flower.
Corolla – the petals and reproductive organs of a flower.
Crozier – the curled top of a young fern frond.
Dioecious – having the male and female reproductive organs in separate plants.
Fastigiate – having the branches more or less parallel to the main stem.
Nectary – a gland which produces nectar.
Panicle – a much-branched inflorescence.
Pappus – the tufts of hairs on the seeds of plants such as dandelions which assist wind dispersal.
Pedicel – a stem that attaches a single flower to the inflorescence.
Perianth – the non-reproductive part of a flower, comprising of the petals and sepals.
Pilose – having soft, long hairs.
Pinnate – shaped like a feather.
Procumbent – lying along the ground, but not putting forth roots.
Scape – stem.
Spathe – a sheathing bract or bracts partly enclosing an inflorescence.
Stigma – the pollen-collecting part of the flower.

Stolon – a horizontal stem or runner.
Style – a long slender stalk that connects the stigma with the ovary.
Tomentum – a felt-like covering of downy hairs on leaves and other plant parts.
Umbels – inflorescences that consist of a number of short flower stalks that originate from a common point, somewhat like umbrella ribs.

ACKNOWLEDGEMENTS

I would like to thank the following, in alphabetical order, for the help provided in the writing of this book.

Barbara Abbs for providing the original manuscript of *A Garden Grew*, information arising from her friendship with Katie, her support for the project, and her hospitality during my visit to East Sussex in September 2024.

Andrew Bennett for making available the recording of Andrew Lusted's December 1991 interview with Katie. Also the other staff at East Sussex and Brighton and Hove Record Office at The Keep for their help in providing documents for me to view in September 2024.

Mary Bonnin (James Ching's daughter) for permission to use the Brighton School of Music advert from her website www.jamesching.co.uk.

The British Newspaper Archive for online access to copies of the *Sussex Express* newspaper.

Alan Edenborough, who now lives in Australia, for permission to reproduce an extract from a 1994 issue of *My Garden* magazine.

Kerry Gniewek at Hearst Publishing for permission to use what is probably a *She* magazine photograph of Katie and Frank in a doorway at Harveys.

Graham Gough for insights into his friendship with Katie.

Sophie Harding, Penzance-based illustrator, for the plan of the garden at Harveys on page 17.

Marjorie Holloway of Cooper & Sons Funeral Directors, Lewes, for information about the funeral arrangements for Katie.

ACKNOWLEDGEMENTS

Andrew Lusted for the information provided on his website www.glynde.info, in his 2008 book *A Guided Tour of Glynde Street,* in numerous e-mails, and during my visit to East Sussex in September 2024. Thanks also for the numerous black and white photos – some of which are included in this book.

Kate Parkin of *The Argus* (previously *The Brighton Argus*) for permission to use the photograph of Katie and Frank in the pet room.

Troubador Publishing. In particular, Lauren Alexander – Production Controller, Lauren Bailey – Customer Services Manager, Stephanie Carr - Digital Marketing Controller, Hannah Cather – Illustration Project Manager and Ella Fennell-Monan – Marketing Controller.

Wikimedia Commons and the contributing photographers for the colour images of plants used throughout the book.

Any errors are my own.

INDEX OF COMMON PLANT NAMES

aconite, winter	72
almond, dwarf	144
Russian	144
alpenrose, hairy	44
alyssum, shrubby	201
anemone, Balkan	72, 172
blue	171
Grecian peacock	172
Japanese	48, 66
yellow wood	172
angelica, garden	141
apple, crab	142
May	161, 209
aralia	165
Japanese	169
archangel	94
artichoke, globe	167
Jerusalem	45
arum, Cretan	78, 167
dragon	172
Italian	172
asarabacca	196
asparagus, Bath	75
asphodel	177
aster, lilac Himalayan	186
auricula	162
baby rubber plant	135
baby's breath	147
bamboo, anceps	33
dwarf	164
barbed wire bush	160
barberry, Darwin's	64
golden	39, 82, 167
barrenwort	161, 209
batchelor's buttons	46
beach bells	126
beetleweed	210
begonia, elephant-ear	120
eyelash	119

hardy	183
king	119
metallic leaf	120
pond lily	120
bellflower, bonnet	107
giant	203
Serbian	54, 203
bellwort, large-flowered	209
bindweed, mallow	56
blackberry	143, 210
bluebell	172
Spanish	172
blueberry	134
blue sausage shrub	43
blue trumpet flower	134
bodkin bush	160
borage, early-flowering	203
box	64
fragrant sweet	44, 200
sweet	44, 153
box tree	194
bramble, Chinese	162
briar, sweet	153
bromeliad, crimson	180
broom	79, 150
butcher's	200
Canary	80
Kew	201
Montpelier	189
Moroccan	151
Mount Etna	199
Spanish	151, 153, 199
winged	101
buckthorn, sea	38
buckwheat, variegated	211
buddleia	38, 82
bugloss, Siberian	203

burro tail	125
bushman's pipe	127
bush monkey flower	184
busy lizzy	120
butterbur, giant	203
buttercup	85, 218
butterfly bush	143, 159
Himalayan	82
buttonweed	54
cacti, orchid	127
cactus, mistletoe	127
rat's tail	127
camassia	177
campion, pink	190
red	190
rose	147
candytuft	59
Cape gold	146
cardoon	167
carnation	201
cast iron plant	135
catmint	51
cedar, japanese	157
western red	27, 59, 199
century plant	125
chalk sticks, blue	125
narrow-leaf	125
chaste tree	195
cherry, bird	38, 41, 157, 221
Christmas	192
Cornelian	41
flowering	60, 199
Jerusalem	192
Nanking	157
winter	189, 203
winter flowering	60

chicory	201	early	53, 70
Chilean potato tree/vine	68, 194	golden bunch	182, 183
Chinese lantern	115	crosswort, Caucasian	153
chrysanthemum	27, 180	crown imperial	174
cinquefoil, shrubby	78, 82, 145	crown of thorns	126
white-flowered	208	cuckoo flower	211
clematis, bush	148	cuckoo pint	172
Chinese	143	currant, flowering	42
golden	65	curry plant	153
pink anemone	205	cyclamen, Cilicean	78
purple	78, 186	false Iberian	182
clog plant	136	Greek	181
clover, bush	147	ivy-leaved	107
Canary	195	Lebanon	130, 181
cock's foot	155	Persian	130, 181
coltsfoot	203	purple	78
comfrey, creeping	203	cypress	54
white	203	false	48, 106, 142, 175
common corn-flag	172	Lawson	27, 58, 143, 144
coral bells	51, 127	Sawara	157
corydalis, yellow	54, 203, 205	standing	81
cotoneaster, wall	204, 205		
cowslip, Cape	131	daffodil	27, 73, 170
Jerusalem	202	angel's tears	170, 171
cranesbill, Armenian	202	autumn	185
Canary Island	142	cyclamen-flowered	170, 171
Caucasian	202	lesser	170
meadow	202	pygmy	170
Wallich	209	Queen Anne's	171
wood	71, 202	rock	171
crassula, spathula-leaf	125	tazetta	171
creeping Jenny	54	Tenby	190
cress, Chamois	107	wild	170, 190
trefoil	94	daisy, African	80
violet	81	African kingfisher	80
crocosmia	169	globe	101
crocus, autumn	74	moon	48

INDEX OF COMMON PLANT NAMES

Mount Atlas	109	
New Zealand	109	
parachute	80	
shasta	48	
daisy bush	151	
dandelion	85, 91, 240	
daphne, February	60, 189, 199	
golden-edged winter	69	
rock	144	
Tangut	143	
twin-flowered	153	
deadnettle, yellow	94	
diamond flower	81	
donkey tail	125	
dragon's teeth	201	
elephants' ears	125	
euonymous, Japanese	189	
everlasting flower	146, 152	
false castor oil plant	199	
fern, button	131	
chain	131	
Chilean hard	210	
hen and chickens	131	
king	134	
ladder	131	
male	207	
mother	131	
ostrich plume	94	
stag's horn	131	
upside-down	211	
fig, creeping	116	
figwort, Cape	152	
firethorn, Chinese	68	
flag, African corn	148	
flax, New Zealand	200	

flower dust plant	125	
flower of an hour	80	
flying goldfish plant	120, 132	
foam of May	42	
forget-me-not	190	
forsythia, Korean	145	
weeping	67	
white	143	
foxglove	205	
climbing	114	
foxtail, golden	155	
fragrant virgin's bower	186	
Fringe cups	161	
fritillary	174, 175	
broad-leaved	182	
pointed-petal	175	
Pontic	175	
Pyrenean	175	
Siberian	175	
fuchsia, Bolivian	123	
brilliant	122	
Californian	56	
Cape	152	
creeping	122	
small-leaved	107	
toothed	122	
trailing	122	
fumewort	54, 203, 205	
garlic, dark blue	190	
keeled	177	
many-flowered	190	
Sicilian honey	177	
witch's	177	
yellow	177	
genista, florists'	180	
gentian, stemless	35	

willow	209	hare's ear	4
geranium, dusky	202	shrubby	159
gouty knee	119	hare's foot	131
night-scented	119	hawksbeard, red	80
white	202	hawkweed, Spanish	108
ginger, western wild	196	hazel, corkscrew	193
ginkgo	157	winter	160
gladiolus, eastern	172	hearts entangled	127
globe flower	97	heath, tree	152
glory bush	130	heather, golden	186
glory of the snow	72, 73, 190	hebe, cypress	146
golden bells	201	large flowered	187
golden bush	186	whipcord	187
golden rod, giant	48	hellebore	203
goldfish plant	136	black false	209
goodnight at noon	80	European false	209
gooseberry, Sierra	42	false	188, 209
granny's curls	195	hogweed, giant	50, 141
grape hyancinth	73, 76	holly	157
common	73	hollyhock, tree	143
paradoxical	74	honesty	49, 172
grass, blue-eyed	54, 109	honeysuckle	82, 193
Bowle's golden	155	Himalayan	198
Chinese fountain	155	small-leaved	27
Chinese zebra	145	trumpet	196
feather	155	winter	39
gold-edged prairie cord	155	honey locust	36, 59, 199, 221
golden-eyed	109	hoop petticoats	170
lyme	155	horehound, Greek	147
pampas	200	horsetail, shrubby	56
ribbon	208	houseleek	101, 102
variegated reed sweet	155	cobweb	102
gromwell, olive-leaved	110	common	102
groundsel	133, 161	Teneriffe	102
climbing	133	waterlily	102
		houseleek tree, dark purple	125
harebell, Australian	116	hyacinth, amethyst	172

INDEX OF COMMON PLANT NAMES

feather		73
grape		208
musk		74, 182
musk grape		74, 182
Spanish		172
summer		177
tassel		73
yellow grape		182
hydrangea		186
climbing		204
ice plant		51, 84
Indian ink plant		164
ink plant		134
inside-out flower, white		208
iris		79, 173
Algerian		64
bearded		68
Danford		182
dwarf bearded		187
foetid		161
orchis		182
snake's-head		70
ivy		153, 165, 169
aralia		165
finger-leaved		154
German		133
parsley-leaved		163
Persian		163
tree		165
jade plant		125
trailing		125
jasmine	115, 116, 130, 133, 136, 180	
Chilean		115
Chinese scented		114
rock		35
woolly rock		107
Jerusalem cross		149
Job's beard		102
Judas tree		60 , 199
juniper, creeping		59
Himalayan		61
Savin		37
kangaroo paw		134
knapweed, giant		50
knotweed, Japanese		41
rock		200
Virginia		211
laburnum, evergreen		143
mock		143
Nepal		143
lace shrub		152
lad's love		145
lady's mantle		147, 203
alpine		147
lady's purse		107
lady's smock		93, 99, 211
lamb's ear		147
laurel, Alexandrian		159
Japanese		158
poet's		159
laurustinus		157, 193
lavender cotton		108, 147
leadwort		55, 114
Cape		114
lead plant		158
leatherwood		150, 153
libertia, golden		196
lilac		41, 141, 159
Californian		45
lily, arum		132

bulb-bearing leopard	131	rose	143
Chinese cobra	172	rough	83
flax	134	shrubby	143
fortune plantain	165	Maltese cross	149
fragrant plantain	166	mandrake	188
ginger	131	maple, flowering	130
Guernsey	186	marguerite	148
Henry's	176	marigold, marsh	93
Jersey	185	marmalade bush	136
kaffir	208, 209	marsh Afrikaner	173
leopard	131	marshmallow plant	196
madonna	176	may apple	161
Natal	130	meadow saffron, spring	209
orange tiger	176	measles plant	136
Persian	175	medick, tree	180
Peruvian	68	mezereon	60, 189, 199
sand	131	milkweed, blue	116
scarlet martagon	176	mimosa	116
St. Bernard's	166	mint, Corsican	107
wavy plantain	166	mirror bush	194
lily of the valley	166	monkshood, climbing	188
lilyturf	208	monkey flower, scarlet	208
spiked	208	montbretia	169
lion's tail, South African	130	giant	166
loosestrife, fringed	145	moonflower	115
lords and ladies	172	moonstone, pink	125
lungwort	202	morisia	110
Bethlehem	202	moschatel	203
narrow-leaved	202	mountain ash, Chinese	210
		mountain everlasting	36
madwort, spiny	205	mourning widow	70
mahoe, thick-leaved	45	mouse plant	172
mahonia, Japanese	158	mullein	49
maidenhair tree	38	muttonbird scrub	186
mallow	50	myrtle	194
hairy	77, 222		
jew's	42, 46	naked lady	186

narcissus	73	wavy	153
watier cliff	171	pear, conference	48, 186
nasturtium, Chilean	132	pelargonium, crisped-leaf	118
tricolor	132	peppermint	118
wreath	190	scented	118
ninebark, common	194	peony, moonlight	161
nutmeg, flowering	195	periwinkle	58, 153
		lesser	187
oat, false	155	phlox	201
oceanspray	45	moss	195
old man's beard	148, 186	pimpernel, blue	80
oleaster, large-flowered	157, 158	pink	58, 101
olive, holly	187	plantain, broad-leaved	63
onion, giant	78, 177	hoary	69
lop-sided	177	plum, cherry	167
ornamental	78	plumbago	55
Persian	78	Chinese	64
twisted leaf	177	poke root	169
orange, Japanese bitter	45	pokeweed	169
mock	141	American	164
trifoliate	186	polka dot plant	136
orange tree	188	polyanthus	162
orchid, lady's slipper	181, 184	polypody, golden	131
showy lady's slipper	184	poppy, dawn	108
osmanthus, Delavay	160	oriental	49
oxalis, fishtail	136	Spanish	71
yellow	136, 182	Welsh	168
ox-eye, yellow	50	poroporo	194, 198
		potentilla	82
pachyphragma, large-leaved	99	primrose	162, 220
paint brush plant	131	dwarf	103
panda plant	125	silver-edged	107
parsley, Cambridge milk	142	primula, candelabra	93
pasque flower	59	princess flower	130
pea, everlasting	153	propeller plant	125
Himalayan	109	purslane, tree	151
spring	149	puya	180

queen's tears	135
quill, zebra	131
quince	32, 37, 158, 189
Japanese	141
ragwort, Barbary	59
climbing	188
Monro's	186
rampion	207
raspberry, creeping	210
red hot poker	131, 167
miniature	148
rohododendron	44
rock brake	130
rockcress	58
rock cress	101
rocket, sweet	49
rock rose, shrubby	109
romulea, crocus-leaved	110, 182
rose, alpine	44, 144
banksia	198
burnet	161, 186, 189
China	38, 188
Damask	188, 196
Guelder	39, 40
Lenten	203
mother's	188
Moyes	188
pink Cherokee	196
red-leaved	109
rock	51, 58, 107
Scotch	161, 186, 189
threepenny bit	160
rose of Sharon	55, 56
rosemary	185, 194
sea	152
roseroot	103
rowan, dwarf	210
saffron, meadow	74, 183, 186
sage, golden	180
Jerusalem	141
Mexican scarlet	137
pineapple	137
yellow	136
salsify	201
sandgrass, early	81
sandwort, mossy	36
savory	107
winter	107
saxifrage, alternate-leaved golden	211
elephant's ear	161
golden	211
opposite-leaved golden	211
purple	107
silver	101
scorpion-vetch, glaucous	194
sedge, Buchanan's	146
cyperus	146
East Asian	146
Gray's	146
sedum	101, 102
senna, bladder	189
shrimp plant	116
siberian pea tree	60
silk tassel bush	153, 207
silverberry, cherry	158
silverbush	116
silverthorn	189
skimmia	194
Japanese	64
smilax	117
snowdrop	72, 76, 174, 205

autumn	167
common	174
Queen Olga's	167
snowflake, autumn	109
rose	110
snow in summer	54
snow pussy	145
soldiers and sailors	172
solomon's seal	210
sorrel	109, 161
Chilean wood	183
sowbread, common	107
eastern	107
spring	78, 107
speedwell, slender	168
spider plant, Brazilian	130
spiderwort, blue	183
cobweb	135
spignel	83
spindle, evergreen	195
flat-stalked	186
spirea, Japanese	201
Kashmir false	167
spruce, Alberta	61
spurge, Japanese	162
marsh	161
Mediterranean	142, 203
Sikkim	161
wood	203
spurge-laurel	189
squill, alpine	76
Portuguese	172
Russian blue	73
Siberian	76
silver	131
stag's horn	131
starfish plant	135
starflower, spring	182
star of Bethlehem	74, 75, 182
spiked	76
star of the veldt	80
starwort, shrubby	186
St. John's wort	146
heath-leaved	107
Hooker's	186
Mount Olympus	107
stonecress	107
iberis-like	108
stonecrop, Caucasian	103
Chinese mountain	102
cliff	102
common	102
pink Mongolian	102
poplar-leaved	103
Siberian	102
Spanish	103
white	54, 102
strawberry tree	34
string of hearts plant	127
sweet spire, holly-leaved	164
sweet William	201
tamarisk	43
thistle, globe	48
thrift	58
thyme	54
mountain	201
toadflax, alpine	107
traveller's joy	148, 186
tree, apple	31, 32, 48, 167
tree peony, Delavay's	161
Ludlow's	161
yellow	59
tree poppy, Californian	196

tridel berry	143, 149	wake robin	208
trillium	208	wax plant	133
tulip	75	whitebeam	167, 169
candia	200	willow, black	204, 205
turkey tangle frog foot	107	Caucasian	107
twinleaf, Asian	107	corkscrew	193
		foot-catkin	164
umbellifer, fine-leaved	78, 222	Gillot's	145
umbrella plant	145	halberd	145, 151
		hoary	194
valerian, red	204	small-leaved	158
verbena, lemon	118	violet	163
vetch, kidney	54	willowherb, rosebay	148
scorpion	135, 180	windflower	171, 172
spring	148	wineberry, Japanese	82
wood	78, 222	wintersweet	67
yellow kidney	108	wire netting bush	68
vibernum, David	200	woodruff	101
Farrer	40, 158		
vine, Chilean potato	68	yarrow	101
chocolate	67	yew	67
grape	67		
kolomikta	164		
Russian	42, 66		
sweetheart	127		
violet, common blue	191		
common dog	191		
dog's tooth	210		
fen	191		
hairy	109		
marsh blue	191		
Missouri	191		
Nuttall's	109		
sweet	190		
sweet white	190		
virginia creeper, Chinese	204		

INDEX OF LATIN PLANT NAMES

Abeliophyllum distichum	143	*Alchemilla alpina*		147
Abutilon megapotamicum	130	*mollis*		147, 203
vitifolium	115	*Allium*		183
Achillea filipendulina	48	*albopilosum*		78, 222
Acis autumnalis	111	*beesianum*		190
rosea	111	*callimischon*		177
Aconitum hemsleyanum	192	*carinatum pulchellum*		178
volubile	188	*cristophii*		83, 223
Actinidia kolomikta	164	*cyaneum*		192
Adoxa moschatellina	203	*giganteum*		78, 177
Aegle	45, 186	*moly*		177
Aeonium arboreum	125	*obliquum*		177
'Atropurpureum'	125	*polyanthem*		190
Aethionema iberideum	108	*pulchellum*		177
'Warley Rose'	108	*schubertii*		78
Agapanthus	177	*siculum*		177
Agave americana 'Mediopicta'	125	*Alopecurus pratensis* 'Aureus'		155
Akebia	69	*Aloysia citriodora*		123
quinata	67	*Alstroemeria ligtu*		68

Althaea	196	*Arachniodes standishii*	211
frutex	143	*Arbutus unedo*	34
hirsuta	77, 222	*Arctotis*	80
Alysum 'Dudley Neville'	58	*Arenaria balearica*	36, 220
spinosum	201	*Argyranthemum frutescens*	148
Amaryllis belladonna	185	*Argyrocytisus battandieri*	151, 155
Amorpha fruticosa	158	*Aria edulis*	169
Anacyclus depressus	109	*Arisaema candidissimum*	172, 173
pyrethrum var. *depressus*	111	*Arisarum proboscideum*	172
Anagallis linifolia 'Phillipsii'	80	*Armeria* 'Corsica'	58
monelli linifolia	83	*Arrhenantherum* var. *bulbosum*	
Anchusa myosotidiflora	203	'Variegatum'	155
Androsace lanuginosa 'Leichtlinii'	107	*Artemisia abrotanum*	145
sarmentosa	35, 219	*Arum creticum*	78, 167
vitaliana	40	*italicum* 'Marmoratum'	172
Anemone apennina	171	*maculatum*	172
blanda	72, 172	*Arundinaria anceps*	33
hepatica	171	*Asarum caudatum*	196
x *hybrida*	66	*europaeum*	196
japonica	48	*Asparagus asparagoides*	117
nemorosa	171	*Asperula arcadiensis*	104
nemorosa 'Allenii'	171	*suberosa*	101
nemorosa 'Robinsoniana'	171	*Aspidistra*	135
nemorosa 'Royal Blue'	171	*Aspidium laserpitium*	211
pavonina	172	*Asplenium bulbiferum*	131
ranunculoides	172	*Aster albescens*	192
ranunculoides 'Seehiana'	172	*pappei*	180
Anigozanthus manglesii	134	*Atriplex halimus*	151
Angelica archangelica	141	*Aubretia*	58
Angiopteris evecta	134	*Aucuba japonica*	158
Antennaria dioica	36, 220		
Anthericum liliago	169	*Ballota acetabulosum*	147
Anthyllis hermanniae	108	*Begonia*	119
vulneraria dillenii	54	*bowerae*	119
Aporocactus	127	'Cleopatra'	120, 123
Aquilega ecalcarata	101	*daedalea*	120
Arabis	58	*feastii* 'Helix'	120

grandis	183	*Calceolaria biflora*	107
haageana	120, 121	*Caltha palustris* 'Flore Pleno'	93
legia	120	*Campanula latifolia* var. *macrantha*	203
'Maphil'	120, 123	*portenschlagiana*	57
metallica	120	*poscharskyana*	54, 203
'President Carnot'	119	*rapunculus*	207
rex	119, 121	*rigidipila*	205
'Ricky Minter'	120	*sarmentosa*	200
scharffii	121, 123	*Caragana arborescens*	60
schmidtiana	120	*Cardamine asarifolia*	93
'Skeezar'	120	*pratensis*	99, 211
Bellevalia paradoxa	76	*trifolia*	94
pycnantha	74	*Carduncellus rhaponticoides*	108
Beloperone guttata	116	*Carex buchananii*	146
Berberis darwinii	64, 65	*grayi*	146
x *stenophylla*	39, 82, 167	*japonica*	146
Bergenia	161	*pseudocyperus*	146
Billardiera heterophylla	117	*Cassinia fulvida*	186
Billbergia nutans	135	*Ceanothus* 'Gloire de Versailles'	45
Bistorta vaccinifolia	205	*Celmisia bellidioides*	109
Blechnum chilense	211	*Centaurea macrocephala*	50
Bongardia	182	*Centranthus ruber*	204
chrysogonum	184	*Cerastium tomentosum*	54, 55
margalla	184	*Ceratostigma plumbaginoides*	55
Brachyglottis monroi	192	*willmottianum*	64
rotundifolia	192	*Ceropegia ampliata*	127, 128
Brimeura amethystina	178	*linearis woodii*	129
Brunnera macrophylla	203	*radicans*	127
Buddleja	38	*woodii*	127
alternifolia	143	*Cersis siliquastrum*	60, 61, 199
crispa	82	*Chamaecyparis* 'Fletcheri'	48, 106, 142, 175
Bulbocodium vernum	183	*lawsoniana*	7, 143, 144, 221
Buphthalmum speciosum	50	*pisifera* 'Squarrosa'	157
Bupleurum baldense	4	*Chamaenerion angustifolium*	
fruticosum	159, 160	'Album'	149
Buxus sempervirens	64, 194	*Chaenomeles japonica*	149, 158

maulei	141	*schleffleriana*	133
Chasmanthe aethiopica	149	x *vedraiensis*	133
vittigera	148	*Coluteaxmedia*	189
Chimonanthus fragrans	67	*Commelina coelestis*	183
praecox	69	*tuberosa*	184
Chinodoxa	190	*Convallaria majalis*	87
Chrysosplenium alternifolium	211	*majalis* var. *rosea*	166
oppositifolium	211	*Convolvulus althaeoides*	56
Cichorium intybus	201	*cneorum*	116
Cistus	158	*Coprosma*	194
Citrus trifoliata	46, 186, 188	*Coriaria terminalis* var.	
Clematis	15, 143	*xanthocarpa*	164
campaniflora	82	*Cornus mas*	41
flammula	82, 186	*Corokea* x *virgata*	68
montana	82	*Coronilla glauca*	180, 194
montana 'Elizabeth'	205	*valentina*	135
montana var. *rubens*	205	*valentina glauca*	184, 198
orientalis	82, 143	*Cortaderia selloana* 'Pumila'	200
recta	148	*Corydalis lutea*	54, 203, 205
recta 'Purpurea'	148	*Corylopsis pauciflora*	160
tangutica	65, 66	*Corylus avellana* 'Contorta'	193
viticella	186	*Corynabutilon vitifolium*	117
vitalba	148, 186	*Cotoneaster horizontalis*	204, 205
Clivia miniata	130	*Cotula acaenifolia*	54
Codonopsis clematidea	107	*Crassula argentea*	125
Colchicum	74, 76	*falcata*	125
x *agrippinum*	74	*marginata*	125
ancyrensis	182, 183	*obliqua*	125
autumnale	74	*ovata*	128
bulbocodium	184	*ovata* 'Obliqua'	128
speciosum	74, 186	*pellucida marginalis*	128
speciosum 'Album'	74	*perfoliata* var. *falcata*	129
variegatum	74	*sarmentosa*	125
Colletia armata	160	*spathulata*	125
hystrix	162	*Crepis rubra*	80
Columnea	120, 132	*Crinum* x *powellii*	148
allenii	133	*Crocanthemum rosmarinifolium*	111

INDEX OF LATIN PLANT NAMES

Crocosmia x *crocosmiiflora*   169
    masoniorum   166
    paniculata   149
Crocus ancyrensis 'Golden Bunch'   71
    asturicus   71
    augustifolius   76
    balansae 'Zwanenburg'   71
    biflorus weldenii 'Fairy'   71
    chrysanthus   71
    etruscus 'Zwanenburg'   71
    kotschyanus   76
    laevigatus 'Fontenayi'   71
    ochroleucus   71
    sativus   71, 72
    serotinus salzmannii   71
    sieberi   71
    speciosus   71
    susianus   71
    tommasinianus   53, 70
    zonatus   71
Crytomeria japonica   157
Cryptanthus   135
Cupressus   54, 59, 150, 151, 201
    lawsoniana fletcheri   58
Curio repens   128
Curtonus paniculatus   148
Cyclamen cilicium   78, 181
    coum   107
    europaeum   78
    graecum   181
    hederifolium   111
    libatonicum   130, 181
    neopolitanum   107
    repandum   78, 107
    persicum   130, 181
    pseudibericum   182
    purpurascens   83

Cydonia oblonga   32, 37, 189
Cynara cardunculus   167
Cypripedium calceolus   181, 183
    reginae   184
Cytisus austriacus   186
    battandieri   151
    x *kewensis*   201
    monspessulana   192
    monspessulanus   189

Dactylis glomerata 'Variegata'   155
Danae racemosa   159
Daphne collina   144
    x *houtteana*   189
    laureola   189
    mezereum   60, 189, 199
    odora 'Aureomarginata'   69
    pontica   153
    sericea   149
    'Somerset'   151
    tangutica   143
Darmera peltata   149
Decaisnea fargesii   43
Decalepidanthus trollii   111
Delairea odorata   134, 192
Dianella intermedia   134
Dianthus   51, 58, 101, 201
    'Mrs. Sinkins'   51
Diervilla 'Florida Variegata'   194
Digitalis purpurea   205
Dimorphotheca   80, 83, 185
Diplacus glutinosus   180, 181
Dorycnium hirsutum   195
Dranunculus vulgaris   172
Drejerella   116
Dryopteris filix-mas   207
Duvallia mariesii   131

Echeveria elegans	125	*palustris*	161
gibbiflora 'Metallica'	125	*robbiae*	203
hoveyi var. *zahni*	125	*sikkimensis*	161
rosea	125	*Fallopia baldschuanicum*	46, 69
Echinops	48, 167	*Fascicularia bicolor*	180
Elaeagnus macrophylla	157, 163	x *Fatshedera lizei*	164, 165
multiflora	158, 159, 163	*Fatsia*	165
pungens 'Maculata'	189	*japonica*	169, 199
Elymus arenarius	155	*Felicia bergeriana*	80
Endymion hispanica	172	*Ficus pumila*	116
scripta	172	*Forsythia* 'Bronxensis'	201
Eomecon chionantha	108	*ovata*	145
Ephedra gerardiana var. *sikkimensis*	56	*suspensa*	67
Epilobium angustifolium 'Album'	148	*Fritillaria*	78
canum	57	*acmopetala*	175
Epimedium	161, 209	*crassifolia*	182
Epiphyllum cooperi	127	*gracilis*	175
crenatus var. *cooperi*	129	*imperialis*	174
Eranthis hyemalis	72	*meleagris*	175
Erica terminalis	152	*messanensis gracilis*	178
Erythronium dens-canis	210	*pallidiflora*	175
Escallonia 'Donard Seedling'	141	*persica*	175
Eucryphia 'Nymansay'	150, 153	*pontica*	175
Euonymus japonicas 'Aureopictus'	189	*pyrenaica*	175, 176
japonicus 'Microphyllus Albovariegatus'	198	*Fuchsia boliviana*	123
		'Chang'	122
japonicas 'Microphyllus Variegatus'	195	*corymbiflora*	123
		corymbosa	122
planipes	186	*denticulata*	123
Euphorbia amygdaloides var.		*fulgens*	122
robbiae	203, 206	*microphylla*	107
characias	203, 204	*procumbens*	122
characias wulfenii	142	*serratifolia*	122
hislopii	126	'Speciosa'	122
milii	126	*splendens*	122
millii var. *hislopii*	129		

Galanthus	205	*Ginkgo biloba*	38, 157
'Atkinsii'	174	*Gladiolus byzantinus*	172
elwesii	174	*communis byzantinus*	178
ikariae	174	*tristis*	173
'Magnet'	174	*Glandora oleifolia*	111
nivalis	72, 174	*Gleditschia triacanthos*	36, 59, 199, 221
octobreasis	167, 169	*Globularia*	101
plicatus	174	*Glyceria maxima* var. *variegata*	155
reginae-olgae	167, 169	*Gypsophila*	147
'Scharlockii'	174		
'Viridapice'	174	*Haemanthus albiflos*	131
Galax aphylla	210	*Hakonechloa macra* 'Alboaurea'	156
urceolata	211	*macra* 'Variegata'	155
Galtonia candicans	177, 178	*Hebe* 'Bowles's Hybrid'	152
princeps	177	*macrantha*	187
Garrya elliptica	153, 154, 207	*Hedera algeriensis* 'Gloire de	
Genista aetnensis	199	Marengo'	153
canariensis	184	*colchica* 'Dentata Variegata'	
cinerea	151, 199		168
fragrans	180	*colchica* 'Variegata'	163
sagittalis delphinensis	101	*helix*	169
tinctoria var. *virgata*	150, 151	*helix* 'Crispus'	163
Gentiana acaulis	35, 219	*helix* 'Cristata'	168
asclepiadea	209	*helix* 'Digitata'	154
Geranium anemonaefolium	142	*helix* 'Glacier'	153
candidum	188	*helix* 'Golden Heart'	154
ibericum	202	*helix* 'Jubilee'	154
pratense	202	*helix* 'Minor Marmorata'	154
phaeum	202	*helix* 'Oro di Bogliasco'	156
psilostemon	202	*helix* 'Parsley Crested'	168
rivulare	202	*helix* 'Silver Queen'	153
saxatile var. *candidum*	192	*Hedychium gardnerianum*	131
'Striatum'	202	*Helianthemum* 'Butter and Eggs'	51
sylvaticum	71, 202	*lunulatum*	109
wallichianum 'Buxton Blue'		'Rose of Leeswood'	51
	209	*rosemarinifolium*	107
Gilia rubra	81	'Wisley Primrose'	51

Helianthus tuberosus	45	'Hidcote'	146
Helichrysum	152	*hookerianum*	186
alveolatum	146	*olympicum* 'Citrinum'	107
angustifolium	153	*olympicum* f. *minus*	111
splendidum	149	*olympicum* f. *uniflorum*	
Helleborus orientalis	203	'Citrinum'	111
Hepatica nobilis	178	*polyphyllum*	107
Heracleum mantegazzianum	50, 141	*Hypocryta glabra*	136
Hermodactylus tuberosus	70	*Hypoestes phyllostachya*	136
Hertia cheirifolia	62		
Hesperantha coccinea	211	*Iberis sempervirens*	59
Hesperis matronalis	49	*Ilex aquifolium* 'Silver King'	157
Hibiscus trionum	80	*aquifolium* 'Silver Queen'	162
Hieracium bombycinum	108	*Impatiens*	120
Hippophae rhamnoides	38, 39	*Iochroma cyaneum*	134
Holodiscus discolor	45	*Ionopsidium acaule*	81
Hormathophylla spinosa	205	*Ipheion uniflorum* 'Wisley Blue'	182
Hornungia alpina	111	*Ipomopsis rubra*	83
Hosta fortunei aurea	165	*Iris* 'Cantab'	173
plantaginea	166	'Clairette'	173
plantaginea var. *grandiflora*	166	*danfordiae*	182
plantaginea var. *japonica*	169	*foetidissima lutea*	161
undulata	165	*foetidissima* var. *lutescens*	162
Hoya carnosa	133	*germanica*	68
Hutchinsia alpina	107	'Green Spot'	187
Hyacinthoides hispanica	178	*histrioides*	182
non-scipta	178	*japonica* 'Ledger'	196
Hyacinthus amethystinus	172	'Joyce'	173
Hydrangea aspera 'Macrophylla'	163	'J. S. Dijit'	173
petiolaris	204	*pumila*	187
Hylotelephium ewersii	104	*stylosa*	64
ewersii var. *homophyllum*	104	'Zia'	187
populifolium	105	*Itea ilicifolia*	164
Hymenanthera crassifolia	45		
Hypericum calycinum	55, 56	*Jasminium polyanthum*	114, 115
coris	107	*Jeffersonia dubia*	107
		Jovibarba heufelii	104

sobolifera	104	*Leonotis leonurus*	130
Juniperus horizontalis	59	*Lespedeza thunbergii formosa*	147
sabina 'Tamariscifolia'	37	*Leucanthemum* x *superbum*	48
squamata 'Meyeri'	61	*vulgare*	48
Justicia brandageeana	117	*Leucojum autumnale*	109
		roseum	110
Kalanchoe manginii	126	*Leymus arenarius*	156
pumila	125, 126	*Leycesteria formosa*	195
tomentosa	125	*Libertia ixioides*	196
uniflora	127	*Lilium candidum*	176
youngensis	126	*chalcedonicum*	176
Kerria japonica	42	*henryi*	176
japonica 'Pleniflorum'	46	*Linaria alpina*	107, 108
Kleinia cylindrica	125	*Lippia*	118
repens	125	*repens*	107
Kniphofia	131, 167	*Liriope spicata*	208
galpinii	148, 149	*Lithospermum oleifolium*	110
triangularis	149	*Lomaria magellanica*	210
Kolkwitzia amabilis	159, 160	*Lonicera*	30, 37, 193
		fragrantissima	39
Lachenalia	131	*nitida*	27
bulbifera	134	x *purpusii*	40
cyaneum	131	*sempervirens*	196
pendula	131	*standishii*	40
Lamium galeobdolon 'Variegatum'	94	*Lotus hirsutus*	198
Lantana camara	136, 137	*maritimus*	205
Lathyrus latifolius	153	*Lunaria annua*	49, 172
latifolius 'Red Pearl'	155	*Lychnis chalcedonica*	148
latifolius 'Rosa Pearl'	155	*coronaria* 'Alba'	147
latifolius 'The Pearl'	153	*dioica* 'Flore Pleno'	190
latifolius 'White Pearl'	155	*Lysimachia ciliata*	145
undulatus	153	*monelli*	83
vernus	149	*nummularia*	54
Lavatera cachermeriana	50		
Ledebouria cooperi	134	*Mahonia*	82
ovalifolia	134	*japonica*	158
socialis	134	*Malus domesticus*	48

'Lane's Prince Albert'	48	*Myrsiphyllum asparagoides*	117
'Laxton Pippin'	48	*Myrtus communis*	194
x *purpurea* 'Eleyi'	142		
Malva cachermeriana	52	*Narcissus asturiensis*	170
Mandragora officinarum	188	*bulbocodium*	170
Mandevilla laxa	117	*bulbocodium romieuxii*	170
suaveolens	115	*caniculatus*	171
Matteuccia struthiopteris	94	'Caniculatus'	171, 178
Maurandya lophospermum	114	'Carlton'	73
Meconopsis cambrica	168	'Cheerfulness'	73
Medicago arborea	180	*cyclamineus*	170, 171
Melicytus crassifolius	46	'Fortune'	73
Mentha requienii	107	x *gracilis*	171
Meum athamanticum	78, 79, 222	'Hesla'	171
Mertensia coventryana	110	'King Alfred'	73
Mibora minima	81	'Mary Copeland'	73
Microglossa albescens	186	*minor*	170
Micromeria corsica	201	'Mme. Krelage'	73
Milium effusum 'Aureum'	155	'Mrs. Backhouse'	73
Mimulus aurantiacus	184	'Mrs. Ernst H. Krelage'	76
cardinalis	208	'Mrs. R. O. Backhouse'	76
Miscanthus sinensis 'Zebrinus'	145	x *odorus* 'Plenus'	178
Morisia monanthos	110	'Orange Queen'	171
Muscari	73, 208	*pseudo-narcissus*	170, 171
ambrosiacum	74	*pseudo-narcissus obvallaris*	
comosum	73		190
comosum 'Plumosum'	73, 75	'Rembrandt'	73
'Heavenly Blue'	73	*romieuxii*	178
macrocarpum	76, 182	*rupicola*	171
moschatum	76, 182	*rupicola watieri*	178
moschatum macrocarpum	74	*tazetta*	171
muscarimi	76, 184	*tazetta laticolor*	178
neglectum	73	'Thalia'	171
paradoxum	74	*triandrus*	170, 171
'Pink Sunrise'	76	*watieri*	171
'Valerie Finnis'	76	*Neillia incisa*	155
Myosotis	190	*Nematanthus strigillosus*	139

INDEX OF LATIN PLANT NAMES

Nepeta x *faassenii*	51
Nephrolepis	131
Nerine bowdenii	186
Olearia x *scilloniensis*	151
Ophiopogon	208
Ornithogalum balansae	182
nutans	75
oligophyllum	184
pyrenaicum	75
umbellatum	74
Orobus vernus	148
Osmanthus delavayi	160
heterophyllus	192
ilicifolius	187
Osteospermum	83
Othonnopsis cheirifolia	59
Oxalis	136
chrysantha	109
conorrhiza	111
corniculata	136
ortgiesii	136
siliquosa	136
valdiviensis	183
vulcanicola 'Siliquosa'	139
Oxypetalum coerulea	116
Ozothamnus rosmarinifolius	152
Pachyphragma macrophyllum	99
Pachyphytum oviferum 'Roseum'	128
roseum	125
Pachysandra terminalis	162
Paeonia delavayi	62, 161
lutea	59
daurica	162
ludlowii	161
wittmanniana	161
Papaver cambricum	169
orientale	49
rupifragum	71
Parachetus communis	109
Paradisea liliago	166
Parthenocissus henryana	204
Pelargonium	114
apiifolia	119
bicolor violaceum	119
crispum	118
'Distinction'	118
fragrans	118
'Friesdorf'	118
gibbosum	119
'Granny Hewitt'	119
'Gustav Emich'	114
'Happy Thought'	118
'Hederinum'	123
'Mabel Grey'	118
'Miss Burdett Coutts'	118
'Miss Stapleton'	119
'Mme. Margot'	119
'Mrs H Cox'	118, 211
'Petit Pierre'	119
'Roi des Balcons'	119
'Schottii'	119
'The Boar'	119
tomentosum	118
triste	119
Pellaea rotundifolia	131
Peltiphyllum peltatum	145
Pennisetum alopecuroides	155
Persicaria	211
viginiana 'Variegata'	211
Petasites japonicas	203
Philadelphus microphyllus	141
Phlomis fruticosa	141, 142

Phlebodium aureum	131, 132	*marginata*	107
Phlox subulata	201	*nana*	105
subulata 'Temiskaming'	195, 197	x *polyantha*	162
		prolifera	93
Phormium tenax	200	*vulgaris*	162
Phuopsis stylosa	153	*Prunus cerasifera* 'Pissardii'	169
Phygelius capensis	152	'Kazan'	60, 199
Phyla nodiflora	111	*padus*	38, 41, 157, 221
Physocarpus opulifolius 'Luteus'	194	*pissardii*	167
Phytolacca americana	164	*subhirtella* 'Autumnalis'	60
clavigera	164, 165	*tenella*	144
polyandra	169	*tomentosa*	157
Picea glauca var. *albertiana* 'Conica'	61	*Pseudodictamnus acetabulosus*	149
Piptanthus nepalensis	143	*Pseudofumaria lutea*	57
Plantago media	63	*Pulmonaria*	202
Platycerium	131	*angustifolia*	202
Pleioblastus pumilus	164	*saccharata*	202
variegatus 'Fortunei'	164	*Pulsatilla vulgaris*	59, 60
Plumbago auriculata	117	*Puschkinia*	107
capensis	114	*Puya alpestris*	180
Podophyllum emodi	209	*Pyracantha crenatoserrata*	68
peltatum	161	*Pyrus aria*	167
Polygonatum	210	*communis*	48, 186
Polygonum baldschuanicum	42, 66		
cuspidatum	41	*Reineckea carnea*	208
vaccinifolium	200	*Reynoutria japonica*	45
Polypodium vulgare	131	*Rhipsalis baccifera*	129
Poncirus trifoliata	45	*cassutha*	127
Potentilla alba	208	*Rhodiola rosea*	105
fruticosa	78, 82, 222	*Rhododendron hirsutum*	44
fruticosa 'Manchu'	82, 149	*Ribes cruentum*	42
fruticosa 'Mandshurica'	145	*roezlii* var. *cruentum*	46
fruticosa var. *veitchii*	82	*sanguineum*	42, 43
fruticosa 'Vilmoriniana'	145	*Romneya coulteri*	196, 197
Primula auricula	162	*Romulea bulbocodium*	110, 182
edgeworthii	103, 104	*Rosa* x *alba* 'Alba Maxima'	160
x *kewensis*	130	'Aglaia'	205

INDEX OF LATIN PLANT NAMES

'Alberic Barbier'	189	*spinosissima* 'Grandiflora'	192
'Albertine'	205	'Tuscany'	188
altaica	189, 192	'William Lobb'	144
banksiae	198	*Rubus*	143
'Belle de Crecy'	164	*bambusarum*	
'Capitaine John Ingram'	188	'Benenden'	149
'Celeste'	160	*fockeanus*	210
x *centifolia*	188	*phoenicolasius*	82
Cecile Brunner'	188	*rolfei*	211
'Charles de Mills'	188	*tricolor*	162
chinensis	38	*Rumex acetosa*	161
'Dorothy Perkins'	38	*Ruscus aculeatus*	200
elegantula 'Persetoa'	162		
'Evangeline'	38	*Salix apoda*	107
'Excelsa'	205, 206	*bockii*	158
'F. J. Grootendorst'	160, 161	*daphnoides*	163
'Frensham'	205	*eleagnos*	194
farreri persetosa	160	x *gillotii*	145
gallica	196	*gracilistyla* 'Kuro-me'	204, 205
glauca	111		
'Golden Showers'	205	*gracilistyla* 'Melanostachys'	
'Hiawatha'	38		204, 205, 206
'Honorine de Brabant'	144	*hastata* 'Wehrhahnii	145, 146, 151'
'Maiden's Blush'	188		
moyesii	188	*magnifica*	164
'New Dawn'	205	*matsudana* "Tortuosa"	193
'Nuits de Young'	188	*Salvia*	185
pendulina pyrenaica	144	*africana-lutea*	180
'Perla de Montserrat'	201	*aurea*	184
'Perle d'Or'	188	*elegans*	139
'Roulettii'	201	*fulgens*	137
rubiginosa	153	*rosmarinus*	194
rubrifolia	109	*rutilans*	137
'Ruth'	205	*Santolina*	108, 147
'Seven Sisters'	230	*rosemarinifolia*	111
sinica 'Anemone'	196	*viridis*	108
spinosissima	161, 186, 189	*Sarcococca confusa*	44, 153

hookeriana var. *digyna*	44	x *rubrotinctum* 'Aurora'	128
ruscifolia	200	*spectabile*	51, 84
Satureia	107	*spurium*	103
subspicata	107	*spurmium* 'Schorbuser Blut'	103
Satureja	111	*Selinum carvifolia*	142
montana illyrica	111	*Semiaquilegia ecalcarata*	104
Saxifraga chrysosplenium	211	*Sempervivum*	101
crustata	101	*arachnoideum*	102
oppositifolia	107, 211	*ciliosum*	102
rotundifolia		*heufelii*	102
chrysosplenifolia	211	*octopodes*	102
Scilla	192	*soboliferum*	102
adlamii	131	*tectorum*	102
bifolia	73, 76	*tectorum* 'Commander Hay'	102
ovalifolia	131	*tectorum* 'Glaucum'	102, 104
peruviana	172	*Senecio mikanoides*	133
sibirica	73, 76	*monroi*	186
'Tubergeniana'	107, 111	*rotundifolium*	186
violacea	131	*scandens*	188, 192
Schizostylis coccinea	208, 209	*talinoides cylindricus*	128
Scorzonera rosea	201	*vulgaris*	161
Sedum acre	102	*Silene chalcedonica*	149
album	54, 102	*coronaria*	149
album var. *murale*	102	*dioica* 'Flore Pleno'	192
amplexicaule	103	*Sinopodophyllum hexandrum*	
cauticola	102	var. *emodi*	211
ewersii	102	*Sisyrinchium*	109, 111
ewersii var. *homophyllum*	102	*bermudiana*	54
floriferum	102	*brachypus*	109
guatemense 'Aurora'	125	*californicum*	111
hybridum	102	*Skimmia japonica*	64, 194
middendorffianum	102	*Solanum aviculare*	198
morganianum	125	*capsicastrum*	189
populifolium	103	*crispum* 'Autumnale'	68, 194
pulchellum	103	*crispum* 'Glasnevin'	69, 198
roseum	103		

pseudocapsicum	192, 203
Solidago gigantea	48, 49
Sollya heterophylla	116
Sorbaria aitchisonii	167
tomentosa var. *angustifolia*	169
Sorbus aria	169
reducta	210
Spartina pectinata 'Aureomarginata'	155
Spartium junceum	153
Spiraea arborea 'Arguta'	143
'Arguta'	42
x *bumalda*	201
japonica 'Walluf'	205
thunbergii	42
x *vanhouttei*	42, 159
veitchii	42
Stachys byzantina	147
lanata	147
Stephanandra incisa	152
Sternbergia lutea	185, 187
Stipa pennata	155
Streptosolen jamesonii	136
Strobilanthes metallica	136
Symphoricarpos orbiculatus	
'Foliis Variegatis'	198
orbiculatus 'Variegatus'	196
Symphytum grandiflorum	203
orientale	203
Syringa 'Bellicent'	159, 160
'Souvenir de Louis Spaeth'	41
Tamarix ramosissima	46
pentandra	43, 44
Taxus baccata	67
Tellima grandiflora	161

Tetragonolobus maritimus	201
Thuya	59
plicata	27, 199
Thymus nitidus	54
richardii nitidus	57
Tibouchina semidecandra	130
urvilleana	134
Tovara virginiana 'Variegata'	211
Trachystemon orientalis	203
Tradescantia	135, 183
sillamontana	135
Trollius	97
Tropaeolum polyphyllum	190
tricolor	132
Tragopogon porrifolius	201
Tulipa batalinii	75
linifolia	75
saxatilis	200
sprengeri	75
tarda	75
Tweedia caerulea	117
coerulea	116, 117
Ursinia	80
Uvularia grandiflora	209, 210
Vancouveria hexandra	208
Veltheimia capensis	131
Veratrum album	188
nigrum	208, 209
Verbascum 'Cotswold Queen'	49
'Gainsborough'	49
'Pink Domino'	49
Verbena	136
Veronica 'Bowles's Hybrid'	155
cupressoides	146
filiformis	168

macrantha	192
ochracea	187
Viburnum davidii	200
farreri	40, 162
fragrans	39, 40, 158
opulus	40
tinus	157, 193
Vicia sylvatica	78, 222
Vinca acutiflora	58
difformis	153
major	58
minor	58, 187
Viola	190
'Alassio'	190
'Amiral Avellan'	190
blanda	190
'Coeur d'Alsace'	190
cucullata	191
elatior	191
hirta	109
labradorica	191
nuttallii	109, 110
odorata	190
persicifolia	192
riviniana	191
riviniana Purpurea Group	192
septentrionalis	191
sororia	192
'St. Helena'	190
'Sulfurea'	190
Vitaliana primuliflora	35, 219
Vitex agnus-castus	195
Vitis vinifera	67
henryana	204
Weigela 'Florida Variegata'	198
Woodwardia	131
Yushania anceps	33
Zantedeschia aethiopica	132
'Green Goddess'	134
Zauschneria	56

This book is printed on paper from sustainable sources managed under the Forest Stewardship Council (FSC) scheme.

It has been printed in the UK to reduce transportation miles and their impact upon the environment.

For every new title that Troubador publishes, we plant a tree to offset CO_2, partnering with the More Trees scheme.

For more about how Troubador offsets its environmental impact, see www.troubador.co.uk/sustainability-and-community